DI063454

Planning and Support for People
with Intellectual Disabilities

by the same author

Ageing with a Lifelong Disability
A Guide to Practice, Program and Policy Issues for Human Services Professionals
ISBN 978 1 84310 077 5
eISBN 978 1 84642 158 7

Group Homes for People with Intellectual Disabilities
Encouraging Inclusion and Participation
Tim Clement and Christine Bigby
ISBN 978 1 84310 645 6
eISBN 978 0 85700 205 1

of related interest

Person Centred Planning and Care Management with People with Learning Disabilities
Edited by Paul Cambridge and Steven Carnaby
ISBN 978 1 84310 131 4
eISBN 978 1 84642 140 2

Active Support
Enabling and Empowering People with Intellectual Disabilities
Jim Mansell and Julie Beadle-Brown
ISBN 978 1 84905 111 8
eISBN 978 0 85700 300 3

Person-Centred Teams
A Practical Guide to Delivering Personalisation Through Effective Team-work
Helen Sanderson and Mary Beth Lepkowsky
ISBN 978 1 84905 455 3
eISBN 978 0 85700 830 5

A Practical Guide to Delivering Personalisation
Person-Centred Practice in Health and Social Care
Helen Sanderson and Jaimee Lewis
ISBN 978 1 84905 194 1
eISBN 978 0 85700 422 2

How to Break Bad News to People with Intellectual Disabilities
A Guide for Carers and Professionals
Irene Tuffrey-Wijne
ISBN 978 1 84905 280 1
ISBN 978 0 85700 583 0

Learning Difficulties and Sexual Vulnerability
A Social Approach
Andrea Hollomotz
ISBN 978 1 84905 167 5
eISBN 978 0 85700 381 2

Planning and Support for People with Intellectual Disabilities

Issues for Case Managers and Other Professionals

Edited by Christine Bigby, Chris Fyffe and Elizabeth Ozanne

Foreword by Jim Mansell

Jessica Kingsley *Publishers*
London and Philadelphia

Published worldwide excluding Australia and New Zealand in 2007
by Jessica Kingsley Publishers
73 Collier Street
London N1 9BE, UK
and
400 Market Street, Suite 400
Philadelphia, PA 19106, USA

www.jkp.com

Published in Australia and New Zealand by
University of New South Wales Press Ltd
University of New South Wales
Sydney NSW 2052, Australia
www.unswpress.com.au

Copyright © Jessica Kingsley Publishers 2007
Foreword copyright © Jim Mansell 2007
Printed digitally since 2014

The right of the editors and contributors to be identified as authors of this work has been asserted by them in
accordance with the Copyright, Designs and Patents Act 1988.

All rights reserved. No part of this publication may be reproduced in any material form (including photocopying or storing it
in any medium by electronic means and whether or not transiently or incidentally to some other use of this publication)
without the written permission of the copyright owner except in accordance with the provisions of the Copyright, Designs
and Patents Act 1988 or under the terms of a licence issued by the Copyright Licensing Agency Ltd, Saffron House, 6–10
Kirby Street, London EC1N 8TS. Applications for the copyright owner's written permission to reproduce any part of this
publication should be addressed to the publisher.

Warning: The doing of an unauthorised act in relation to a copyright work may result
in both a civil claim for damages and criminal prosecution.

Library of Congress Cataloging in Publication Data
Planning and support for people with intellectual disabilities : issues for case managers and other professionals / edited by
Christine Bigby, Chris Fyffe, and Elizabeth Ozanne ; foreword by Jim Mansell.
p. cm.
Includes bibliographical references and index.
ISBN 978-1-84310-354-7 (alk. paper)
1. People with mental disabilities—Services for. 2. Social work with people with disabilities. I. Bigby, Christine. II. Fyffe,
Chris, 1954- III. Ozanne, Elizabeth, 1944-
HV3004.P55 2007
362.3'532—dc22

2007005852

British Library Cataloguing in Publication Data
A CIP catalogue record for this book is available from the British Library

A catalogue record for this book is available from the National Library of Australia
Bigby, Christine, Fyffe, Chris and Ozanne, Elizabeth (editors)
Planning and Support for People with Intellectual Disabilities: Issues
for Case Managers and Other Professionals

ISBN 978 1 84310 354 7 (Worldwide excluding Australia and New Zealand)
ISBN 978 086840 950 4 (Australia and New Zealand)
eISBN 978 1 84642 617 9

Contents

Tables

Boxes

Case studies

Foreword

Jim Mansell, Professor, Tizard Centre,
University of Kent, UK

For people with severe or complex disabilities, such as intellectual disabilities, redistribution of resources, for example money, housing and employment, is usually not enough to obtain equality of opportunity. The nature of people's impairments means that they need help from others in order to realise the opportunities that life presents. Thus, the relationship between helper and helped is the most important relationship in providing services to disabled people. It is the place where money and resources are turned into the kind of life the person wants to live.

The nature of this task includes helping to identify and prioritise appropriate goals; finding, organising and allocating resources; and then using those resources to achieve the person's goals. This is often a long-term process, and so reviewing and revising arrangements is required. These are the tasks that have come to be called 'case management'. They differ from social work in that the case manager, at least ideally, controls resources and can use his or her own judgement to arrange them in a way best suited to help the disabled person.

Case management has been a central component of the development of social services in many western countries since the growth of community-based services in the 1970s and 1980s. Writing in the 1980s, Applebaum and Austin (1990) pointed out that 'case management has become omnipresent, even when there is limited consensus about just what it is'. They attributed its rise to the move away from institutional care, in which all of a person's needs were intended to be addressed in one place, to community-based services. These were, they argued, fragmented and complicated. People with substantial needs required services from different agencies and, therefore, faced a difficult task of obtaining and coordinating their access and delivery – a task that may be beyond the personal resources of the individual. Adding a coordination role addresses this need

(Moxley 1989). Case management, therefore, has grown out of a recognition that effectively meeting individual needs requires a tailored, person-centred approach to planning and organising the care and support offered.

A second aspect of the rise of case management has been steadily rising expectations about the breadth and degree of what services ought to aspire to achieve. This is particularly clear in the field of intellectual disability, where a narrow focus on skill development in order to increase independence extended to other domains of life, such as personal relationships, activity, choice and social integration, until, as person-centred planning, the focus is the quality of a person's life in every aspect. Person-centred planning – now defined as a continuous process and so in a sense the same thing as case management – has ended up embracing the widest range of outcomes, including aspirations and needs; the provision of support at a range of levels so that people with greater needs can aim for the same goals; every aspect of service delivery and design; and the organisation of the informal social network in so far as it relates to support for the individual (Mansell and Beadle-Brown 2004).

Case management, therefore, has expanded its focus to include all of a person's life and all the potential sources of formal and informal support available to that person. It therefore has an absolutely fundamental role in service provision. As such, it deserves study.

The tasks involved are complex. Effective case management requires the assessment of individual needs and aspirations of people who may have limited ability to express themselves, limited experience of possible alternatives and low expectations. It requires that the results of assessment are weighed against human rights and people's entitlements to service. It entails wide knowledge of the range of possible kinds of support to help people achieve their goals, the negotiating skills to acquire and organise these resources, and the skills of monitoring, reviewing and adapting the range of support provided as people's goals change. Understanding what is involved in each of these tasks, and how they can be done well, is an important prerequisite of effective case management.

Case management also deserves study for a second reason. The tasks of case management are demanding not only because of the complex nature of individual goals and the kinds of support people require. They are demanding because these tasks are carried out against a background of pressures and influences arising elsewhere in the welfare system. Case management is the arena in which conflict between these forces is worked out at the individual level. The most obvious pressure is on resources. Part of the motivation for adopting individual case management was to improve the efficiency of services (Davies and Challis 1986), both by providing only those services needed in just the right amount to meet individual goals, and by harnessing and augmenting less expensive forms of care such as informal support from neighbours and family. So, case managers have to ration resources (or work within systems that ration resources for them), and this creates conflict between what the people served need and what the case manager can deliver. A similar example is the growth of risk assessment and management, where risks to the organisation may be given priority over those to the service user, creating conflict for the case manager.

The way in which these external pressures bear on case management differs in different jurisdictions. Rationing is much more important in liberal welfare states, which see the goal of welfare as a limited safety net for those who cannot fend for themselves, than it is in a social democracy where the goal is equal rights or a conservative system where entitlement is based on status (Esping-Andersen 1990). So, although the language of case management and the kinds of tasks carried out may be similar, the way in which case management works is likely to be different, depending on the context in which it operates.

This book brings together, for the first time, perspectives on these different aspects of case management. It focuses on aspects of the work of case managers in a detailed and critical way, addressing the tasks that they do. It also attends to the context in which case management takes place and the conflicts that are played out as the work is done. And it is comparative in approach. Thus, it avoids the trap of claiming to offer a blueprint for what case managers should do, but instead offers a set of thoughtful reflections on aspects of the task.

Case managers will find this book invaluable as a guide to thinking through how they should work. Many other people will find the arguments presented here relevant to their own practice, as professionals working alongside case managers, as teachers of professionals, as policymakers and as service users, advocates and representatives. In short, it should be read by everyone concerned with improving services for people with intellectual disabilities.

References

Applebaum, R. and Austin, C.D. (1990) *Long-term Care Case Management*. New York: Springer.

Davies, B. and Challis, D. (1986) *Matching Resources to Needs in Community Care*. Aldershot: Gower Publishing.

Esping-Andersen, G. (1990) *The Three Worlds of Welfare Capitalism*. Cambridge: Polity.

Mansell, J. and Beadle-Brown, J. (2004) 'Person-centred planning or person-centred action? Policy and practice in intellectual disability services.' *Journal of Applied Research in Intellectual Disabilities 17*, 1–9.

Moxley, D.P. (1989) *The Practice of Case Management*. London: Sage.

The Contributors

Susan Balandin is Associate Professor at the University of Sydney, Australia. Her research interests focus on people with lifelong disability who have little or no functional speech and require augmentative and alternative communication (AAC) systems to communicate.

Christine Bigby is Reader and Associate Professor in the School of Social Work and Social Policy at La Trobe University, Victoria, Australia. She is joint editor of *Australian Social Work*. Her research interests are ageing with an intellectual disability, case management and intellectual disability policy.

Brenda Burgen is currently completing her PhD at the School of Social Policy and Social Work at La Trobe University, Melbourne, Australia. She has worked with people with intellectual disabilities as a social worker and educator in women's health, sexuality and sexual health, social skills and relationships, and parenting, across community health and public hospital sectors.

Eric Emerson is Professor of Disability and Health Research at the Institute for Health Research at Lancaster University, Lancaster, UK. He has written several books and numerous articles in academic and professional journals on issues related to the health and social inequalities faced by people with intellectual disabilities.

Margaret Flynn is Principal Researcher at Sheffield Hallam University, Sheffield, UK. In her non-university time, she undertakes work for organisations such as Skills for Care, IDeA and the Local Government Association.

Peter Flynn lives in Manchester. He undertakes voluntary work in local hospitals. He loves singing and is a valued member of his local church.

Chris Fyffe has worked as a psychologist, a manager of disability services and an academic. For the past decade, as Director (together with Jeffrey McCubbery) of her own specialist disability consultancy firm (Grimwood Pty Ltd), Mandurang, Victoria, Australia, she has completed service evaluations, research and policy development projects and consultations with people with disabilities and their families.

Estelle Fyffe is a Psychologist and the Chief Executive Officer of annecto – the people network, a not-for-profit community organisation based in Victoria, Australia, with a mission to increase choices and opportunities for people with disabilities.

Susana Gavidia-Payne has been involved for nearly 30 years in the human service and disability field. From a career that spans Australia, the USA and Peru, she has extensive experience as a practising psychologist and research expertise in the family, children and disability areas and in the planning, delivery and evaluation of services. She currently holds a dual position as Director of the EPIC early childhood intervention programme and is Senior Lecturer in the Division of Psychology, RMIT University, Melbourne, Australia.

Lesley Gough has worked in the disability field for the past eight years. For the past three years she has been employed as a Disability Case Manager for Melbourne Citymission, Victoria, Australia. She completed a Master's degree in social work by undertaking research looking at the relinquishment of children with disabilities, which is a direct result of her experiences as a case manager and practice concerns around the issue.

Gordon Grant is Research Professor in the Centre for Health and Social Care Research at Sheffield Hallam University, Sheffield, UK. His research interests lie in the identity constructions of vulnerable groups, family caregiving over the life course, and participatory research. He is an editor of the *British Journal of Learning Disabilities*.

Philip Graves is a developmental paediatrician, Head of the Developmental Disabilities Clinic, Monash Medical Centre, Victoria, Australia, and Honorary Senior Lecturer at Monash University Department of Paediatrics.

David Green teaches Social Work at La Trobe University, Melbourne, Australia. He has over 40 years' management and operational experience in a number of human service sectors. He served as Victoria's public advocate, the guardian of last resort, in which role he developed a keen interest in risk and disability.

Colin Hiscoe has been a self-advocate working with people with intellectual disabilities in Australia for a long time. He works for Reinforce, a self-advocacy organisation based in Melbourne, Australia, and has been involved in research projects, education and campaigns that try to make life better for people with intellectual disabilities.

Kelley Johnson is Senior Lecturer at RMIT University, Melbourne, Australia, and is currently a Marie Curie Fellow at the Institute for Intellectual Disability, Trinity College Dublin, Ireland. She has worked as a researcher and an advocate with people with intellectual disabilities for more than 15 years and has written extensively in the field.

Marie Knox is Senior Lecturer and Assistant Director (Teaching and Learning) at Queensland University of Technology, Brisbane, Australia. She is the parent of a young man with a significant disability. Her research interests centre around families, social networks and research paradigms that promote people with disabilities as critical players in the research agenda.

Gary W. LaVigna is Clinical Director of the Institute for Applied Behavior Analysis (IABA) in Los Angeles, USA. He spends much of his time consulting with organisations on establishing non-aversive behaviour support plans for individuals exhibiting severe and challenging behaviour and presenting seminars on the topic throughout the world. His work is reported in numerous articles and books.

Gwynnyth Llewellyn is Dean of the Faculty of Health Sciences, University of Sydney, Sydney, Australia. Her multidisciplinary research team, the Australian Family and Disability Studies Research Collaboration (www.afdsrc.org), focuses on disability concerns for parents, families and their children.

Elizabeth Ozanne is Associate Professor and Head of the School of Social Work at the University of Melbourne, Victoria, Australia, where she is involved in research and teaching in the areas of ageing and disability.

Paul Ramcharan is Lecturer in the Division of Disability Studies at RMIT University, Bundoora, Australia. Paul has spent 17 years researching national policy initiatives in Wales as well as coordinating with Gordon Grant a national research initiative to support the implementation of Valuing People, the national policy for people with intellectual disabilities in England.

Janet Robertson is Lecturer in Health Research at the Institute for Health Research, Lancaster University, Lancaster, UK. She has completed work on a Department of Health funded evaluation of the impact of person-centred planning for people with intellectual disabilities in the UK.

Margaret Spencer is a Registered Nurse and a catholic religious sister and has over 20 years' experience providing community care to individuals and families living in the inner city of Sydney. Margaret has degrees in theology and social work and is undertaking doctoral studies on the topic of assessing the supports needed by parents with intellectual disabilities.

Tim Stainton is a former service broker with the Community Living Society. He is currently an Associate Professor of Disability Policy, Theory and Practice at the University of British Columbia School of Social Work, Vancouver, Canada. He is author of numerous works on disability rights, individualised funding, history, ethics and theory.

David Sykes is the Manager of Policy and Education at the Victorian Office of the Public Advocate in Australia. Before this, David worked as an advocate at the Office of the Public Advocate, coordinated a citizen advocacy programme and worked in the areas of volunteer management and work-care rehabilitation. His doctoral thesis developed a model of advocacy practice for use with people with cognitive disabilities.

Thomas J. Willis is Associate Director of the Institute for Applied Behavior Analysis (IABA) in Los Angeles, USA. With over 25 years' experience as a behavioural consultant and workshop leader, he has co-authored numerous articles on providing person-centred behavioural support to people with severe and challenging behaviour. He is an internationally recognised authority and lecturer in the field.

Introduction: contexts, structures and processes of case management

Christine Bigby, Chris Fyffe and Elizabeth Ozanne

With the shift from institutional to community care in the 1980s, case management or care management became the dominant service delivery mechanism in the UK and Australia for older people and people with disabilities. The aim was to have more responsive services tailored to individualised needs and meeting the neo-liberalist agenda for more efficient and effective service systems.

Since the early experimental UK programmes that demonstrated the effectiveness of this mode of service delivery, case management has, however, lost some of its distinctive characteristics of small caseloads, devolved control over budgets and tight targeting to people with long-term complex needs. Case management now exists in many guises, from models with a more supportive or clinical orientation to those with a more organisational processing and dispositional focus (Stalker and Campbell 2002).

In this book, we have conceptualised case management very broadly as the overarching set of functions in a service system that seeks to organise comprehensive individually tailored packages of support for people with intellectual disabilities. These functions are:

- information collection, assessment, planning and prioritisation of needs
- allocation, development and negotiation of resources
- implementation, monitoring and review of support plans.

The way in which these three sets of functions are assembled, their separation or clustering together, and the locus of decision-making can differ significantly between models. New models are continuously evolving to reflect the shifting goals of policy and the nature of the service systems of which case management is one part.

Although the field of intellectual disabilities has a long tradition of planning for individuals, this usually occurs within the confines of specialist programmes or services. As Robertson and Emerson demonstrate in Chapter 18 of this book, there is a dearth of descriptive or evaluative literature about case management in this field. This is changing, however, as the focus of attention shifts from specialist disability services to planning for inclusion of people with intellectual disabilities across all aspects of their lives, using both formal and informal supports. Two publications have explored these broader issues. Cambridge and Carnaby (2005) examine the connections between person-centred planning and broader care management systems, while Concannon (2005) explores the challenges of involving people with intellectual disabilities in planning their own services. Our book adds to this growing literature seeking to understand how to plan most effectively in concert with people with intellectual disabilities and their families to work across the seams of government (Castellani 1996), to enable access to responsive person-centred support from both mainstream and disability-specific services as well as informal networks of support made up of family, friends and community organisations. Our purpose is not to get caught up in an examination of particular models of case management or tools for planning; rather, it is to contribute to the development of good case management practice by illuminating its complexities, the tensions and dilemmas practitioners must negotiate every day, and the multiple sources of knowledge on which they need to draw in order to do so.

Three key dimensions mediate the outcome of case management for people with intellectual disabilities: the context of the broader social welfare system in which a case management programme is located; the structure of the case management programme; and case management practice – the processes used by practitioners, including the skills and knowledge on which they draw that shape these processes.

Context

Contemporary neo-liberal ideology in Australia and the UK tends to restrict eligibility and conceive of welfare as residual, standing in stark contrast to the rights-based, person-centred ideology of the disability movement. People with intellectual disabilities have few enforceable rights to services that match their needs, and the process of rationing – weighing up individual needs against available resources – compromises the capacity of case managers to deliver on visions of individual choice. The constraints imposed on case management practice by context are illustrated by Mansell and Beadle-Brown (2004, p.5) 'through the introduction of waiting lists, the use of standardised procedures for assessment (prix fixe rather than à la carte), the bureaucratisation of management processes and the reservation of funding decisions to higher-level managers removed from direct contact with service users'. The impact of the broader welfare system was evident in Robertson *et al.*'s (2005) evaluation of person-centred planning, which suggests the need to complement such planning with the removal of structural barriers to achieve inclusion in employment and access to mainstream housing. Green and Sykes in Chapter 3 of this book, and other writers (Beck 1992; Kemshall 2002), draw attention to the 'risk society' as a relatively new context of case management and suggest that increasingly the day-to-day operations of the helping professions and service providers are restricted by imperatives to avoid or manage risk. The intangible risks to the quality of life of people with disabilities are often accorded less weight than more tangible and easily measured risks or those associated with staff occupational health and safety. Practitioners need to be aware of the tensions that arise in their practice from the broader context in which they work if they are to have any chance of negotiating the impact of these at the organisational and individual levels.

Structure

It is important too that case managers have an understanding of the nature of the programme in which they work and the particular issues inherent in its structure and/or organisational base. The model of case management adopted determines the way in which work is structured and operational factors such as administrative requirements, caseloads, staff qualifications and supervision arrangements. Grant and Ramcharan in Chapter 7, for example, illustrate the way in which a purely administrative model can hamper the development of empathic relationships with families and the problems case managers encounter in having no command or control over resources. Increasingly, too, attention is drawn to the potential for case managers' conflicting interests to undermine an individual's self-determination. For example, Stainton in Chapter 5 suggests that if assessment, funding and provision of services are linked directly in an organisation, then a structural incentive is generated for case managers to understand need in line with available services, which leads to service- rather than user-led assessment. New models of case management that separate these functions and place control of budgets in the hands of consumers are suggested as a means to preserve a rights perspective, to avoid such conflicts and to shift power from professionals to people with intellectual disabilities and their families. Although these models, such as direct payments and consumer-directed budgets, may tackle structural tensions for case managers, the transfer of power to consumers may also be illusionary, as it does not solve the problem of demand exceeding supply and the need to ration resources. These models do attempt, however, to make the process more transparent.

Process

The values of self-determination and choice that underpin case management practice with people with intellectual disabilities are common to work with many vulnerable populations. We argue, however, that it is particularly complex to infuse these values into practice with people with intellectual disabilities, who, despite having many strengths, are likely to have complex communication needs, impaired social interaction, limited experience of choice and difficulty making informed decisions for themselves. For example, as LaVigna and Willis illustrate in Chapter 12, a more thorough and comprehensive approach to information collection, assessment and planning is required when people cannot easily articulate their own needs, express their feelings or explain the source of their distress. As Chapters 7 and 11, by Grant and Ramcharan and Spencer and Llewellyn, respectively, exemplify, significantly more time is required to both establish a relationship and devise and use an array of alternative forms of communication with people who have limited expressive or receptive skills. Efforts to obtain information from multiple sources should be a key process in case management with people with intellectual disabilities. A significant challenge is to identify those who know the person well and whose knowledge is partial. Case managers must ensure they draw on all potential sources of knowledge about the person and their social environment in order to ensure all perspectives and possibilities are taken into account in the formulation of plans. Grant and Ramcharan suggest this must include case knowledge, system knowledge, biographic knowledge, communicative knowledge and community knowledge. Important too are sensitivity to and a recognition of the impact of wider social networks in terms of socioeconomic status, ethnicity and culture. Many of the chapters in this book will assist case managers to explore these different sources of knowledge, including the differing ways of understanding the nature of intellectual disabilities, knowledge related to health, communication and the life course.

Reconciling different perspectives is part of the art of assessment and priority-setting. Maintaining a person-centred stance rather than the more expedient one of professional ascendancy is a source of constant tension for case managers who work with people who cannot easily challenge their decisions or judgements and who may have no one else to do so for them. Margaret and Peter Flynn describe in Chapter 9 the long-term and detrimental effects of decision-making that excludes those who know the person well but are located outside the service system. How and by whom decisions are made are central practice questions. For many people with intellectual disabilities, transparent informal mechanisms are required to ensure their rights are upheld and preferences acknowledged. This requires identification and recognition of those who are best able to stand in the person's shoes to make decisions rather than professional judgements about the person's best interests. If conflict exists, and open dialogue and negotiation around differing views fails, then case managers must have the skills to use formal legal frameworks for alternative decision-making.

Relationships with families are a core issue in case management practice with adults with intellectual disabilities and form a thread running through this book. Many adults, whether they live with their parents or elsewhere, remain important members of their families and part of a unique system of reciprocal relationships. Family members may not have legal rights to make decisions on behalf of their adult member with intellectual disabilities. They may not provide hands-on care and yet many care deeply and have a lifelong involvement as staunch allies and advocates. Few other relationships can replace the long-term commitment of parents and siblings in ensuring that the interests of the family member with a disability, rather than the service system, are uppermost in all decisions. The complex task of the case manager is to support and nurture family relationships while identifying and resolving conflicting needs and interests between adults and their families. In Chapter 7, Grant and Ramcharan provide a useful way of tackling this by thinking about the coexistence of intrapersonal, interpersonal and intergroup empowerment.

This book is intended for case management practitioners and human service professionals who, although not labelled as such, are involved in the function of case management. Its primary focus is adults with intellectual disabilities and their families, although Chapter 17 by Gavidia-Payne explores case management issues from the perspective of children and their families. The book grew out of the suggestion of a government department that a manual was required to guide practice and our realisation that the practice of case management with people with intellectual disabilities and their families is too multifaceted and complex to be captured in that way. Rather, we set out to write a book that discussed some of the diverse elements that impact on practice and the unique and complex processes that are needed to retain a person-centred approach in working with people with intellectual disabilities and their families in order to achieve inclusion, choice and participation.

We have retained the nomenclatures used by authors that stem from the context of their writing, and thus some chapters refer to 'case management' while others use 'care management'. Contributors are drawn from Australia, the UK, Canada and the United States of America. The contributors are academics, parents, people with intellectual disabilities, service providers and case managers, reflecting the many different perspectives on case management.

Outline of chapters

Chapter 1 provides the background for other chapters by tracing the origins of case management and its policy context. The original defining characteristics of case management, its conflicting purposes and the way it is conceptualised in this book are set out. This chapter considers some challenges to case management practice and the various ways in which its performance might be critiqued. These issues are examined further by Emerson and Robertson in Chapter 18. The chapter concludes with some ideas about best practice in case management and questions to be resolved in evolving models.

In Chapter 2, Chris Fyffe uses the World Health Organization (WHO) framework (WHO 2001) to draw attention to the different ways in which intellectual disabilities can be understood from a medical, functional and rights perspective. Fyffe argues that although rights should provide the overarching framework, the other perspectives make an important contribution to building a picture of a person's support needs. This chapter establishes a foundation for understanding intellectual disabilities and the subsequent chapters that individually delve further into rights and specialised supports for community living.

The focus of Chapter 3 is the increasing prominence given by both government and non-government organisations to risk management. Green and Sykes argue risk management has become dominant in case management practice and use the Australian Standards risk framework (Standards Australia 2004a,b) to illustrate the way it is impinging. The authors highlight how risk management can pose a threat to people's quality of life by giving priority to risks associated with occupational health and safety, focusing on hazards and worst-case scenarios. They suggest the importance of articulating risk and integrating it into individual planning. Using a series of case vignettes, they illustrate the impact of ill-considered or unbalanced risk management and suggest strategies by which risk can be creatively managed and shared between organisations involved in supporting an individual. The last part of their chapter discusses the need for legal mechanisms if restriction of personal liberty or rights is necessary to manage severe risk. They provide as an example legislation from Victoria, Australia, that provides a legal framework for compulsory detention and treatment for those judged to be a severe risk to themselves or others.

Chapter 4 is a short chapter about the experiences of the contributor, Lesley Gough, as a case manager. Gough illustrates vividly the impact of the broader context of unmet needs and the shortage of long-term accommodation on the adequacy of her case management practice and the trauma this causes to the lives of the children and families with whom she works. She describes how dealing with crisis and finding short-term stopgap measures diverts attention from more proactive preventive work with families and children.

Chapter 5 begins by explaining the fundamental importance of a rights perspective and the impact of programme and organisational structures in upholding rights. Tim Stainton argues that many of the tensions inherent in case management can be dealt with by organisational change, and he provides two examples – one from the UK and the other from Canada – where attempts have been made to implement such reforms.

In Chapter 6, Estelle Fyffe, the chief executive officer of a non-government organisation, explores the importance of organisational relationships for the case manager both within the employing organisation and within external organisations. Fyffe illustrates how organisational culture and practices can support or undermine good practice, and she highlights the challenges of working across organisations and sectors where organisations and case managers may hold very different values and understanding of intellectual disabilities.

In Chapter 7, Gordon Grant and Paul Ramcharan draw on research that examines case managers' experience in putting into practice person-centred practice with families of adults with intellectual disabilities. The authors highlight the interdependence between adults and their families and the invisibility of much care and the difficulties experienced by case managers in understanding family coping mechanisms. They reframe tensions between adults and their families by setting out a model of family empowerment that pays attention to the empowerment of self as well as acknowledging interdependence among family members and the need to empower the family as a group to address wider social change. They conclude by noting the need for practice research and the absence of hard evidence as to how empowerment practice can work effectively, for whom and in what circumstances.

In Chapter 8, Marie Knox, who is both an academic and a parent of a young man with high support needs, describes a common case management model where a worker in an accommodation service doubles as a case manager. Knox demonstrates the role of parents as advocates in case management processes while also illustrating the care required to ensure it is the voice of her son and his views, rather than her own, that dominate. She traces the fine line parents and case managers must tread between upholding a person's right to autonomy by ensuring their wishes and needs are met and that of protecting the individual from poor choices and harm. Importantly, too, she draws attention to the fear of retribution confronted by parents and other allies when they challenge or push a service system that potentially wields much power over the life of the person they seek to represent.

The importance of including families in case management processes is illustrated vividly in Chapter 9, written by Margaret Flynn with her brother Peter. This chapter poignantly describes how failure to recognise the long-term relationships within families that are not defined by daily contact led to disastrous changes for Peter. The assumption that the 'system knows best' pervades the chapter and demonstrates the ease with which biographical knowledge can be lost and the person simply becomes a 'case'. The chapter conveys powerfully the disempowerment and frustration that result for family members when this occurs. It highlights the importance of responsive, accessible checks on professional power and the failure of professionals to challenge poor practice and poor services or remedy errors once made.

Chapter 10 is written by Colin Hiscoe, with Kelley Johnson. The life events that Colin recalls illustrates the lack of power many people with intellectual disabilities have over their lives. Colin tells of his expectations of case managers – that he is respected and listened to and is the priority for a case manager, regardless of what 'the system says'.

Chapter 11 by Margaret Spencer and Gwynnyth Llewellyn proposes a collaborative approach to working with adults with intellectual disabilities, drawn from mainstream theories of family systems, critical reflection and a strengths-based approach. The chapter illustrates the application of this approach to long-term work with a young mother with intellectual disabilities and the iterative dynamic nature of case management practice. The example, drawn from the experience of Spencer, uses discussions between a parent and a case manager to demonstrate the importance of respect and skilled, carefully adapted means of communication to understand the priorities and assumptions of each individual. The chapter also illustrates the role of a case manager in interpreting intellectual disabilities and resourcing mainstream services to foster attitude change and enable them to provide more appropriate adapted support to people with intellectual disabilities.

Chapter 12, by Gary LaVigna and Thomas Willis, although focused on people with mental illness and problematic behaviour, illustrates a comprehensive model of biopsychosocial assessment that covers all possible dimensions of a person's life, sources of knowledge and perspectives. It demonstrates too the development of a plan that seeks to tackle underlying causes of an individual's problems rather than short-term manifestations. The authors elegantly describe the role of positive behaviour support in furthering the participation of people with complex behaviours and mental health issues in community living. Without such assistance, the promise of community living can be unavailable to some people. Some readers may be critical of the professional stance taken by the writers, but careful reading demonstrates clearly the value of such an approach to informing and organising practice to ensure multiple perspectives and sources of information about a person are taken into account. The chapter highlights the value of monitoring and review, functions that are often neglected.

Chapter 13 by Brenda Burgen and Christine Bigby focuses on the non-practical issue of friendships, which are too often neglected in work with young adults and yet are crucial to their self-worth, growth and emotional development. The chapter draws on Burgen's research, which demonstrates that experience of friendships can build skills and highlights the importance of structured activities and segregated environments in creating opportunities for the formation of friendships between young people.

Chapter 14 by Christine Bigby considers a range of issues that stem from the increased life expectancy of people with intellectual disabilities. Issues include making the transition from living with parents, differentiating between middle and old age and dealing with age-associated expectations and stereotypes. The chapter highlights the continuing importance of families as people age and the importance of including siblings, parents and the person themselves in planning for the future. It stresses the importance of an understanding by case managers of likely age-associated change to enable planned adaptations in support and to raise questions about potentially discriminatory service practices regarding retirement and 'ageing in place'.

In Chapter 15, Susan Balandin explains the importance of communication in expressing needs and choices and highlights the high proportion of people with intellectual disabilities whose communication is difficult to understand and who have difficulty understanding verbal and print communication. She demonstrates the extent to which professionals frequently overestimate the capacity of people with intellectual disabilities to understand verbal communication and the potential this has to exclude people from decisions about their lives. The chapter discusses strategies to simplify verbal communication and other options that require alternative or augmentative communication and the importance of committed communication partners. The use of Talking Mats™ is presented as one relatively simple tool to enable the expression of feelings and preferences, although to maximise its potential considerable biographical knowledge of the person is required.

Chapter 16 is written by Philip Graves, a medical practitioner, who sets out the case for the importance of high-quality healthcare for people with intellectual disabilities and argues they must have rights to the same quality of care as the general community, delivered in the same contexts and using the same clinical rules and levels of urgency. The chapter details the reasons why an understanding of the causes of disability is important for people with intellectual disabilities and their families and explains the key medical conditions associated with intellectual disabilities. The final part of the chapter uses four case studies to illustrate the importance of diagnosis, equal access to treatment and the obstacles that can be encountered.

Chapter 17 by Susana Gavidia-Payne is one of the two chapters with a focus on children rather than adults. The author attempts to explain the dominance of a family support versus a case management orientation. The chapter provides a comprehensive critique of case management from the perspective of a family with young children.

Chapter 18, by Janet Robertson and Eric Emerson, discusses the dearth of evaluative literature on case management with people with intellectual disabilities and approaches the analysis by identifying the core functions that come under the rubric of both case management and individualised planning. In presenting a succinct summary of research that has evaluated individualised planning, the authors point to the vital connection required between preparation and implementation and suggest that the real test of the planning process is the impact on an individual's lifestyle and quality of life. The chapter provides a blueprint for the development of quality plans and highlights how few actual plans reflect best practice. The last part of the chapter discusses the authors' evaluation of the person-centred planning initiative in the UK, suggesting that the results indicate that person-centred planning builds on the existing capacity of services rather than representing a radical departure from previous practices. They conclude that person-centred planning has had a positive impact on the life experiences of the 70 per cent of people with intellectual disabilities in the study who had a plan prepared during a 12-month period, noting 30 per cent of people in their study did not have a plan prepared. Positive outcomes were increases in the size of social networks, greater chance of having active contact with family and a member of family in their social network, a higher level of contact with friends, more community-based activities, and increased hours per week of scheduled daily activities. The authors found no apparent impact on some of the stronger measures of social inclusion, however, such as more inclusive social networks and employment.

Significantly, the case managers interviewed for Robertson *et al.*'s study cited tensions stemming from the competing purposes of their work and organisational structures as obstacles to person-centred practice and attempts to find innovative solutions to the problems thrown up by person-centred planning. It is these very tensions, together with the multiple sources of knowledge that can inform practice, that this book seeks to illuminate in order to support case managers to negotiate the complexities of person-centred case management practice.

References

Beck, U. (1992) *Risk Society: Towards a New Modernity.* London: Sage.

Cambridge, P. and Carnaby, S. (eds) (2005) *Person-Centred Planning and Care Management with People with Learning Disabilities.* London: Jessica Kingsley Publishers.

Castellani, P. (1996) 'Closing institutions in New York state.' In J. Mansell and K. Ericsson (eds) *Deinstitutionalization and Community Living: Intellectual Disability Services in Britain, Scandinavia and the USA.* London: Chapman & Hall.

Concannon, L. (2005). *Planning for Life: Involving Adults with Learning Disabilities in Service Planning.* London: Routledge.

Kemshall, H. (2002) *Risk, Social Policy and Welfare.* Philadelphia, PA: Open University Press.

Mansell, J. and Beadle-Brown, J. (2004) 'Person-centred planning or person-centred action? Policy and practice in intellectual disability services.' *Journal of Applied Research in Intellectual Disabilities 17*, 1–9.

Robertson, J., Emerson, E., Hatton, C., Elliott, J., *et al.* (2005) *The Impact of Person-Centred Planning.* Lancaster: Institute for Health Research, Lancaster University.

Stalker, K. and Campbell, I. (2002) *Review of Care Management in Scotland.* Edinburgh: Scottish Executive Central Research Unit.

Standards Australia (2004a) *Australian and New Zealand Standard: Risk Management.* AS/NZS 4360 Risk Management. Sydney: Standards Australia.

Standards Australia (2004b) *Risk Management Guidelines.* AS/NZS 436:2004. Sydney: Standards Australia.

WHO (2001) *International Classification of Functioning, Disability and Health.* Geneva: World Health Organization.

1

Case management with people with intellectual disabilities: purpose, tensions and challenges

Christine Bigby

This chapter provides a background to the later chapters by setting out our understanding of case management. The chapter identifies the origins of case management and its competing purposes. It considers various critiques of case management and suggests that the apparent inability to deliver envisioned outcomes for people with intellectual disabilities may be due to some of case management's inherent tensions, the social context in which it operates and the complexities involved in working with this disadvantaged, socially excluded group. Finally, the chapter highlights some of the key issues that confront case management practitioners that make case management practice with people with intellectual disabilities so complex and demanding. The focus is case management with people with intellectual disabilities and their families, although the chapter draws on both the extensive generic case management and community care literature and the more limited research in this area that focuses specifically on people with intellectual disabilities.

Origins of case management

Many factors influenced the development of case management as a model of service provision, including growth in complexity of services systems, ideological shifts in approaches to welfare, growth of a rights perspective and traditions of individualised planning in intellectual disabilities. These factors are diverse, reflecting different and often contradictory value positions, and they provide some insights into the inherent tensions within case management.

Growth of complexity and ideological shifts in welfare

At the simplest level, the need for case management emerged from the evolving nature of service systems and a growth in size, complexity and fragmentation that made it difficult for people with long-term care needs and multiple disabilities to negotiate access (Austin 1990; Intagliata 1992). Changes to the organisation and delivery of welfare that led to this variable, fragmented approach to service provision and created the need for coordination stemmed from the ideological shifts in the role of government and welfare in Europe and Australia that occurred in the last two decades of the twentieth century, although these shifts were largely presaged by the rapid development of case management systems in the USA in the mid and late 1970s. These shifts also brought to the fore the tension between meeting individual needs and the economic costs involved in doing so. Neo-liberalism aimed to reduce the role of government in welfare, to integrate economic and social criteria and contain costs. Collective commitments to vulnerable populations were reduced and greater emphasis placed on private and community responsibilities, mainly those of individuals and families. Emphasis was placed on choice, individual risk and responsibility and explicit recognition of informal support. The delivery of welfare services was shifted to reflect business principles of efficiency and effectiveness, greater accountability and control of budgets. Mechanisms such as quasi-markets were introduced to separate purchasers from providers, and services were competitively tendered and contracted out to the non-government and private sectors. A managerial approach to the delivery of community services replaced the control and dominance of social work and other human service professions in service delivery (Baldock and Evers 1991; Ife 1997).

Deinstitutionalisation

Allied to neo-liberal reforms in welfare delivery was a shift in the balance of care from institutions to the community. Although it can be argued that deinstitutionalisation was driven by economic imperatives of shifting the cost of care from the state to families, it was also driven by the ideology of normalisation that sought to close inhumane, abusive institutions and achieve a more valued life for people with intellectual disabilities in the least restrictive environment. Institutions were essentially a group-based approach to support for people with intellectual disabilities, across the whole of their lives. Closure of institutions and the values associated with normalisation required that support be provided not only to those affected by closure but also to the larger proportion of people with intellectual disabilities who had always lived in the community. This brought with it greater attention to family support and the coordination of formal and informal sources of support. Like neo-liberalism, but for different reasons, deinstitutionalisation fostered more individualised approaches to people who needed long-term support across different phases of their lives.

A rights perspective

The disability and human rights movements that gained strength in the 1980s emphasised the rights of people with disabilities as citizens, while neo-liberalism focused on their rights as consumers of services. Both, however, emphasised individual choice, autonomy and control over services, although the rights movement also continued to be concerned with collective interests of vulnerable and disadvantaged groups. Although for different reasons, both perspectives contributed towards shifting the balance from professionally defined or mediated needs towards self-defined wants and aspirations, and influenced the development of consumer-driven models adopted by the independent living movement for people with physical disabilities. The rights perspective also emphasised a support model derived from the social model of disability that focused on external support and environmental change to enable participation rather than more traditional individual skills training and preparation based on medical and functional models of disability that previously had dominated the field of intellectual disabilities.

Traditions of individualised planning

The origins of case management are also found in the strong tradition of individualised planning at the micro-service level for children and adults with intellectual disabilities. This type of approach was seen as a key way to meet individual needs in group-based services, such as schools, day centres and institutions. Many schemes were founded on the principles that people with intellectual disabilities and their families should be involved in decisions about their own lives and have a say in setting goals and strategies. For example, Greasely (1995) refers to the gradual shift in the nature of individual planning from service- to user-led, and from a deficit to strengths-based approach. He cites Brechin and Swain's (1987) model of 'shared action planning', which conceptualised planning as a continuous process of discussion, shared experiences, observations and negotiations between individuals, family members and professionals. The model was underpinned by a

> commitment to those people who usually have least opportunity to develop and express their views about what should happen next; people such as parents or unqualified staff, who may be closely involved but lack the power or information to make key decisions; and people with learning difficulties themselves, who may these days be 'consulted' but lack the time or opportunity to develop their ideas properly. (Brechin and Swain 1987, p.viii)

Community care policy reforms

In the UK, case management has been a key part of policy reform and the development of community care for vulnerable populations since the late 1980s. The early experimental programmes in the UK that targeted elderly people demonstrated the viability of case management, both for individuals and the service system, not only facilitating continued community living for older people but also accomplishing this at a lower cost than institutional care, and increasing the efficiency of social care provision (Challis and Davies 1986). The early pilot programmes became part of a huge national experiment after the 1989 White Paper 'Caring for People' mandated the development of case management systems by local authorities delivering community care services (Department of Health 1989). Although termed 'individual planning', the core functions of case management were embedded in the All Wales Strategy for the Development of Services for Mentally Handicapped People in 1983 (Felce et al. 1998). Similarly, in Australia, at the federal level, case management programmes such as Linkages and Community Options formed the backbone of community care reform for people with disabilities and elderly people that grew out of the Home and Community Care Act 1985 (Ozanne et al. 1990). At a state level, case management programmes were central to the implementation of the common state-based Disability Services Acts in the form of programmes such as Options in South Australia and Making a Difference in Victoria.

Distinguishing characteristics of case management

In the early UK experimental models, case management was clearly distinguished from other human service work intervention in several ways. The organisation of support was separated from its provision, and performance of tasks such as assessment and planning were cast as being needs-led and expected to involve both users and carers, rather than service-led and dependent on the availability of formal services. Organisationally, budgets were devolved and case managers had control or at least decision-making authority over available resources, whether funding or access to services. Case managers had small caseloads, freedom to spot purchase resources, highly tuned assessment skills, and good information about local resources. Case managers were expected to span the boundaries of service systems, and programmes were highly targeted and differentiated by a commitment to durable intensive but variable support aimed tightly at people with long-term complex needs that crossed diverse life areas (Challis 1999). Outcomes of these early case management experiments in the UK were better quality of life for older people, prolonged residence at home, reduced dependency on congregate care and lower per-capita costs. But as Stainton points out in Chapter 5 of this book, individuals did not always feel they had a greater degree of control over their own lives (Challis and Davies 1986).

The growth of case management, however, has been characterised by diverse organisational and operational arrangements that has meant many of the key features of earlier models are not always present. The diversity has become so great that Challis (1999) suggests little evidence now exists of a shared definition of case management. There can be little doubt that, at times, case management is used simply as a blanket term for the way in which any individual is processed through a care agency (Rubin 1985; Stalker and Campbell 2002). Various dimensions are used to characterise different types and models of case management (Weiner *et al.* 1992). Challis (1999), for example, distinguishes between generic and intensive models of case management, arguing that the centrality of a differentiated response has been lost, such that in some systems case management has become a generalist response to all potential clients. Generic models are not targeted tightly and tend to be concerned more with service coordination. In contrast, intensive models remain targeted more tightly at individuals with complex needs and take a broader, longer-term, more intensive approach that seeks creatively to build support and to gain access to services. Challis (1999) suggests that the more differentiated models of care management typically are found to be more effective. Using another dimension, the distinction is made between professional/clinical and managerial/administrative models. The former recognises the importance of professional knowledge and judgement, the individual and their unique issues, and the importance of a supportive relationship between the client and case manager; the latter model, on the other hand, is more task-oriented, focusing on the implementation of formal procedures and processes (Challis 1994). Processes for allocating resources and the pattern of clustering case management tasks are also used to distinguish models of case management. Stainton (see Chapter 5), for example, suggests that models that allocate funds directly to individuals and separate planning from resource allocation are more likely to enhance the power of people with intellectual disabilities and their families.

In the field of intellectual disabilities, more attention has been paid to models of individualised planning, such as individual program and educational plans and, more recently, person-centred planning, than to ideas about case management. Cambridge *et al.* (2005), however, use the locus of responsibility for case management to distinguish four types of case management available to people with intellectual disabilities relocated to the community from an institution: (i) provider marginalised, (ii) consolidated mainstream, (iii) diluted mainstream and (iv) fragmented. Although they are specific to the UK context, these models resonate with the situation of people with intellectual disabilities in Australia. The provider-marginalised model excludes residents of group homes from the case management services available to older people and people with disabilities living with their families in the community, and leaves both programme-specific and broader lifestyle planning to their main (usually accommodation) service provider. This model is very common in Australia for residents of shared supported accommodation services provided by government and large multi-programme non-government agencies (see Chapter 8). In consolidated and diluted models, residents are integrated into case management services available to others living in the community, which are hugely variable in organisation and operation and have often lost a professional focus. In the fragmented model, individuals are caught between the community care and health systems, with a lack of any real clarity as to which system takes responsibility for case management functions (Cambridge *et al.* 2005).

Common functions of case management

The purpose of this chapter is not to get caught up in an examination of particular models of case management, as these will vary by jurisdiction and the nature of the system of which they are a part. Rather, the aim of the chapter is to illuminate the challenges that confront frontline practitioners of case management with people with intellectual disabilities and their families. Therefore, case management is conceptualised very broadly as the overarching set of functions undertaken in a service system that seeks to organise comprehensive individually tailored packages of support for people with intellectual disabilities. In the current systems of mixed economies of welfare in the UK and Australia, these functions are:

- information collection, assessment, planning and prioritisation of needs

- allocation, development and negotiation of resources

- implementation, monitoring and review of support plans.

How these three sets of functions are put together depends a great deal on service histories, interagency working and linkages with local communities. Even nomenclatures can vary; for example, a service might be named 'case management', 'service coordination', 'care management', 'support and choice', 'local-area coordination', 'linkages' or 'community options'. Points of difference concern the locus of responsibility for resource allocation, plan implementation and review. For example, in some systems, all functions rest primarily with the case manager, while in others, assessment and planning occur separately from the allocation of resources and plan implementation. The separation or clustering of functions, and the locus of decision-making, affects the balance of power between professionals, the individual and their informal network.

This approach proposes that the varied ways of organising case management functions form a continuum rather than being distinct types of service provision. At one end of the continuum is the traditional professional model, where all the functions are vested in a professional case manager, who, in conjunction with clients and families, formulates and implements plans for support. At the other end of the continuum is a self-directed individualised funding model, whereby the person with intellectual disabilities is allocated a budget based on assessed needs or other formulae. The person and/or their family formulates, implements and manages the plan by purchasing support and services from their individual budget. This continuum is evolving continuously as models of case management are refined and new models adopted. In both the UK and Australia, current developments indicate a shift towards the individualised and self-managed end of the continuum.

Outcomes for individuals

Case management is a service-delivery mechanism and is a means to an end rather than an end in itself (Austin 1990). At its simplest, case management is a process to enable an individual to get the support and services they need in a coordinated, responsive, effective and efficient manner (Intagliata 1992). It is generally part of a broader system of state welfare provision, the capacity of which determines what can be achieved for individuals and their families. From the perspective of the individual, the purpose of case management is 'tailoring services to individual need' (Department of Health 1991), and its functions are the assessment and prioritisation of needs and wants;[1] allocation, development and negotiation of resources from informal and formal support systems; and implementing, monitoring and reviewing support plans over time. Ideally, it is an iterative rather than a linear process and is responsive to changing needs and wants.

Functions may involve tasks such as challenging poor-quality services, developing the capacity of informal support networks, blending formal and informal sources of support, taking proactive and preventive action in order to avoid crises, responding to changing life circumstances and aspirations, building on individual strengths, undertaking advocacy and system change, coordinating support across service areas and different phases of life, and providing a point of access to a complex system of support.

Expectation of what case management will deliver for people with intellectual disabilities is often seen as far-reaching and sometimes confused with broader policy visions. Outcomes can be protecting the rights of people with intellectual disabilities, enabling them to achieve a quality of life in the community that reflects their choices and meets their needs and aspirations. Mansell (personal communication, 2006) sums up the benefits to individuals as individualisation, responsiveness and control over the services they receive. Outcomes for families and/or carers are support to continue caring with increased satisfaction and reduced stress and to enjoy a full and rewarding life outside caregiving.

Case management is one formal mechanism for ensuring people with intellectual disabilities have the long-term support they need to live in the community. Many of its functions may be undertaken competently by family or others in the informal network of the person with intellectual disabilities (Seltzer, Ivry and Litchfield 1992). Conversely, case managers, as paid workers, are not able to replicate many of the functions that informal support plays in people's lives. Case managers cannot have the long-term commitment that characterises close family relationships; nor do they occupy an unfettered position to advocate unequivocally or have the flexibility to take on totally non-routine idiosyncratic tasks that are more likely to characterise informal relationships (Bigby 2000; Litwak 1985). While individual case managers inevitability come and go and confront conflicting responsibilities as employees within organisations, families and other informal network members are typically there for the 'long haul'.

Outcomes for service systems

From a systems perspective, case management is a means to manage intractable policy and practice dilemmas that arise in a mixed economy of care. Case management acts as a mechanism to negotiate the competing social and economic objectives that surface as resource constraints in care services at the micro-level. Case management processes are where social and economic criteria are integrated, and the claims between needs and resources, scarcity and choice are weighed and determined (Cambridge 1999; Challis 1999). Central to case management systems is decision-making about access to and allocation of resources, whether undertaken directly by the case manager or via formal organisational processes. Hence, it plays a significant role in rationing scare resources among those with potential claims on them. In systems that work well, the individual decisions taken within the case management system also inform and influence strategic and population needs planning. Some writers, too, point to the role of case managers, through consultation and education of other sectors, to increase the capacity of the overall system. Core to case management is the aim of increasing the overall efficiency and effectiveness with which resources are used within the system, by ensuring responsiveness to individual need.

Person-centred planning and case management

Whether and where person-centred planning fits into the continuum of a case management described above is subject to debate in both Australia and the UK (Cambridge and Carnaby 2005; Robertson et al. 2005). The relationship between person-centred planning and case management was not articulated well in the UK White Paper 'Valuing People', which mandated the centrality of the former in support for people with intellectual disabilities (Department of Health 2001) or in its subsequent implementation (Robertson et al. 2005). It appears, however, that person-centred planning was not intended to replace or be a form of case management.

Person-centred planning may be focused only on the day-to-day micro-experiences of a person's life rather than comprehensively across all aspects.

Person-centred planning generally is not linked to any mechanisms for the allocation of formal resources that are a central component of case management. Cambridge and Carnaby (2005) suggest various juxtapositions between the two, preferring a model whereby person-centred planning is incorporated into case management as an additional strand of the information-gathering and assessment process that adds to the understanding of the perspectives of the person with a disability and their family and potential sources of support. This appears to be the position of some who argue that person-centred planning is not a new paradigm of practice but, rather, adds to the multiple perspectives necessary to understand and support people with intellectual disabilities by focusing attention on their gifts and capacities and both the informal and formal support necessary to enable these to be expressed (O'Brien, O'Brien and Mount 1997). Commentators such as O'Brien (2004) also suggest that person-centred planning is, in many ways, the antithesis of case management, as it is centred on informal circles of support and cannot therefore be systematised as a part of formal service systems.

The absence of a mechanism that ties resources to a plan is one element that distinguishes person-centred planning from case management. The centrality of 'person-centredness', which is not prominent in all models of case management, is the other element. Brewster and Ramcharan (2005, p.491) suggest, 'the idea of being "person-centred" has a warm ring to it'. Although person-centredness is variously defined, Brewster and Ramcharan suggest its essence is placing the person, rather than professionals, at the centre of all processes and placing the person, their advocates and supporters in control rather than professionals, understanding and acting on what is important to the person, acting in alliance with their family and friends, taking into account their gifts and capacities to judge the supports they need, and drawing on informal shared commitments and formal services to realise plans. Although such an approach has underpinned the practice of many case managers, person-centredness has not been a defining feature of all case management models or practice.

Critiques of case management

Case management has been the subject of considerable criticism from the perspectives of practitioners, families, advocacy groups and architects of various models. Although most of the issues can be traced to the inherent tension in case management itself, critiques fall into three broad areas: resourcing, design and implementation.

Resource issues

Perhaps most commonly identified is the failure of case management to deliver expected outcomes: services are either not available or those that are accessed are not individualised but merely reflective of restricted supply (Parry-Jones and Soulsby 2001; Spall, McDonald and Zetlin 2005). Such poor outcomes are thought to stem from the quantum of resources available or the limited control or influence that case managers exercise over resources. Limited purchasing power means that case managers cannot always develop individual contracts with services but must rely on block purchases made elsewhere. In some systems, a case manager's influence over access to services is limited by the separation of case management from the service purchasing function, quality control or regulatory systems (Cambridge *et al.* 2005). Placing too much reliance on the sum of individual case management decisions alone to drive the development of innovative services that can respond to demand, however, has also be criticised as problematic. For example, Felce (2004) suggests the importance of population-based service planning utilising identifiable targets to complement the influence of individual decisions over what is available.

Design of case management systems

Many of the criticisms of case management and its inability to deliver outcomes relate not only to limited resources but also to the design of the case management system and its relationship with health and community services systems. Poorly targeted case management systems are seen as responsible for spreading resources too thinly and pushing systems towards short-term crisis work. In Victoria, Australia, for example, the Disability Clients Services case management system is criticised as being too episodic, with the absence of meaningful monitoring and review functions. This makes the system reactive to crisis rather than having the long-term capacity to respond proactively to changing needs and circumstances (Auditor General 2000; Bigby and Pollet 2001). Lack of role clarity, an unduly narrow focus on the intellectual disabilities sector and poorly defined relationships with other sectors can obstruct access to wider health and welfare services. For example, in Victoria, Australia, practitioners considered that the case management system lacked clearly defined relationships with other sectors, such as child and family welfare, child protection, health, mental health, criminal justice, housing and education (Bigby and Pollet 2001), leading not only to difficulties in leveraging resources from other sectors but also to coordination problems. One complicating component of this was the absence of a single point of access and coordination for individuals across all these sectors.

Some commentators criticise case management for being too professionalised, while others consider that it has become too managerial and proceduralised. For example, Rothman's (1994) model of case management with vulnerable populations takes for granted its underpinning by professional social work, while Cambridge *et al.* (2005) pose questions about the non-professional skills base of UK care management and its unclear connection to the social work profession.

In some systems, concern is expressed about administrative and bureaucratic requirements that redirect priorities and interfere with the achievement of client outcomes. Poorly designed managerial tools such as performance indicators lead to means, such as the preparation of a case plan, becoming an end in themselves. For example, the indicator may be the number of cases opened or closed or the number of plans prepared, meaning that a count of these may take priority over implementation and client-oriented outcomes (Bigby and Pollet 2001).

Process and implementation issues

Failure to achieve system-wide implementation of case management programmes has been a recurrent issue in the literature. For example, in Wales, individual planning at best covered only 33 per cent of the potential population (Felce *et al.* 1998). Allied to this is a commonly low level of plan implementation and a stance that regards plans only as exercises on paper rather than working documents that inform the delivery and coordination of services and support. Plans have also been criticised as having poorly constructed goals that cannot be measured or having goals that are easily achieved but more akin to strategies (Mansell and Beadle-Brown 2004b) – for example, goals such as putting a person's name on a waiting list, which are achievable but do not meet relevant or important personal needs. Plans are also criticised for placing too much emphasis on deficits, being framed by a skill development rather than a citizenship/rights approach. They may be dominated by particular points of view, be these of professionals or families, rather than those of the person concerned (Williams and Robinson 2000). Questions have also been raised as to whether plans should be aspirational or realistic, as this may determine the extent to which plans can be implemented.

As explored further by Emerson and Robertson in Chapter 18, compared with the fields of ageing and mental health, few evaluative or research projects have examined the nature of case management models and practice with people with intellectual disabilities. Much of the work in this area falls into the grey, unpublished, often inaccessible literature comprised of internal and confidential service reviews (Bigby and Pollet 2001; Jackson *et al.* 1998).

Current context and challenges

Case management systems do not stand alone but operate in conjunction with the wider community care system and other health and welfare systems. The context of the case management that Emerson and Stancliffe (2004) refer to as 'system architecture' includes elements such as the nature of health and community care budgets, the constellation of available services and service infrastructure such as core funding mechanisms, pre-service education and training for human service workers, the regulatory regime and the consumer rights framework. All of these components influence outcomes from case management.

The tensions found in the origins and purposes of case management are added to by the current community care context in which it operates and the characteristics of the population of people with intellectual disabilities with whom case managers work. In both the UK and Australia, forward-looking visions about equality, rights and inclusion in society for people with intellectual disabilities are embedded firmly in legislation and policy. These are supported insufficiently, however, by resources for implementation and prevailing cultural mores. In these countries, apart from income-support payments, people with intellectual disabilities and their families have no enforceable rights to services, support or funds to meet their additional disability-related needs. Demand from those eligible outweighs the supply of discretionary resources. Demand management is left to the service system, this often being case managers. Demand is fuelled by demographic changes, such as increased life expectancy, the impact of medical technologies and the emergence of new disability groups, such as people with acquired brain injury (Australian Institute of Health and Welfare 1996, 2002; Emerson *et al.* 2001; Felce 2004). For example, Stancliffe (2002) notes the significant underprovision of residential support services for people with intellectual disabilities in Australia compared with the UK and the USA and illustrates the problem further by pointing out that these two countries fall far short of meeting demand, such that expenditure would have to increase by 27 per cent and 19 per cent, respectively, in order to meet known demand. The Auditor General (2000) concluded that despite Victoria, Australia, having the highest per-capita expenditure on disability services in Australia, residential service provision alone would have to expand by 19 per cent in order to meet the needs of those currently on waiting lists. As these figures suggest, resource allocation is plagued continuously by competition between preventive, proactive and crisis approaches. Similarly, in the climate of privatised risks, the rights of people with intellectual disabilities to choice or support may be compromised by the perceived risks to providers of litigation for negligence and regimes imposed by occupational health and safety insurance and legislation (Sykes 2005).

The thrust towards inclusion and participation of people with intellectual disabilities is occurring in an increasingly individualistic society, built on consumer interests rather than social solidarity. Indicative of this are concerns with social capital and the rediscovered need for community development to combat social exclusion (Bryson and Mowbray 2005). The prominence of individual needs and choice has overshadowed the visibility of collective needs and issues shared by all members of a particular group.

A generic approach to disability policy and programmes that is dedifferentiated and no longer uses diagnosis to inform policy and service delivery is being adopted in Australia and the UK. As Fyffe notes in Chapter 2, this creates obstacles to the recognition and acquisition of specialist knowledge about people with intellectual disabilities and implementation of the often differentiated strategies necessary to enable communities and services to adapt to people who are different (Bigby and Ozanne 2001; Mansell and Beadle-Brown 2004b).

Despite significant reform of community care policy over the past two decades towards individualised funding models in both Australia and the UK, the bulk of intellectual disability resources are still tied to services. The dominance of block-funded day and residential services leaves little scope to resource alternative creative supports for individuals.

Working with people with intellectual disabilities presents complex challenges to case managers, particularly in hearing the voice of the person with intellectual disabilities and ensuring that assessment and planning are person-centred rather than simply professional- or family-dominated. Mansell and Beadle-Brown (2004a), for example, draw attention to characteristics such as complex communication needs, impaired social interaction, and limited experience of choice- and decision-making among people with intellectual disabilities. Accommodating these requirements demands a lot from care managers in terms of time, commitment and skill. It also raises important ethical issues about the determination of a person's 'best interest' when the person cannot make informed decisions for themselves. Mansell and Beadle-Brown (2004a) point, too, to the small social networks of people with intellectual disabilities, many of whom are not known well by anyone, which adds considerably to the challenges of achieving social inclusion. As a UK national survey illustrates (Emerson et al. 2005), people with intellectual disabilities are one of the most socially and economically disadvantaged and excluded groups in society. Many individuals have no avenues other than statutory health and welfare services to meet their needs (Saunders 2005).

Conclusion

The competing purposes of case management, the challenges of its social context and the complexity of working with people with intellectual disabilities create many challenges for case management practice. Central to these are the ways in which the tensions that result from competing perspectives, needs, views and interests are explored and weighed, and how judgements are made about what should take priority in order to achieve person-centred ends. For example:

- How can personal, familial and professional perspectives be accommodated within decision-making in case management in an accountable way?

- How is mental incapacity incorporated within case management to ensure the protection of a person's best interests?

- Can attention to strengths also take account of deficits and the need for skill development?

- Can a person's wishes and dreams be achieved with limited resources?

- How can individuals and families be empowered through care management experiences?

- What is the role of independent advocacy, and how can its absence be compensated?

- How can individual planning drive strategic planning?

- How can meaningful links be maintained between case management, strategic planning and benchmarking?

The challenge of case management in this field and the outcomes sought are captured well by Mansell and Beadle-Brown (2004a), who suggest that helping people with intellectual disabilities requires

> a sustained commitment and engagement with them as individuals to find out what it is they need and want, and to work with them at the difficult complex process of putting it into place… [T]his should be done a in a way which sustains and, if possible, extends family and community ties rather than just relying on public services… [T]his is a process of discovery and

iteration as people grow and develop. (Mansell and Beadle-Brown 2004a, p.33)

Those few studies that have considered good practice in this field point to elements underpinning good case management as being:

- integration of a range of knowledge and perspectives
- a strong value base from which to represent the person and their interests
- formation and maintenance of empathic relationships
- recognition of the social rather than individualised nature of people's lives
- recognition of the reciprocities and interdependence of everyday lives and the need to build and work with alliances (Bigby and Pollet 2001, 2002; Cambridge 1999; Cambridge *et al.* 2005; Grant *et al.* 2004a,b).

Case management systems that foster these ways of working are considered to be those that are targeted with the capacity for continuity of involvement of variable intensity over time, with small caseloads, that have the capacity to draw on independent advocacy. Both Challis (1999) and Cambridge *et al.* (2005) suggest that the coherence of the case management system is the most important element in its design, the logic of relationships between its parts and its fit with the wider system of managing resources and building service infrastructure and capacity. The aim of this book is to explore the knowledge, skills and approaches that will support good case management practice with people with intellectual disabilities and their families.

References

Auditor General (2000) *Services for People with an Intellectual Disability.* Melbourne: Government Printer.

Austin, C. (1990) 'Case management: myths and realities.' *Families in Society 71*, 398–405.

Australian Institute of Health and Welfare (1996) *Commonwealth State Disability Agreement Evaluation: The Demand Study.* Supporting paper no. 2. Canberra: Australian Institute of Health and Welfare.

Australian Institute of Health and Welfare (2002) *Unmet Need for Disability Services: Effectiveness of Funding and Remaining Shortfalls.* Canberra: Australian Institute of Health and Welfare.

Baldock, J. and Evers, A. (1991) 'Innovations and care of the elderly: the front line of change for social welfare services.' *Ageing International xv111/1*, 8–21.

Bigby, C. (2000) *Moving on Without Parents: Planning, Transitions and Sources of Support for Middle-Aged and Older Adults with Intellectual Disability.* Sydney: Maclennan and Petty.

Bigby, C. and Ozanne, E. (2001) 'Shifts in the model of service delivery in intellectual disability in Victoria.' *Journal of Intellectual and Developmental Disability 26*, 205–18.

Bigby, C. and Pollet, J. (2001) *Redevelopment of a Case Management Framework for Disability Services. Phase 1. Report. Review of the Current Disability Client Service Case Management Model.* Melbourne: Department of Human Services.

Bigby, C. and Pollet, J. (2002) *Redevelopment of the Case Management Framework for Disability Services. Phase 2. Report. A Framework for Individualised Planning and Support Coordination.* Melbourne: Department of Human Services.

Brechin, A. and Swain, J. (1987) *Changing Relationships: Shared Action Planning with People with a Mental Handicap.* London: Harper & Row.

Brewster, J. and Ramcharan, P (2005) 'Enabling and Supporting Person-Centred Approaches.' In G. Grant, P. Goward, M. Richardson and P. Ramcharan (eds) *Learning Disability: A Lifecycle Approach to Valuing People.* Maidenhead: Open University Press.

Bryson, L. and Mowbray, M. (2005) 'Community, social capital and evidenced based policy.' *Australian Journal of Social Issues 40*, 91–106.

Cambridge, P. (1999) 'Building care management competence in services for people with learning disabilities.' *British Journal of Social Work 29*, 393–415.

Cambridge, P. and Carnaby, S. (eds) (2005) *Person-Centred Planning and Care Management with People with Learning Disabilities.* London: Jessica Kingsley Publishers.

Cambridge, P., Carpenter, J., Forrester-Jones, R., Tate, A., *et al.* (2005) 'The state of care management in learning disability and mental health services 12 years into community care.' *British Journal of Social Work 36*, 1039–62.

Challis, D. (1994) 'Case Management: A Review of UK Developments and Issues.' In M. Titterton (ed.) *Caring for People in the Community: The New Welfare.* London: Jessica Kingsley Publishers.

Challis, D. (1999) 'Assessment and Care Management: Developments Since the Community Care Reforms.' In M. Henwood and G. Wistow (eds) *Evaluating the Impact of Caring for People. With Respect to Old Age: Long Term Care – Rights and Responsibilities, Community Care and Informal Care Research.* Leeds: Nuffield Institute for Health, University of Leeds.

Challis, D. and Davies, B. (1986) *Case Management in Community Care.* Aldershot: Gower.

Department of Health (1989) *Caring for People.* London: HMSO.

Department of Health (1991) *Care Management and Assessment: Managers Guide.* London: HMSO.

Department of Health (2001) *Valuing People: A New Strategy for Learning Disability for the 21st Century.* London: The Stationery Office.

Emerson, E. and Stancliffe, R. (2004) 'Planning and action: comments on Mansell and Beadle-Brown.' *Journal of Applied Research in Intellectual Disabilities 17*, 23–6.

Emerson, E., Hatton, C., Felce, D. and Murphy, G. (2001) *Learning Disabilities: The Fundamental Facts.* London: Foundation for People with Learning Disabilities.

Emerson, E., Malam, S., Davies, I. and Spencer, K. (2005). *Adults with Learning Disabilities in England, 2003–04.* London: Health and Social Care Information Centre.

Felce, D. (2004) 'Can person-centred planning fulfil a strategic planning role? Comments on Mansell and Beadle-Brown.' *Journal of Applied Research in Intellectual Disabilities 17*, 27–31.

Felce, D., Grant, G., Todd, S., Ramcharan, P., *et al.* (1998) *Towards a Full Life: Researching Policy Innovation for People with Learning Disabilities.* Oxford: Butterworth Heinemann.

Grant, G., Ramcharan, P. and Flynn, M. (2004a) 'Development of person-centred support for people with learning disabilities: retrospect and prospect. Part 1: the literature.' Unpublished manuscript. Sheffield: University of Sheffield.

Grant, G., Ramcharan, P. and Flynn, M. (2004b) 'Development of person-centred support for people with learning disabilities: retrospect and prospect. Part 2: early practitioner experiences.' Unpublished manuscript. Sheffield: University of Sheffield.

Greasely, P. (1995) 'Individual planning with adults who have learning difficulties: key issues – key sources.' *Disability and Society 10*, 353–63.

Ife, J. (1997) *Rethinking Social Work*. Melbourne: Longman.

Intagliata, J. (1992) 'Improving the Quality of Community Care for the Chronically Mentally Disabled: The Role of Case Management.' In S. Rose (ed.) *Case Management and Social Work Practice*. White Plains, NY: Longman.

Jackson, A., Ozanne, E., Bigby, C. and King, C. (1998) *Patterns of Case Management Utilisation in Disability Services*. Melbourne: Department of Human Services.

Litwak, E. (1985) *Helping the Elderly*. New York: The Guilford Press.

Mansell, J. and Beadle-Brown, J. (2004a) 'Person-centred planning or person-centred action? Policy and practice in intellectual disability services.' *Journal of Applied Research in Intellectual Disabilities 17*, 1–9.

Mansell, J. and Beadle-Brown, J. (2004b) 'Person-centred planning or person-centred action? A response to the commentaries.' *Journal of Applied Research in Intellectual Disabilities 17*, 31–6.

O'Brien, J. (2004) 'If person-centred planning did not exist, valuing people would require its invention.' *Journal of Applied Research in Intellectual Disabilities 17*, 11–16.

O'Brien, J., O'Brien, L. and Mount, P. (1997) 'Person-centred planning has arrived…or has it?' *Mental Retardation 35*, 480–88.

Ozanne, E., Howe, A. and Selby-Smith, C. (eds) (1990) *Community Care Policy and Practice: New Directions in Australia*. Melbourne: Faculty of Economics and Politics, Monash University.

Parry-Jones, B. and Soulsby, J. (2001) 'Needs led assessment: the challenge and the reality.' *Health and Social Care in the Community 9*, 414–28.

Robertson, J., Emerson, E., Hatton, C., Elliott, J., *et al.* (2005) *The Impact of Person-Centred Planning*. Lancaster: Institute for Health Research, Lancaster University.

Rothman, J. (1994) *Practice with Highly Vulnerable Clients: Case Management and Community-Based Service*. Englewood Cliffs, NJ: Prentice Hall.

Rubin, A. (1985) 'Case Management.' In National Association of Social Workers (ed.) *Encyclopedia of Social Work*, 18th edn, Vol. 1. Silver Spring, MD: National Association of Social Workers.

Saunders, P. (2005). *Disability, Poverty and Living Standards: Reviewing Australian Evidence and Policies*. Sydney: Sydney Social Policy Research Centre, University of New South Wales.

Seltzer, M., Ivry, J. and Litchfield, L. (1992) 'Family Members as Case Managers: Partnerships between Formal and Informal Support Networks.' In S. Rose (ed.) *Case Management and Social Work Practice*. New York: Longman.

Spall, P., McDonald, C. and Zetlin, D. (2005) 'Fixing the system? The experiences of service users of quasi-market in disability services in Australia.' *Health and Social Care in the Community 13*, 56–63.

Stalker, K. and Campbell, I. (2002) *Review of Care Management in Scotland*. Edinburgh: Scottish Executive Central Research Unit.

Stancliffe, R. (2002) 'Provision of residential services for people with intellectual disability in Australia: an international comparison.' *Journal of Intellectual and Developmental Disability* 27, 117–24.

Sykes, D. (2005) 'Risk and rights: the need to redress the imbalance.' *Journal of Intellectual and Developmental Disabilities* 30, 185–8.

Weiner, K., Stewart, K., Hughes, J., Challis, D. and Darton, R. (1992) 'Care management arrangements for older people in England: key areas of variation in a national study.' *Ageing and Society 22*, 419–39.

Williams V. and Robinson C. (2000) '"Tick this, tick that": the views of people with learning disabilities on their assessments.' *Journal of Learning Disabilities 4*, 293–305.

2

Understanding intellectual disabilities

Chris Fyffe

The opportunity to support people with intellectual disabilities to live the lifestyle of their choosing underpins the personal motivation of many case managers. Although at first glance this intent is seemingly straightforward, the environment in which case managers operate demands consideration of multiple perspectives and fulfilment of often conflicting roles. These demands make the task of promoting personal empowerment more complex than simply responding to the preferences of an individual with intellectual disabilities. For example, as well as commitment to the people they are supporting, case managers have organisational responsibilities as decision-makers about resource allocation, classifiers of need and priority-setters that may reflect different priorities or perspectives from those underlying the client relationship. In addition, the very nature, if not the existence, of a paid professional–client relationship establishes an inequality of power that is arguably inconsistent with notions of client empowerment (Ife 1997) or person-centred practice (Kincaid 1996).

This chapter argues that many of the pressures faced by case managers in their daily work stem from the different understandings of the nature of intellectual disability embedded in policies and models of support that inform decisions at many levels. Such differences are implicit in the perspectives of the individuals involved in a person's life and generate conflicting prescriptions for action. Exposing and understanding the perspectives that underpin the views of others enables case managers to enter into dialogue that leads to better representation and support for people with intellectual disabilities. Adoption of a multifaceted approach to understanding intellectual disabilities can compensate for the inherent weaknesses of each perspective. This chapter explores these different perspectives, all of which can contribute to everyday case management practice. By describing these perspectives in detail, the chapter aims to enable case managers to recognise and draw on the strengths of each. Too often, theoretical and practice-based change is perceived as linear, with the new replacing the old. This chapter aims to exemplify the coexistence of three perspectives for understanding intellectual disabilities, each of which has its origin at a different point of history.

The World Health Organization model of disability

Successive definitions of disability have emphasised the relationship between individual functioning and supports, with increasing recognition of the importance of context, individual strengths and development (AAMR 2002). The broader World Health Organization (WHO) framework of functioning, disability and health brings together three key perspectives that are often considered independently (WHO 2001). 'Disability' is described as involving marked and severe problems of functioning stemming from capacity, ability and/or opportunity to function. Its three main elements are:

- 'capacity to function', which has its origins in body function and structure and the impairment of these as the basis for understanding limitations

- 'ability to function', which relates to limitations of activity or difficulties in executing tasks or actions that stem from impaired capacity

- 'opportunity to function or participate', which considers restrictions on community and economic participation that stem from the impact of broader social forces and the availability or accessibility of resources, adaptations and supports.

These different ways of thinking about functioning stem from a central focus on the body, or the individual or the society, while acknowledging they are mediated by personal, psychological, physiological, environmental and health factors such as history, gender, age and lifestyle (WHO 2001). The WHO model provides a useful framework for further specific exploration of issues and ideas because it acknowledges the coexistence and contributions from all of these elements.

Although the model is ordered conceptually, in practice different perspectives about disability are generally hidden and have a differential impact. This chapter explores the implications for the role of case managers working with people with intellectual disabilities when these different perspectives are adopted. It seeks to highlight that other people in a person's life, policies and services may rely on only one perspective, while others may apply various understandings more flexibly. The stance taken can mean that very different decisions are made with and/or on behalf of an individual with an intellectual disability. The goal for case managers must be to consider and draw on the strengths that each perspective has to offer for any given individual.

Capacity of the body: the 'medical model'

Description

A focus on capacity to function emphasises impairment in physiological and psychological body functions and anatomical or biological structures. Impairments include any significant deviation, deficit or loss of bodily function or structure. This perspective concentrates on diagnosis and description of the characteristics of people with intellectual disabilities, such as measures of IQ, genetic makeup and associated health-related conditions. Intervention or treatment is from a medical perspective, with outcomes focused on health and illness.

From this perspective, people with intellectual disabilities are understood and grouped in terms of impairments of body functions and biological structures. The individual is deemed to be incompetent, impaired or deficient when assessed against various measures of physical or biological normality. Understanding of individual deficits in capacity is based on a generalised understanding of the group and specific subgroups of people with intellectual disabilities to which they belong. For example, a diagnosis of Down syndrome, or a psychometric assessment of IQ less than 60, is sufficient according to this approach to reach conclusions about the individual, their (limited) potential and their group membership. The impairment is a diagnosed medical condition for which there is no 'cure'. The response offers a description of limitations and impairments and consideration of how to best provide care, as distinct from how growth and development might be achieved. This perspective has, most typically, been represented as the medical model of disability (e.g. Fulcher 1989) and has historically shaped services for people with intellectual disabilities.

Strengths

Although this perspective was rejected as a dominant paradigm for understanding intellectual disabilities in the 1970s, an emphasis on the body and its biological functioning remains an important contribution in understanding the needs of the person with intellectual disabilities. The medical model illuminates the medical and health characteristics associated with intellectual disabilities, alerts the individual, family members and workers to the possibility of such conditions and their treatment, and identifies group-based health-related needs that are relevant for service planning, staff training and individual support plans. For example, it is important for case managers and service planners to know that fragile X syndrome is inherited and that genetic counselling may be appropriate for family members, and that the life expectancy of people with Down syndrome is increasing but such people have an increased incidence of early-onset dementia.

The medical model remains the basis for service eligibility and targeted service development. An individual qualifies for services and support on the basis of diagnosed or assessed incapacities or differences compared with people in the general population who do not require such support. Hence, a diagnosis of intellectual disability is often the entry point to agencies specialising in supporting people with specific disability types and as a basis for budget allocations. The medical model may be critical for the individual, as many other lifestyle issues depend on the understanding and attention to factors affecting health and wellbeing. Such considerations should not be sidelined.

Weaknesses

A drawback of the application of the 'medical model' to people with intellectual disabilities is the assumed differences between those with a specific diagnosis or impairment and the general population and the assumed similarities among people with a specific diagnosis or impairment. Global assumptions such as these often mean that individual differences, aspirations and circumstances are not considered relevant and little attention is paid to the voice of the individual with intellectual disabilities.

This view dominated service design at the beginning of the twentieth century, when people with intellectual disabilities were diagnosed, deemed incurable and recommended for 'care' in segregated and congregated living arrangements. As a consequence of their diagnosis, all people with intellectual disabilities were assumed unable to manage in the general community because of their difference. Their incapacity to function provided the rationale for services based on isolation and protection from typical human experience and lifestyles.

There was no individualised service response within a medical worldview, as intellectual disabilities could not be cured. Care and protection were the only option.

Discussion

Global assumptions about the nature of a person based on their membership of a particular group that shares common biological, medical or psychometric characteristics is unsustainable as a starting point for understanding and supporting an individual who happens to have an intellectual disability. The restricted usefulness of the medical model on its own becomes evident when the myriad differences between people with similar impairments or medical conditions are recognised. For example, although two people with trisomy 21 (Down syndrome) have additional chromosomal material (impairment of body structures), differences exist between them in their ability to function in day-to-day life and their interests, preferences and preferred ways of learning. Even more dramatic are the differences between two people with the same IQ. For example, one person with an IQ of 55 may be very talkative about day-to-day events and require lots of assistance with personal care; another person with the same IQ may be particularly interested in numbers and enjoy completing daily set routines independently. Nevertheless, although reliance on the diagnosis of impairment alone is very limiting, it is not completely irrelevant. The medical model, however, does not deserve the total rejection that has been common in recent years. The poor health profile of many people with intellectual disabilities attests to the need for accurate health diagnosis. Positive examples exploring this perspective for conditions associated with intellectual disabilities are given in Table 2.1.

Ability of the individual to function in the environment

Description

Intellectual disabilities involve all aspects of development, including learning and memory; physical, sensory, social and behavioural development; and speech and language. The implications are different for different people. This functional perspective focuses on the ability of the individual to undertake and be part of everyday situations and considers how best to support people in carrying out everyday tasks. A central assumption is that difficulties can be compensated for, sidestepped or overcome by appropriate intervention such as aids, environmental adaptations, educational strategies and an emphasis on the individual's strengths and abilities. For example, cooking can be taught in small steps using pictorial

Table 2.1 Contemporary examples of the application of the capacity to function perspective

The examples here emphasise health-related issues pertaining to diagnosis and medical treatment

Diagnostic issues	Health related issues
• Describing a behavioural phenotype for Rett syndrome	• Treating reccurent respiratory tract infections in people with Down syndrome
• Diagnosing personality disorders in people with intellectual disability	• Researching osteoporosis in women with Down syndrome
• Identifying bipolar disorders in people with intellectual disability	• Treating oesophageal obstruction in man with pica and Lennox Gastaut syndrome
• Observing compulsive behaviour and tantrums in children with Prader–Willi syndrome	• Identifying and treating risk factors for low mineral bone density of residents in an intellectual disability facility
• Recording different presentations of late-detected phenylketonuria in two brothers	

cookbooks, or the task may be understood differently by the use of preprepared meals and a microwave oven. Essentially, however the task is approached, the outcome for the individual is the same – in this case, competence in preparing meals. This perspective was first characterised as the 'getting ready model', where skill attainment has been the basis for people with an intellectual disability being 'allowed' to commence non-segregated opportunities.

This functional model recognises that people with intellectual disabilities, despite the absence of a medical 'cure' – except when they are unwell – can learn and develop. The importance of understanding what and how people with intellectual disabilities can learn led, in the 1970s, to the creation of special learning technologies and environments designed to maximise development. As a result, best practice was perceived to be in the special settings where superior competence could be demonstrated. Typical community settings that were less structured and predictable could not reproduce the possibilities for personal skill and behavioural achievement offered by these controlled and special settings.

From this perspective, service provision relies on expert, professional and technical decisions about eligibility and diagnosis; specialist environments that traditionally have been well separated from a typical life in the community; and professional judgements from therapists, educators and psychologists about the extent and type of support, including assessed 'readiness' to move to less restrictive or less isolated options and opportunities. Examples include judgement about the readiness of people working in a sheltered workshop for open employment, and the readiness of children attending a special school or early-intervention programme for regular school or preschool experiences. The assumption is that the way in which an individual manages in the special setting is a predictor of how they will manage in a more typical or mainstream situation. This may be the legitimate basis for short-term rehabilitation programmes where people are recovering from accidents and illness, but it has dangers for people with intellectual disabilities who risk never being judged 'ready' for community life.

Strengths

Attention to maximising each individual's ability to function, rather than the assumed limitations that arise from a global diagnosis about capacity, brought with it recognition that people of all abilities can learn and develop and that this may occur in different ways. Various professional disciplines can make contributions to improving a person's life experience through interventions that increase independence, competence and coping and minimise limitations of learning, memory, behaviour, communication, social development and mobility that may arise from intellectual disabilities. This approach also recognises the importance of minimising secondary handicaps. Secondary handicaps are additional disabilities that can develop because the person is supported poorly; for example, a person with an intellectual disability who is not involved in typical daily social experiences will exhibit even more marked difficulty with meeting new people or making choices, as a consequence of the social isolation, combined with a slow rate of learning about social relationships; likewise, a person with cerebral palsy may develop permanently reduced joint flexibility because of limited opportunities to move around and a lack of physiotherapy. Specialist information is needed to train staff and as a source of information for individuals and families.

More recently, it has been recognised that there is no reason why interventions of this nature should be restricted to specialist or separate environments. They can occur in the settings and processes of everyday life. The recognition that various specialists have a role in promoting community living has been slow, however.

Weaknesses

The focus of the functional model is on the individual's lack of ability and the role of experts in enhancing that ability and making judgements about appropriateness for life in the community. Initially, support was understood along a continuum of settings, and failure to make the transition from special to community settings was often understood as a failure of the individual rather than of the surrounding support systems. The transition from segregated settings to community living was described in terms of readiness or ability – defining, measuring and promoting the core skills that a person needed to 'make it'. The effect has been that some people with intellectual disabilities remain isolated from the community as they are deemed unable to function and are never judged to be ready to integrate or are returned to isolated settings because of judged failures of community placements. This remains most common for people with high behavioural or medical support needs. From this perspective, there is no right to be part of the community, irrespective of ability or capacity – transition and access are earned by the individual, monitored by experts and deemed inappropriate for some.

An implicit and underlying assumption of the functional perspective is that people with intellectual disabilities should be 'like everyone else' before they can be part of their local communities. Controlled development in isolation from other community members was judged to be more relevant than everyday life experiences. For example, an adult with an intellectual disability may have been part of an independence training programme during the day, where cooking, cleaning and bed-making were taught. Opportunities to be part of these activities during the usual times of the day may never be planned for and may never occur. The assumption has been of difference until adequate intervention achieves change, and only then can 'entry' to typical community settings be planned. This has resulted in an emphasis on the developmental model, learning and skill development separated from the meaningful situation and failure to recognise the importance of participation, social inclusion and belonging, regardless of skills. For example, learning social skills, how to prepare meals or how to cross the road might be important only if the person has friends and the opportunities to go out or invite friends and family home; the importance of being part of a meal in a restaurant was not recognised. Furthermore, some goals may be irrelevant for some people, even though such goals may be developmentally appropriate.

As interventions typically followed a set course as understood by various professionals (teachers, therapists, psychologists), the recipients of the intervention – people with intellectual disabilities – rarely had an opportunity to express views and preferences or direct the course of the intervention. There has been little opportunity for people with intellectual disabilities to set their own goals for specialist support.

Discussion

Many professional groups owe their identity and *raison d'être* to people with developmental and acquired disabilities. The therapies and special education in particular were established in response to moves to determine competence and readiness for participation in the community and devise programmes for (re)habilitation to promote the transition from special settings to ordinary home, work and community settings. These professionals recognised that people with intellectual disabilities could benefit from (re)habilitation and education, and became the assessors of the capacity to function and the gatekeepers to integrated and what is now regarded as more everyday human experiences.

The recognition of the limitations and rejection of the 'getting ready model', however, has also led to a rejection of the input from professionals. It is arguably the exclusive role of professionals in decision-making and approval of community living that requires review, rather than a total rejection of the contribution of specialist knowledge to supporting people with an intellectual disability to live in the community. For example, there remains a need for specialist knowledge available for people with an intellectual disability who have sleeping, mental health, mobility or communication difficulties. Table 2.2 lists examples relevant to the application of this perspective.

Table 2.2 Contemporary examples of the application of an ability to function perspective

These examples emphasise interventions designed to improve abilities and minimise disabilities to enable a person to more readily participate in daily life

- Teaching daily living skills at a shared community house
- Learning approaches based on implicit and explicit learning and memory
- Providing alternative communication systems through technology
- Teaching decision-making with young adults with intellectual disabilities in the workplace
- Identifying skills needed for successful inclusion in preschool
- Designing exercises to improve motor coordination and mobility that can be undertaken during daily exercise routines
- Designing houses and workplaces to maximise people's independence, such as visual and sensory cues to the pathways to move around a building
- Staff activity in community housing to promote increased resident engagement

Opportunities and society

Description

The right to live in the community is relatively new and is the foundation for the third way of understanding intellectual disabilities. This approach has much in common with the social model of disability and locates the barriers and enablers to community participation for people with disabilities in social processes and structures. Restrictions on participation stem from the nature of society and are, therefore, external to the characteristics and efforts of the individual. Participation has been defined as:

> the individual's involvement in real life situations, denotes the degree of involvement, including society's response to the level of functioning. Participation restrictions are interaction problems due to hampered availability or accessibility of various resources. Participation restrictions are disadvantages that limit the fulfilment of social roles that are typical for the individual. (AAMR 2002, p.107)

Participation restrictions imposed by society limit the achievement of typical social roles, for example employee, graduate, citizen, consumer and friend. Other concepts associated with participation are self-determination, social justice and individual choice (Reinders 2002).

The origins of the social model lie in the disability rights movement founded by people with physical disabilities (e.g. Oliver 1996). This has focused exclusively on the disabling effects of society, the factors external to the individual creating disability – such as absence of human rights, poor physical access and lack of personal assistance – and discrimination across all life areas. The defined solutions have been in terms of political strategies to establish human rights and reform of social structures. The social model of disability proposes that it is the nature of macro-environments and the structure of societies that create disability. Atypical or segregated environments where people with intellectual disabilities have spent much of their time have also reinforced or created difference, failed to guarantee safety and protection, and created unreal life experiences and situations that have exacerbated the consequences of impairment.

Best practice from this perspective means that people with intellectual disabilities should live like other community members and fulfil typical social roles, and various barriers to community acceptance and inclusion should be overcome. There is a growing expectation that society needs to change in order to include people with intellectual disabilities. People with intellectual disabilities should not have to earn or demonstrate their capacity to be included or be asked to 'be like everyone else' in order to be accepted.

The social mode of disability, with its associated recognition of the rights of people with an intellectual disability to citizenship and community living, has triggered the rise of (self)-advocacy and rights-based legislation as mechanisms to protect people's rights. Such society-wide processes had been noticeably absent from the two preceding perspectives.

The social model of disability tends to reject the relevance of an individual's lack of capacity, assuming all people can be self-determining, and rejects any focus on activity restrictions if these establish a continuum of options for services and supports culminating in community living as only one option rather than a right.

Strengths

The preferences and views of the person with intellectual disabilities are central to this perspective. The perspective starts with the individual participating in the community and calls for services and supports designed to promote each person's chosen lifestyle. This is the only understanding of disability that stipulates a relationship between people with intellectual disabilities and other community members as peers. Service design is derived from supporting typical or ordinary life experiences. The strength of this approach is the emphasis on a flexible and wide-ranging response from the community and broader system. This perspective challenges earlier assumptions that all difficulties and barriers faced by people with disabilities can be attributed solely to the individual's capacity or ability to learn and develop.

Weaknesses

This approach is limiting when the nature of impairment does affect social participation, such as fatigue or illness, which are not determined socially and will not be resolved through political action. The social model has neglected the barriers to inclusion faced by many people with intellectual disabilities, who may experience major difficulties with personal choice, exercising rights and limits on their ability to self-determine. Insistence on the place of people with intellectual disabilities within the community has been used as a rationale to override any contribution from early understandings of intellectual disabilities, which were centred more narrowly on the (in)capacity and (in)ability to function of the individual.

The social model has been much stronger on ideology than its translation into everyday practice.

Discussion

There is a growing recognition of the limitations of a rights-only viewpoint (Reinders 2002). Many rights, such as the right to informal social relationships, cannot be legislated. The immediate environment that mediates the impact of intellectual disabilities includes informal support from friends and family and other social networks, in addition to the more public physical environment. Ways to influence these informal supports and individual attitudes, which lie beyond the scope of human rights and anti-discrimination legislation, are not understood well. Ironically, proponents of the other views that focus on the individual's lack of capacity and inability to function implicitly resist community living, precisely because of negative experiences or expectations that community members will not support individuals with intellectual disabilities. The solution of these approaches, however, was the withdrawal of people with intellectual disabilities from the general community, rather than engagement with the wider and more complex task of tackling community and social structures. In combination with the social model, these other perspectives provide the insights to make social inclusion more of a reality. Table 2.3 sets out some of the approaches that have been used in furthering the rights approach.

Table 2.3 Contemporary examples of the application of the opportunity to function perspective

The examples here emphasise the right of people to be part of the community and experience a full quality of life irrespective of their skills and abilities and the nature of their disability

- Citizenship rights of people with intellectual disability
- Campaigns to promote positive attitudes of community members about disability
- Policies that require information to be provided in plain English
- Quality-of-life assessment
- Life satisfaction of people with intellectual disability living in community residences
- Equal-opportunity legislation
- Self-advocates in partnership in research with university researchers
- Staff selection for support staff by service users
- Person-centred planning

Opponents of the social model have argued that solely considering broad social structures ignores the reality and experience of intellectual disabilities for each individual. The social model potentially would be strengthened if it also took advantage of the legitimate contributions from the previous two perspectives – the 'medical model' and the 'getting ready model'. For example, alone, the right of a person to attend a football match or go shopping does not guarantee that the individual understands what is happening, has a say in what is decided or is assisted to be part of what is going on. If an individual is not able to make decisions to direct their life course, then to be meaningful, their inclusion in society as a right will depend on specialised assistance from others to make decisions, communicate, ensure engagement, experience different situations and ensure safety.

Implications for case managers

A narrow understanding of a rights perspective of intellectual disability risks failing to use information and approaches that could improve people's lives in the community. It is important to adopt a multifaceted approach to intellectual disabilities, and it is shortsighted to limit understandings to one perspective, as each alone will identify only some of the possibilities, limitations and solutions for each person.

It is the case manager's task to harness the best contributions from these three perspectives for each individual. The medical model and the functional model are sensitive to the vulnerabilities and incapacities of people with intellectual disabilities but risk ignoring talents, preferences, interests and rights. For example, protection of an individual by ensuring that skilled professionals, family and friends decide on their behalf whether they are judged as less than competent is an important contribution arising from these perspectives. This must be tempered, however, by a rights framework that establishes the right to exercise choice and experience an ordinary life and puts in place processes and safeguards to ensure the preferences of each individual are ascertained as clearly as possible and drive the actions of professionals, families and the service system. It is important to guard against limited experiences of community participation that have been mediated by expert or professional judgements about the individual's capacity (Ericsson 2002) rather than by rights. A rights-based perspective focused on inclusion and opportunities to participate must be the starting point. Lack of recognition of the other two perspectives, however, can be a denial of the rights of people with an intellectual disability to be well-supported as part of community life.

Too often, the field of intellectual disabilities has managed these conflicting perspectives by assuming that only one was legitimate at a time and therefore represented best practice. This has meant that the more recent emphasis on inclusive communities and human rights strategies (opportunity to function) has diverted attention from, for example, health diagnosis (capacity to function) and developments in education and therapy (ability to function). The implications of these restricted visions detract from what potentially may be available to each individual and has influenced service- and support-system design. For example, the spotlight on community participation has been accompanied by a decline in practice and research in relation to psychological issues such as memory and learning for people with an intellectual disability.

Multiple perspectives in practice

The application of all three perspectives is illustrated by considering the preferred support for Rob, a 30-year-old man with physical and intellectual disabilities and who is not able to live independently. If the starting point is maximising Rob's opportunities and, therefore, how he can live a typical and preferred lifestyle (given his age, culture and gender), then he might be living in a shared house with friends, or with a partner or with a family member. Rob may have a job, hobbies or recreational pursuits that take him into different community settings, as well as things he likes to do at home and household chores. That opportunity alone, however, will not maximise his ability to function – that is, do things in his daily life. Understanding how Rob learns best, and what aids and equipment maximise his communication and mobility, are important. This individualised assistance depends on an accurate understanding of Rob's abilities, including minimising the impact of any health-related conditions. Relying solely on externally creating opportunities for a typical lifestyle will mean Rob may be unable to understand, learn from or have maximum autonomy in these situations. In addition, foundation health and wellbeing factors (such as medication impact, genetic implications for the family, likelihood of sensory impairments, chronic illness) may be overlooked.

Key questions to be explored when deciding Rob's support needs are outlined in Table 2.4. The starting questions relate to Rob's participation in the community – the opportunity to function. The other perspectives of disability provide some of the how-to to make Rob's lifestyle goals a reality.

Table 2.4 Questions arising with regard to Rob with each perspective of disability

Opportunity to function	Ability to function	Capacity to function
What sort of a life does Rob want to live, given his age, culture and gender?	How can Rob's differences be minimised?	What is the aetiology of Rob's physical and intellectual disability?
What will he be doing at home, for leisure, for education and for work?	How can Rob's developmental delays be minimised?	Are there medical or genetic issues to be responded to now and over time?
Who are his important friends and family?	What is the best way for Rob to communicate?	What is the likelihood of hearing impairment, neck injury, Alzheimer's disease and thyroid deficiency in people with Down syndrome?
How can Rob have the main say in his life?	What does Rob need to learn about friendship and relationships?	
What support does he need for this?	How does Rob learn best?	
What is the role of this support?	What can Rob learn to be as independent as possible? What can Rob not do until he is more independent?	
How can engagement, skill development, protection, personal care and community modelling be promoted?	What interventions can maximise Rob's development, e.g. mobility, communication, behaviour?	
How can social structures be altered to support his participation?		
How can Rob have more friends?		

Negotiating the milieu

Case managers provide the gateway to services and supports for many people with intellectual disabilities through an individual relationship with each person and their family, as appropriate. At the micro-level, the case manager analyses and negotiates based on the often unspoken beliefs and attitudes about intellectual disabilities from various stakeholders. The consequence of these different attitudes and beliefs about intellectual disabilities may be critical or benign, depending on who holds the view and what decision it mediates. The intended result from case management is more flexibility and choice for the individual in the context of coherent whole-of-life planning, community participation, less service fragmentation, and the provision of appropriate supports (Austin 1990). Ironically, individualised approaches, although offering the hope of increased flexibility, may leave individuals vulnerable to the frequently unspoken tensions and battles between the three perspectives about intellectual disabilities. All of the perspectives discussed in this chapter have as a stated aim a better life for each person with intellectual disabilities. Each perspective judges 'best' in a different way. Different stakeholders – service systems and individual – argue for 'best' based on their preferred perspective. The case manager can strive to apply the perspectives that are optimum for each individual's situation and to recognise the concurrent contribution of these perspectives in system-wide and stakeholder-specific views and decisions. A planned approach that results in relevant contributions from the three perspectives about intellectual disabilities will form the optimum basis for effective case management for people with intellectual disabilities, provided the rights to citizenship and a typical life are the pre-eminent, but not exclusive, starting assumptions.

References

AAMR (2002) *Mental Retardation, Definition, Classification and Systems of Support,* 10th edn. Washington, DC: American Association on Mental Retardation.

Austin, C.D. (1990) 'Case management: myths and realities.' *Families in Society: Journal of Contemporary Human Services 71,* 398–405.

Ericsson, K. (2002) *From Institutional Life to Community Participation: Ideas and Realities Concerning Support to Persons with Intellectual Disability.* Uppsala: Uppsala University.

Fulcher, G. (1989) *Disabling Policies? A Comparative Approach to Education Policy and Disability.* London: Falmer Press.

Ife, J. (1997) *Rethinking Social Work: Towards Critical Practice.* Melbourne: Longman.

Kincaid, D. (1996) 'Person-Centred Planning.' In L.K. Koegel, R. L. Koegel and G. Dunlap (eds) *Positive Behavioral Support: Including People with Difficult Behavior in the Community.* Baltimore, MD: Paul H. Brookes Publishing.

Oliver, M. (1996) *Understanding Disability: From Theory to Practice.* London: Palgrave Press.

Reinders, J.S. (2002) 'The good life for citizens with intellectual disability.' *Journal of Intellectual Disability Research 46,* 1–5.

WHO (2001) *International Classification of Functioning, Disability and Health.* Geneva: World Health Organization.

3

Balancing rights, risk and protection of adults

David Green and David Sykes

Introduction

Risk, safety and protection have always been central considerations in the provision of services to people with intellectual disabilities. In the past two decades, however, the management of risk has become much more central to the provision of these services, particularly for people living in the community. Two different forces have produced this change. First, within the field of disability services, policies leading to deinstitutionalisation, community care, self-determination and, more recently, person-centred planning introduce new risks and new opportunities for service users, workers, local communities and organisations. These policies bring into sharp focus the wide range of tensions facing human service organisations: protection of vulnerable people, their rights to take risks and access opportunities for a more fulfilling life, the rights of workers to safe workplaces, the requirements of organisations to fulfil their duty-of-care obligations, and the wellbeing of the community. In the context of these tensions, risk assessment and risk management have become vital and complex elements of service-planning and provision and central to the work of case managers.

Second, we have entered a new era of risk, which some writers call the 'risk society' (Beck 1992; Giddens 1990, 1991, 2000). Increasingly, the day-to-day operations of governments, the helping professions, businesses and service providers are being managed through the frameworks and technologies of risk. The major corporate collapses and scandals of the last two decades of the twentieth century have demanded attention to governance issues and the management of risk in the corporate, public and not-for-profit sectors (Kemshall 2002; Lupton 1999; Rose 1999). Identification, control and transfer of risk now represent political imperatives for most governments and their contracted agencies. Although these imperatives are much wider than the focus of this book, developing effective responses to the impact of risk in intellectual disability services is informed by an understanding of the heightened significance of risk in contemporary society.

Case managers in frontline health, protective and community services are in the thick of this change. The demand on these case managers to manage and control risk can become a dominating factor shaping their practice. The tensions between controlling risk and assisting people with intellectual disabilities to live more fulfilling and meaningful lives are central to both the planning and the provision of services. Understanding risk today requires a complex analysis of the real and possible risks for service users, workers, provider organisations and the community, arising from both traditional and emerging models of care.

Further, more and more jurisdictions are changing their policies to favour person-centred planning and enabling people with intellectual disabilities to make their own decisions about how they live and what services they will use. As people develop their own preferred living arrangements and use a wider range of services, new risks emerge that require different approaches. Individual case managers and, of course, their clients now take on the management of risks that were once embedded in the routines and structures of the institution, the group home or the day programme.

The focus of this chapter is on these contemporary issues from the point of view of the case manager. We examine briefly the changing nature of risk and its significance for people with intellectual disabilities and those who support them. Then we discuss the major elements of today's risk-management strategies and make some suggestions as to approaches to practice that reconcile the competing demands of rights, protection and risk. This analysis is based on the standpoint that the experience of taking risks is of critical importance to both people with intellectual disabilities and their case managers. Finally, we examine briefly the particular issues arsing from the need to use legislation and coercive measures to manage risk.

Contemporary risk management

The emergence of the risk society has produced a wide range of policies, practices and regulations regarding the management of risk, which impact on all sectors of the economy. In Australia, leadership came from the Standards Associations of Australia and New Zealand, which published the first joint Australian/New Zealand Standard, *Risk Management*, in 1995. The current standard is accompanied by detailed generic guidelines that are used by organisations from all sectors, including many disability services (Standards Australia 2004a,b). The Australian Standard defines risk as 'the chance of something happening that will have an impact on objectives' (Standards Australia 2004b, p.4). This broad approach means defining a wide range of events that might positively or negatively affect the key goals of the organisation or enterprise and, indeed, the client. Similar guidelines and procedures for risk management are available in most western nations, but the agencies that auspice them vary considerably, according to the different history and structures of each regulatory regime. Alongside this national standard for risk management, related regulatory regimes, such as those for occupational health and safety, professional indemnity, and common-law provisions for duty of care and negligence, are all part of the regulatory environment for services to people with intellectual disabilities.

The contemporary challenge for organisations is to manage risk in ways that protect service users, workers and the community, without compromising the values and ideals that are central to the service goals and activities. It is increasingly more complex, however, to achieve this objective for people with intellectual disabilities living in the community. Most services, including case management, are delivered from a wide range of unregulated private and public sites, including service users' homes, public housing estates, group housing, the streets and many other places. These sites are not subject to the same controls and routines as the hospital, institution and factory floor. As a consequence, case managers operate in changing and unpredictable environments. Furthermore, person-centred planning and associated individualised service and funding models increase the diversity and complexity of the case manager's responsibilities. Contemporary case management requires complex collaboration and partnerships between services, service users and case managers. For these relationships to work effectively, the most sensitive and sensible of all approaches to risk management is required, namely the development of trust and the willingness to share risk. Although risk-sharing has become a well-established practice in business and major capital projects such as public–private partnerships, it is a new and often problematic concept for community services and their funders.

Risk management has become central to the organisation and practices of community services working with vulnerable adults in the community. It has led to innovations that help safeguard the rights and safety of the community and reduce the exposure of workers to injury and hazard, while also increasing the safety of clients. Despite these gains, however, a growing body of evidence suggests that risk management has led to reduced availability of some services, reduced flexibility within and between services, a decline in quality, infringement of user rights and failure to address the long-term interests of users (Kemshall 2002; Kemshall *et al.* 1997; Rose 1996, 1998). Notwithstanding the requirement that the objectives of risk management are to improve service delivery, enhance efficiency and foster innovation (Standards Australia 2004a), it appears that many risk strategies in community services are focused narrowly on a number of low-frequency adverse events or outcomes. Such strategies produce major unresolved tensions between the goals of community services for individuals with a disability and the perceived imperatives of risk management for staff and organisations (Alaszewski, Harrison and Manthorpe 1998; Kemshall 2002).

Risk is 'increasingly embedded in organisational rationales and procedures for the delivery of services and relationships with users and clients'; it has assumed an important role in determining priorities, shaping the 'focus of professional activities' and 'judgements about the quality of performance' (Kemshall *et al.* 1997, p.214). The impact of risk on priority-setting in a context of declining resources and increasing demand for services can effectively push aside service users' needs as the major determinant of service delivery. If services are stretched for resources and have limited capacity to respond to need, then people assessed as low risk increasingly become low-priority clients, irrespective of their needs (Kemshall 2002; Rose 1998). At the same time, organisations with the authority to do so may elect to reject high-risk clients, also irrespective of their needs.

The process of defining, controlling or preventing adverse incidents has the potential to take priority and dominate the perspectives of the organisation and its case managers. The identification of a risk forces case managers to become what Beck (2000, p.214) calls 'risk decision-makers' and to embark on a journey to control that risk. Risk is 'transforming professional subjectivity', as its assessment and management become the practitioner's central professional obligation (Rose 1996, p.349).

Many disability services are developing their own risk-assessment and risk-monitoring procedures. They are looking for systematic and responsible ways to assess and protect the safety and wellbeing of the clients, workers and the community, while achieving their service goals. In the next section, we examine some of the ways in which services can use risk strategies to achieve both safe and responsible risk-taking services.

A framework for 'managing' risk

In addressing the development of policy and practice guidelines for managing risk, we have adopted a commonly used framework, which is spelt out in the Australian Standard (Standards Australia 2004a). The recommended steps for establishing a sound risk-management programme that balances the promotion of ordinary living against practical issues of safety (Manthorpe *et al.* 1997) include:

- defining goals and establishing the context
- identifying, assessing and evaluating risk
- treating risk through risk avoidance, risk reduction and risk sharing.

Establishing the goals and defining the context

All aspects of risk management take place within three broad domains – societal, organisational and individual:

- *Societal:* Services must work within the prevailing societal and cultural understandings of the rights of the person, and the obligations of service providers to that person and the community. Alongside these broadly ethical factors are the legal and regulatory requirements that guide responsible decision-making, such as duty of care, occupational health and safety, privacy, confidentiality, service standards and specific professional codes of ethics. All of these constitute the general context for the management of risk and frame an approach to the operational tasks of identifying, assessing and treating risk.

- *Organisational:* The management of risk is significantly affected by the organisational context, in particular the values, mission, goals, capabilities and culture of the particular service (Standards Australia 2004b). Specific requirements of funding and regulatory bodies must also be considered in the way an agency approaches risk.

- *Individual:* The individual context, the needs and goals of the client with an intellectual disability, the client's family, and the contractual and subjective relationships between them must be considered. The knowledge, experience, values and beliefs of the case manager are also critical factors in the way in which risk is assessed and approached.

Therefore, the key decisions that have to be made regarding rights, safety and protection are always framed by the interplay of environmental factors, the organisation's values, ethos and culture, and the meaning of these for each case manager and service user. In this context, risk is seen from both an objectivist and subjectivist perspective, suggesting that the experience of risk for all of us is not only professional, legal and administrative in nature but also deeply personal (Beck 1992).

In setting the context for the management of risk, services and case managers need to recognise subjective and personal issues as well as the formal, rational and legal issues. Understanding and defining the context for risk management is an essential task that places the operational aspects of risk management at the centre of planning and service delivery for each client. It requires clear definition of key goals at the organisational and client levels, articulation of the decisions that have to be made, and the activities or interventions necessary to realise these goals safely and effectively (Standards Australia 2004b). This work sets the stage for effective risk assessment and risk management.

Risk identification, analysis and evaluation

If risks are not identified and understood at critical stages, then they may be excluded from consideration in case-planning and case-management decisions. A common approach to initial risk assessment is to identify high-, medium- and low-impact risks and to estimate the likelihood and severity of any possible adverse outcomes. For case managers working with vulnerable people, however, this process, although helpful, is too static, because risk must be understood in the context of the constantly changing daily needs, routines and preferences of the client. To counter this problem, Alaszewski (1998) and Carson (1995) recommend an extended definition of risk, which allows risk to be considered not only as hazards but also in the context of service goals and the client's changing life situation. As the focus is on improving individual lives, quality of life and needs become central to risk assessment, alongside the dangers that may threaten the safety and wellbeing of the significant people involved.

Very high-risk commercial organisations, such as those involved in the production of energy and chemicals, usually adopt a complex classification of risks, including risks to their capacity to deliver profits and meet the expectations of their shareholders and their responsibilities to meet safety standards for their workers and the community. Such businesses recognise that at the very centre of the risk-management process is the resolution of conflicting demands and choices about production, quality and profitability. A similar approach should, and can, be adopted by disability services. Given that hazards and dangers can easily push aside needs and quality of life, effective risk assessment must confront the total context and all the service objectives, not only safety and security.

One approach to this imperative is the use of lifestyle interview formats for the initial stage of risk identification and assessment, which includes in the planning process the naming of risks that are necessary for the achievement of a balanced and fulfilling life and the risks that threaten these goals. The focus of this approach is on the client rather than on the worker or the organisation, which sets the stage for an overall resolution of any conflicting goals directed to quality of life, or protection, or safety and rights.

Organisations that do not take this broad client-focused approach tend to give priority to a small number of high-profile adverse incidents (Alaszewski and Manthorpe 1998). Such organisations are in danger of being preoccupied with 'hazards rather than risk' (Alaszewski 1998, p.147). As a consequence, other real risks to key organisational and client goals are understated or ignored. This kind of approach focuses on the worst-case scenario and inevitably leads to more restrictive practices for the client.

A broad approach to risk identification and assessment will be dynamic and changing. As the client's lifestyle preferences change, new risks emerge. A continuing assessment and evaluation of risk must be integrated into the processes of preparing, implementing and reviewing plans for each client. Changing service goals usually means different risks and triggers the need to rethink the risk-management strategies to maintain safety and enhance opportunity. Jenny's story elaborates this process (see Case study 3.1).

To this point in the process of planning for Jenny's housing, the identification, analysis and evaluation of the risks incorporates the client's goals, the philosophy of the case management service, and the safety and wellbeing of the workers. Jenny's short-term interests are overruled, but her rights are protected through a transparent process appointing a substitute decision-maker to make some key decisions. There is a clear resolution based upon a shared understanding of a range of different risks.

Following the industrial clean-up of Jenny's house, however, a new case manager commenced the planning of Jenny's return home with the required support services. This case manager eventually refused to provide support, even though the house was now clean, because Jenny had a practice of heaping stones on the pathway to her home. The new case manager considered this to be an occupational health and safety risk for workers visiting the house.

This case demonstrates the difficulties that arise from different interpretations of what constitutes the most important risks, even in relatively straightforward situations. Increasingly, some service providers are interpreting obligations under health and safety legislation as the elimination of all potential risks to

Case study 3.1 Identifying and assessing risk

Jenny is 48 years old and has intellectual disabilities. She has lived at home with her parents all her life. Both of her parents died recently, and an interim case manager was appointed to assess her situation. Her living situation had deteriorated, with the house being in a very squalid state, partly as a result of having a number of cats living inside all the time. The case manager understood that Jenny very much wanted to remain at home, but if this was going to occur the place would need to be substantially cleaned. Jenny had limited capacity to understand or give informed consent regarding moving out of home, even if this was on a temporary basis, and so a guardian was appointed to make this decision for her. The guardian decided that she should move out while the house was cleaned, as this was likely to be less traumatic for her. Jenny was asked to make clear which items she wanted to keep. Due to the large number of cats, some of these had to be removed; again, this was done in consultation with Jenny. All of this was undertaken with the clear understanding that the overriding objective was to enable Jenny to continue to reside in her parents' house for as long as possible. In all these decisions, the case manager was working within the context of agency goals to promote the autonomy and independence of the client and respect her wishes.

workers, a practice reinforced by the increases in insurance premiums they face when injuries occur. This approach leads to a proliferation of risk-assessment tools and procedures that require workers entering people's homes to first survey potential risks to themselves. In the case of Jenny, the risk-assessment process required by the case management service led to an identification of one of a number of designated risks; as a result, the service was automatically refused. Such an approach to risk management highlights the problems that arise when one risk, or one category of risk, albeit of limited likelihood and severity, takes precedence over the needs and quality of life of the service user.

Treating risk

Avoiding risk

The first option considered in the risk-treatment stage is generally avoidance, which is 'deciding not to start or continue with an activity which gives rise to the risk' (Standards Australia 2004b, p.70). Traditionally, the easiest means of avoiding risk are to change, contain or cease the scope and frequency of risky activities. This strategy has been a routine and time-honoured approach used by disability services for almost two centuries, particularly by services that fail to identify risks to client goals as central to the process.

Risk avoidance is often preferred in situations where services are under pressure or are unable to fund the costs of other strategies. In Tran's story (see Case study 3.2), however, as in the case of Jenny, avoiding risk negates other goals for the client's care, stability and support. Although some risks have to be avoided because of their likelihood and/or the potential severity of their impact, in these instances the implications of withdrawing a service are greater than the consequences of the risk itself. Avoiding risk by withdrawing a service should be a last-resort approach. Unfortunately, however, some services also use risk as a reason not to provide a service to clients who may be considered unpleasant or difficult to deal with in some way. In these situations, different strategies and different approaches to controlling risk are required.

Case study 3.2 Avoiding risk

Tran is a young man with a mild intellectual disability and a mental illness. He lived at home with his parents until the recent death of his father. His mother is quite frail and can no longer manage to support Tran. Tran was close to his father, whose death had a profound impact upon Tran. A case manager was engaged to assist Tran to find more suitable accommodation.

The case manager arranged for Tran to be placed in a respite house in his local area until a permanent place could be found. Tran continued to attend the day placement that he had attended for the past ten years. One day, when he arrived home from the day placement, one of the other residents in the house alleged that Tran had assaulted him. The police were called, but they considered that Tran was unfit to be interviewed and no further action was taken. The house supervisor, however, demanded that the case manager immediately find Tran alternative accommodation, as he posed a risk to the other residents and they were having difficulty finding staff members who were prepared to work with him after the alleged incident. The case manager spoke with staff from the day programme who knew Tran well, and they reported that nothing like this had ever happened before. Further enquiries indicated that even if the assault had occurred, then it was unlikely to be repeated. Despite this, the community service organisation providing the respite care was still adamant that Tran had to be removed. The case manager managed to find a house on the other side of town and, after discussing the option with Tran, moved Tran to this new location. Tran still attended the day programme, as this was one of the few constants in his life at that time, even though this meant travelling for several hours in a taxi across town. Eventually, accommodation closer to the day programme was found, and Tran moved one more time.

Reducing risk

The preferred risk-management strategy in community services seeks to reduce the likelihood and/or the severity of risks, rather than to avoid them (Standards Australia 2004b). In fact, reducing risk may be the only strategy available to services supporting people with intellectual disabilities, because some risks are inherent in the provision of community care and cannot be avoided or transferred. The objective must, therefore, be to continue the identified activity but to address the likelihood of risk and its potentially negative consequences. A common example of this approach is the use of safety equipment to protect against hazards in the form of injury to a client or worker. Even the impact of safety equipment may not be neutral, however, as it can alter an activity and change the quality of the experience for the client. For example, using a hoist rather than requiring a worker to lift or move a person with a disability is an effective risk-reduction strategy but not necessarily favoured by all clients. Such decisions about reducing risk in travel, sport, recreation, participation, relationships, work and many other activities are central to the risk-management work of most services and their case managers. Risk-reduction strategies inevitably involve compromises that alter or adapt activities to reduce risks. Wherever possible, such decisions should be made with the participation of the person with the disability.

Effective decision-making in these situations includes an analysis of both the likelihood and the severity of an adverse outcome arising from a particular activity. The case manager also needs to be confident that the reduction strategy proposed will be effective – that is, that it will eliminate or reduce the risk. On this basis, workers and their clients are able to formulate operational strategies for guiding and supporting an individual's day-to-day activities and experiences while controlling risk.

The approach taken in Case study 3.3 demonstrates an attempt to reduce risks and achieve the major goals directing Allan's care. Allan's greatest wish was to live in a flat on his own. With the support of his case manager and some active outreach, the service was able to work together with Allan to help achieve this goal, even though Allan found the presence of the worker in the evening intrusive at times. This plan was reviewed regularly in order to identify what was and was not working and to ensure that Allan's changing needs were being responded to appropriately.

Case study 3.3 Reducing risk

Allan had left home at an early age and been placed in a series of foster homes before moving to his own flat. He had a mild intellectual disability and epilepsy. The epilepsy was getting worse because he forgot to take his medication, and on two occasions had been found unconscious on the floor of his flat. He has been in prison several times for minor assaults and stealing offences to help feed an illicit drug habit. Upon his release from prison, a specialised case management service was engaged to provide support to Allan. Arrangements were made for him to live in a one-bedroom flat because of his tendency to irritate other people and initiate or provoke aggressive outbursts. Although the case management service could do little to stop Allan's abusive behaviour, beyond a behavioural-modification programme, the service did discover that most of his offending behaviour occurred at night. They found that if Allan got into the routine of taking his medication before he went to bed, he was more likely to sleep through the night and function better during the day because his epilepsy was controlled better. A staff member stayed with Allan in the early evening and made sure that he had a shower, his dinner and his medication before the staff member left. This approach had a dramatic impact on reducing Allan's abusive behaviour, which had the benefit of making his accommodation more stable, even though Allan did not want workers in his flat.

Sharing risk

This risk-management strategy can be defined as 'sharing with another party the burden of loss, or benefit gained from a particular risk' (Standards Australia 2004b, p.5). Contemporary developments in community care open up the possibility of sharing risk both between service providers and, more significantly, with clients who have the capacity to make judgements about risk. Services may enter into complex shared arrangements to meet their own and client goals. In such situations, implicit sharing of risk can occur, although this rarely has any formal legal or administrative basis and it requires a high degree of trust between services. Case study 3.4 illustrates this kind of arrangement.

Case study 3.4 Sharing risks with other services

Serge is 36 years old, lives alone and has both an intellectual disability and a personality disorder. He suffers from a vascular disease caused by diabetes, which has led to the removal of part of his toes. Serge will accept some services offered by district nursing but not others. This is often despite experiencing a significant amount of pain and discomfort. At times, he has been found on the floor in an unconscious state as a result of a hypoglycaemic attack. Serge also believes that the health service discriminates against him and will sometimes refuse to enter an ambulance. He has even threatened suicide if any attempt is made to take him to the local hospital.

Although Serge had a guardian appointed who consented to treatment on Serge's behalf, Serge could still make it difficult for the treating team to assist him. This situation demonstrates the importance of both consent and compliance in providing treatment and interventions. Serge has a case manager to assist him to remain living in the community and to help him cooperate with the services necessary to maintain his independence. The case manager has liaised closely with the mental health crisis assessment and treatment team in his area, so that the team is aware of his situation and can advise on appropriate responses to Serge when he is refusing services or his medication.

The case manager has managed successfully to negotiate with all the services in order to maintain their ongoing involvement and maintain a consistent approach to supporting Serge. This was achieved through regular and comprehensive case-planning meetings and the development of a written document detailing responsibilities in the event of specific incidents occurring. This document helped to clarify the respective roles and responsibilities of each organisation. These processes gave the services the confidence to persevere with a high-risk situation, based on shared responsibility for managing the risks. The range of services included the mental health team, two hospital outpatient departments, the ambulance service, the general practitioner and the disability support service.

This case highlights the important role of case management in maintaining a delicate balance between risk protection and rights, through the sharing of significant risk. The case manager was critical to keeping the services engaged and facilitating the collaborative relationships necessary to achieve the client's goals. Had any of the services chosen to withdraw, the level of risk for the others would have increased, perhaps to the point where they may have felt too exposed and may have withdrawn, jeopardising the ongoing living situation for Serge.

Research has highlighted the importance of sharing risk decisions with the people who are most affected by them but suggests that service users often have little involvement in the risk-assessment and risk-management strategies adopted on their behalf (Langan 1999; Manthorpe 2000; Stalker 2003). Risk-assessment processes are potentially very intrusive, and it is argued that service users should be seen as experts in their own protection and risk avoidance (Parsloe 1999; Waterson 1999). An ethical practice would start from the position that people with appropriate capacity should be free to make their own decisions about risk. Even services strongly committed to advancing service users' control of their own lives, however, may still be very uneasy about their liability and exposure if key risk decisions are left to, or based upon, the judgement of their clients. Even in situations where the service user has undisputed capacity to make the necessary decisions, restrictive action may be taken on the basis of possible adverse outcomes for both services and the client. The involvement of relatives who are seeking interventions to control danger may add to the complexity of decision-making about risk. In such situations, many provider organisations experience a high degree of uncertainty about the implications of vulnerable service users sharing decisions about risk.

Central to these debates is the capacity of individuals to make their own informed decisions about taking risks. As with other aspects of case management, steps must be taken to support decision-making by establishing effective means of communication with clients so they can explore and understand the full range of options and the possible consequences, both positive and negative, of adopting these options.

Where a case manager cannot be satisfied that a person is able to make informed and reasoned decisions, the case manager, together with the person's guardian or relative if available, must weigh up the risks and benefits associated with a particular course of action or inaction on behalf of the client. Depending upon the level of risk involved and the probability of its occurrence, the situation may require specific assessments and additional services to become involved. Often, case managers are involved in situations where the client is unable to make an informed decision about the risk and its consequences, and there is no formal guardian or family available. In such situations, when the impacts of the risk are judged to be extensive and the probability of the risk being realised is high, consideration must be given to seeking a formal substitute decision-maker, such as a guardian. The legislative solutions and processes involved in such situations differ in each jurisdiction; the situation in Victoria, Australia, is discussed briefly later in this chapter.

Case study 3.5 illustrates in dramatic terms some of the issues involved in sharing risk.

Case study 3.5. Sharing risks with clients

Marie was adamant that she wanted to spend some time alone in her bath without having to have a staff member present. Her case management agency considered this request from a number of perspectives. First, they established that the client understood the risks and had the capacity to make the decision. They also reviewed the likelihood of the activity leading to harm and decided it was low, while acknowledging that the potential severity of the risk was high. Eventually, it was agreed to institute arrangements that would allow Marie to be alone, but with some precautions. Tragically, after a number of successful occasions, Marie slipped under the water and subsequently died.

At the following coronial inquiry, the court found that the service had acted reasonably and responsibly in managing both Marie's wishes and her care. This affirmation for the approach of the agency depended on the clear documentation of their shared decision-making with Marie and the precautions taken, even though these precautions were, in the end, ineffective.

Without doubt, the management of risk in the community and people's homes is becoming more complex and demanding. Providers of services to people with intellectual disabilities living in the community must recognise their limited capacity to control many aspects of the environment. As more jurisdictions move towards independence and choice for the users of care services, the complex issues arising from the sharing of risk, in conjunction with a wider understanding of the sources of risk, will become more central to the practice of the case manager. This complexity requires more than generalised rules and procedures. Services with a clear commitment to improving the lives of people with intellectual disabilities will be not only using reliable risk-assessment instruments and risk-reduction strategies to assist this process but also facilitating and strengthening their clients' capacity to make their own judgements about risk and risk-taking.

Legislative frameworks and the management of severe risk

Substitute decision-making, rights and risk

The first significant international recognition of the rights of people with disabilities occurred in 1981 through the United Nations International Year of Disabled Persons. The programme for this year focused on 'full participation and equality', defined as the right of people with disabilities to take part fully in the life and development of their societies, enjoy living conditions equal to those of other citizens, and have an equal share in improved conditions resulting from socioeconomic development. As a result of this emphasis, two types of legislation were enacted in many jurisdictions. The first sought to ensure that the provision of support services for people with a disability was based upon their rights to participation in the community. The second sought a legislative framework to protect the right of people with a disability to make their own life descisions, by clearly outlining the conditions that needed to be satisfied before appointing a substitute to make decisions on their on behalf. This legislation was important because it started from the premise that people with disabilities can make their own decisions. One such condition for the appointment of a substitute decision-maker is exposure to a significant level of risk.

In the Australian state of Victoria, the Guardianship and Administration Act 1986 provides for the appointment of a guardian as a substitute decision-maker when a person with a disability is found to be unable to make a decision and there is no other, less restrictive way of resolving a situation. In this context, it is important for case managers to be aware of the difference between supported and substitute decision-making. Supported decision-making is providing the necessary information and support to assist a person to make a reasoned, well-informed decision. Substitute decision-making, while involving consultation with the individual, means that someone else is appointed to make decisions on behalf of that person and should never be confused with the role of case management. Once appointed, the guardian, particularly in making risk-related decisions, must take an approach that is least restrictive of the person's freedom of action (Gardner and Glanville 2005).

In the current climate of risk aversion, sometimes there is a tendency by agencies to seek the appointment of a guardian to carry the risk and thereby reduce the extent to which the service provider is exposed to risk. This is particularly the case where a person may exhibit challenging behaviours that potentially put others at risk. Removal of a person's right to make decisions is a major step and should be preceded by a thorough exploration of alternatives which allow people with intellectual disabilities to be involved in the decisions that affect them.

Involuntary care and detention

Mental health legislation in Victoria, in common with many other jurisdictions, has provisions for the involuntary care and treatment of people suffering a mental illness. However, legislation for people with intellectual disabilities, while enacted at the same time, was based on the premise that the person can choose whether or not to receive assistance. Over an extended period of time it was found that the absence of any *legal* framework for compulsory intervention, together with a growing concern about the management of risk in community care, led to decisions that lacked transparency, were not subject to appeal, and did not ensure that the decision-makers were held to account for ensuring that the least restrictive solutions to risk problems were sought and used (Gardner and Glanville 2005).

For example, in Victoria, a secure residential service was established to provide treatment to assist people with intellectual disabilities, who were also sex offenders, to modify their behaviour. However, when a criminal justice order or sentence, which lawfully held such people, expired, and the person did not give or was unable to give consent to his or her ongoing detention and treatment, there was no basis for it other than a decision of a guardian. This situation led to a problematic conflict in the decision-making of appointed guardians, caught between the apparent necessity for ongoing detention and treatment and their obligation to make the least restrictive decisions in the best interests of the person with a disability. Guardians effectively became involved in criminal justice decisions.

As a result new disability legislation will come into force in Victoria during 2007 that addresses this problem by providing a more transparent framework for involuntary care of people with intellectual disabilities who are considered to

Case study 3.6 Involuntary care

John lives with four other residents in a house with staffing support. He came to the house because his parents were unable to manage his levels of violence and aggressive behaviour. In order for John to move to this residence, adaptations were made to the garage so that he could have his own living space away from the other residents. Since moving to the house, he has assaulted other residents and staff. Consequently, many of the residents choose to stay in their own rooms for fear of being assaulted if they venture into the lounge or dining room.

Although a behaviour-management plan was developed for John, he still continued to assault people on occasions. One response to John's circumstances that had to be considered was limiting his freedom of movement in order to protect the other residents. Ideally, such a restriction of his rights should occur by a procedure that explored all possible options and offered a transparent process, open to appeal and review. Before the 2006 legislation, the only mechanism for this to occur in Victoria, Australia, was through the appointment of a guardian. This is inherently problematic, for not only does the guardian have to make decisions in the best interests of the client and not others, but the guardian's decisions are not open to appeal or review.

Under the Victorian Disability Act 2006, once the service has exhausted the less restrictive options, the service is able to make an application to the Victorian Civil and Administrative Tribunal for a supervised treatment order, which would allow John to be detained because he represents a significant risk of harm to others. To effect this intervention, the legislation provides that a treatment plan must be submitted to and approved by the senior practitioner before an application for the order is made.

The treatment plan must state clearly the expected benefits to John arising from the intervention and treatment, any restrictive interventions proposed, the level of supervision required to ensure John participates, and a process for transition of John to less restrictive levels of supervision and, if appropriate, to living in the community without a supervised treatment order. If the tribunal is satisfied that these requirements are met, then it can make an order. This order is subject to regular periodic review and appeal (Disability Act 2006, Victoria).

present unacceptable risks. The new legislation avoids the previous distortion of the role of guardianship and offers protection to the rights of the person with disabilities if the person is detained for the purposes of care or treatment. This later feature emerged from the recognition that at times, community-based services are required to place restrictions upon an individual's rights and freedoms as part of a risk-management strategy. Case study 3.6 illustrates how these restrictions may need to be imposed when other, less restrictive options have been pursued.

Conclusion

This chapter has sought to capture some of the theoretical policy and practice understandings that will inform effective risk management for and with people with intellectual disabilities. Managing risk is central to the work of case managers and one of the most challenging parts of their practice. Managing risk will become increasingly complex in the context of changes in service models and the growing need for collaborative approaches to practice. Consequently, the level of support and supervision that the case manager receives in their assessment and management of risk is important, particularly if a reflective and effective practice is to be encouraged and promoted in relation to this issue.

In this context, Parton (1998, p.22) observes that 'our contemporary conceptualisations of risk have predominantly assumed that the world can be subject to prediction and control'. The pressure to minimise risk will continue as governments become increasingly convinced that matters of safety and security are their key administrative and political imperatives (Kemshall 2002; Rose 1999). This pressure adds further to an expectation that risks, particularly social risks, can be reliably predicted and controlled. The reality is, however, that notwithstanding increasing knowledge and research informing practice, case managers will continue to face ongoing uncertainty in the management of risks, particularly as more clients direct their own services. For this reason, it is important that clients and their representatives be engaged and supported in any assessment and treatment of risk.

References

Alaszewski, A. (1998) 'Health and Welfare: Managing Risk in Late Modern Society.' In A. Alaszewski, L. Harrison and J. Manthorpe (eds) *Risk, Health and Welfare*. Buckingham: Open University Press.

Alaszewski, A. and Manthorpe, J. (1998) 'Welfare Agencies and Risk: Formal Structures and Strategies.' In A. Alaszewski, L. Harrison and J. Manthorpe (eds) *Risk, Health and Welfare*. Buckingham: Open University Press.

Alaszewski, A., Harrison, L. and Manthorpe, J. (eds) (1998) *Risk, Health and Welfare*. Buckingham: Open University Press.

Beck, U. (1992) *Risk Society: Towards a New Modernity*. London: Sage.

Beck, U. (2000) 'Risk Society Revisited: Theory, Politics and Research Programmes.' In B. Adam, U. Beck and J.Van Loon (eds) *Risk Society and Beyond: Critical Issues for Social Theory*. London: Sage.

Carson, D. (1995) 'Calculated risk.' *Community Care*, October–November, 26–7.

Giddens, A. (1990) *The Consequences of Modernity*. Cambridge: Polity Press.

Giddens, A. (1991) *Modernity and Self-Identity: Self and Society in the Late Modern Age*. Stanford, CA: Stanford University Press.

Giddens, A. (2000) *The Global Third Way Debate*. Malden, MA: Polity Press.

Gardner, J. and Glanville, L. 2005, 'New Forms of Institutionalization in the Community.' In K. Johnson and R. Traustadottir (eds) *Deinstitutionalization and People with Intellectual Disabilities: In and Out of Institutions*. London: Jessica Kingsley Publishers.

Kemshall, H. (2002) *Risk, Social Policy and Welfare*. Philadelphia, PA: Open University Press.

Kemshall, H., Parton, N., Walsh, M. and Waterson, J. (1997) 'Concepts of risk in relation to organisation, structure and functioning within the personal social services and probation.' *Social Policy and Administration 31*, 213–32.

Langan, J. (1999) 'Assessing Risk in Mental Health.' In P. Parsloe (ed.) *Risk Assessment in Social Care and Social Work*. London: Jessica Kingsley Publishers.

Lupton, D. (1999) *Risk*. London: Routledge.

Manthorpe, J. (2000) 'Risk Assessment.' In M. Davies (ed.) *The Blackwell Encyclopaedia of Social Work*. Oxford: Blackwell.

Manthorpe, J., Walsh, M., Alaszewski, A. and Harrison, L. (1997) 'Issues of risk practice and welfare in learning disability services.' *Disability and Society 12*, 69–82.

Parsloe, P. (1999) 'Introduction.' In P. Parsloe (ed.) *Risk Assessment in Social Care and Social Work*. London: Jessica Kingsley Publishers.

Parton, N. (1998) 'Risk, advanced liberalism and child welfare: the need to rediscover uncertainty and ambiguity.' *British Journal of Social Work 28*, 5–27.

Rose, N. (1996) 'The death of the social? Reconfiguring the territory of government.' *Economy and Society 25*, 327–56.

Rose, N. (1998) 'Governing risky individuals: the role of psychiatry in new regimes of control.' *Psychiatry, Psychology and Law 5*, 177–95.

Rose, N. (1999) *Powers of Freedom*. Cambridge: Cambridge University Press.

Stalker, K. (2003) 'Managing risk and uncertainty in social work.' *Journal of Social Work 3*, 211–33.

Standards Australia (2004a) *Australian and New Zealand Standard: Risk Management*. AS/NZS 4360 Risk Management. Sydney: Standards Australia.

Standards Australia (2004b) *Risk Management Guidelines*. AS/NZS 436:2004. Sydney: Standards Australia.

Waterson, J. (1999) 'Redefining community care social work: needs or risks led?' *Health and Social Care in the Community 7*, 276–9.

4

Walk a day in my shoes: managing unmet need on a daily basis

Lesley Gough

I work as a disability case manager for Melbourne Citymission. My job entails working with families who have children with disabilities to assist in maintaining the child within the family home and wider community. This chapter describes how a shortage of services can reduce the role of the case manager to a daily chasing of placements, which can contribute to stress and distress for people with intellectual disabilities and their families.

Jane[2] was 11 years old and not able to remain at home with her parents, as they found it too difficult to care for her on a day-to-day basis. Jane's care consumed the lives of her family. Jane's mother felt she had lost her identity as a person and that her life was meaningful to others only in terms of her relationship to her child with a disability. Jane's family found their situation so desperate that they decided not to pick up Jane from a respite facility after a weekend stay – in effect, relinquishing her care to the state.

Respite care is defined as a temporary intermittent service aimed at providing families with relief from the day-to-day care of their child with a disability (Levy and Levy 1986). For some children, however, it has also become the only foresee-able pathway to long-term out-of-home care. Families such as Jane's, unable to obtain the long-term support they need, seek relief from full-time caring by electing to leave their child in out-of-home respite services. Through my work as a case manager, I have found most out-of-home respite facilities have at least one individual who is classed as homeless, generally as a result of being left in the facility by their family, who felt unable to continue to care for the disabled person.

Estimates suggest that in Victoria, Australia, between 40 and 100 children with intellectual disabilities live on a full-time basis in respite facilities (O'Brien 2005). Jane was part of those statistics that attest to the inadequate support to the family, the shortage of alternative care options and the difficulties of planned transition to longer-term out-of-home care. Her unplanned crisis placement typifies the additional pressure on the respite care system that reduces its capacity to support continued family caring. Her relinquishment illustrates the way in which the aims of case management are undermined by urgent needs generated by inadequate resources in the disability support system.

> The doors opened and I stepped out of the lift on to the third floor of the hospital. I made my way down the corridor, towards the nursing station I could see in the distance. As I was walking, a small girl came up beside me, grabbed my hand and held it. She said hello to me and continued to hold my hand as we both headed towards the nursing station. When I reached the group of nurses behind the counter, I introduced myself as Jane Clarey's case manager. I told them I had been contacted and informed that Jane was ready to be discharged. I asked if they could show me to her room. One of the nurses looked at me oddly and said: 'That's Jane', pointing to the child beside me. 'Why don't you ask her to show you her room?' I turned and looked properly at the child by my side. I had never met the girl for whom I had been advocating over the past six months.

How could I not know Jane after working with her family for six months? Bad practice? Bad case management? If I am honest, I have worked with several children whom I have never met or have met on only one occasion. The bulk of my work was done with families who cared for a child with a disability. That doesn't mean that I wasn't working for the interests of the child – just that I mostly supported parents to support their child. Our practice was termed 'family-centred', meaning our work aimed to recognise parents as the key experts in planning for their child with a disability, taking account of the family's needs and aspirations. A study by Mahoney et al. (1998) into family-centred practice raised concerns that the 'child can become lost' in the way that this model is implemented. Research has concluded that there is a considerable need for practice strategies in order to ensure that the needs of both the family and the person with disabilities are addressed (Owen et al. 2002). Time limitations meant that I relied on parents to explain the needs of their child. I had a caseload of 17 families, many of whom required daily support; there was just so much need! I never had time to go to day placements, respite houses or families' homes in the evening to meet 'the client'. I barely had time to keep up with my day-to-day workload, let alone find space to really get to know the children who were my clients.

I knew a lot about Jane – the child I had never met. I could write an eight-page briefing in an hour describing her family situation, personality, behaviour, likes, dislikes, daily routines, emotional stability, medical history and on and on… Unfortunately, due to pressure and time constraints, I did not really *know* her. I just knew *about* her, and that had to be enough.

> Jane looked small for an 11-year-old. She had olive skin and a mound of dark curls that fell around her shoulders. As I looked at her, I could see a strong resemblance to her father. I asked Jane to show me her room. I asked her how she was feeling and she said 'good'. She led me to a large room with a single hospital bed in the middle. The room was dull and in need of a coat of paint. There were no pictures on the walls or bright colours. Jane had been dropped at the hospital two days ago by her grandmother, who had visited her in respite. It was the January school holidays – just after Christmas – and it had been extremely difficult to find Jane a place to stay each night. She had spent some time in a respite facility, some time with a foster family. She had stayed with her grandmother for a few days and had then been looked after by paid carers, whom she had never met previously. She was admitted to hospital with a severe case of asthma and spent two days by herself.

With Jane's family unable to care for her and her grandmother too frail to take her into her home, it was my responsibility, as Jane's case manager, to find Jane a 'placement'. It is not usually called a home. There are huge demands for out-of-home placements within the disability field. Australian statistics show that formal requests for placements between 1995 and 2000 went up by 300 per cent (Owen *et al.* 2002). Finding a placement for this child meant negotiating the system and competing with all the other professionals and parents trying to secure a stable home for people with disabilities. O'Brien (2005) suggests it can take years to find a new home for a child who has been relinquished and reports on conversations with parents who have been waiting years for foster families to be found for their children.

My case management role was reduced to Jane's placement coordinator, whereby it became my daily responsibility to find her a roof under which to sleep every night. At times, the pressure was so great and the situation so hopeless that I would have considered taking her home to my place, despite the professional boundaries that were in place. I felt personally responsible for this child.

Knowing that you have five hours in which to find somewhere for a little girl to stay is unbelievably stressful.

It was difficult to explain to Jane's grandmother that I did not have a place for Jane to stay on any particular night. As a case manager, one becomes the face of the service system. One has to explain and justify the service system's limitations and inadequacies and often has to bear clients' frustrations and disappointments about the system's treatment of them. How do you explain adequately to a child's grandmother that you have nowhere for her grandchild to stay? How can you expect her to understand this? Lack of resources, high demand and need, red tape and bureaucracy? All Jane's grandmother wanted was for her granddaughter to be safe and cared for. I couldn't guarantee this.

Jane's grandmother was an important support to both Jane and Jane's mother. In my experience, many families did not receive the type of support that Jane's grandmother provided. Having a child with a disability can be an isolating experience for the family. Research suggests that families who have a child with an intellectual disability receive only limited support from informal networks such as immediate and extended family, friends and neighbours (Cummins and Baxter 1997). Relatives, particularly grandparents, may not be able to offer support because of their grief over the situation. Sometimes parents may mistakenly see their intentions as judgemental and critical of their parenting skills (Bennett, DeLuca and Allen 1996). Accepting that a grandchild has a disability can be very difficult (Meyer 1986). Jane's grandmother defied these research findings. She took on the responsibility of liaising with me about Jane's placement issues. Jane's parents found this task just too tough to cope with.

It was very difficult to rally support from other service providers when advocating for a stable placement for Jane. At times, it seemed that no one wanted to take responsibility for finding this child a placement. I was told by one respite manager that her service did not want to offer too much support to Jane, as she feared the resultant pressure to care for Jane on a full-time basis. Respite facilities are not designed for longer-term placements, and their use by children who have become homeless through family relinquishment disrupts opportunities for other families who need short breaks from caring for their children. I could understand the respite agency's dilemma. There were probably 100 other children like Jane who needed a place to sleep, and the service system was dealing with such incredible need with limited resources (O'Brien 2005).

I told Jane that a lady called Jo would be coming to meet her soon and she would look after her for a few days. Jane said 'Good'. I asked her if she had any clothes to put on so we could change her out of her pyjamas. She didn't answer. A woman walked into the room and introduced herself as Jo. She yelled Jane's name and gave her a big hug. She told me that she had helped Jane's grandmother care for Jane, just for the day, while she was staying with her a few weeks before. She then proceeded to tell me all about Jane. She told me her likes and dislikes. She told me her behaviour was easy to manage and she could not understand why her family would 'give her up'. She said she felt so sorry for this girl that she would be willing to adopt her herself. She said that the rest of her family wouldn't mind and she would be able to manage Jane easily. She asked me to inform the Department of Human Services that she was ready and willing to go ahead and organise the adoption.

We left the hospital with Jane still in her pyjamas, as that was all she had. Jo chatted away to her and told her she was going to take her for a ride in her car. I was driving separately and meeting them at an empty residential unit that was currently being sold by the Department of Human Services. I left them at Jo's car and headed off to the house.

Jo's reaction to Jane's family's decision to relinquish care of her is interesting. It seems to reflect common perceptions of the issue. The literature on relinquishment demonstrates clear shifts in the way the service system responds to children and families in this situation. Deinstitutionalisation has meant parents are no longer encouraged to relinquish care of their child and are expected to meet all their daily needs at home. The emphasis on empowering families of children with disabilities has led to the expectation that parents become therapists, policy-makers, case managers and advocates (Fewell 1986; Mallory 1986). In the absence of adequate services and support, such expectations create additional stresses for parents on top of their everyday caring role (Mallory 1986). Families that reach the difficult conclusion that they can no longer care for their child at home, and consider relinquishment, face blame and persecution about their decision and judgements such as those expressed by Jo. Research concerning the service system's judgements about families with disabilities states: 'Professionals need to recognize and respect the diversity of parents' and families' situations and of the strategies they develop for responding to and managing disability in a child' (Baldwin and Carlisle 1994, p.44). I felt that Jane's parents were not understood or respected in their decision – relinquishment is not seen as an acceptable strategy for dealing with a child with a disability.

I reached the house and spent 40 minutes waiting for Jo to arrive with Jane. I was starting to get worried, as the drive to the house took me only 15 minutes. Just as I was contemplating ringing Jo's mobile, I received a call from her manager at the respite agency asking me to contact Jo straight away, as she was having difficulty with Jane. When I rang Jo, she informed me that Jane had begun banging her head on the dashboard of the car while in the passenger's seat. She said that Jane's nose had begun to bleed and she had then grabbed the steering wheel. Jo had pulled over to the side of the road, calmed Jane and then placed her in the back seat. Jo finally arrived at the house and I went to the car. Jane's face and lips were covered in dry blood and her pyjamas were stained. I lifted her into my arms and walked with her into the house.

Jo stayed with Jane for two nights in the house. After the first night, she asked for another carer to be rostered on to help, as she found Jane's behaviour too difficult to manage. At the end of the second night, she contacted me saying that she could not continue to work with her. Jane was back with me again.

References

Baldwin, S. and Carlisle, J. (1994) *Social Support for Disabled Children and their Families: A Review of the Literature.* Edinburgh: Social Work Services Inspectorate.

Bennett, T., DeLuca, D.A. and Allen, R.W. (1996) 'Families of children with disabilities: positive adaptation across the life cycle.' *Social Work in Education 18,* 31–44.

Cummins, R.A. and Baxter, C. (1997) 'The influence of disability and service delivery on quality of life within families.' *International Journal of Practical Approaches to Disability 21,* 2–8.

Fewell, R.R. (1986) 'A Handicapped Child in the Family.' In R. Fewell and P. Vadasy (eds) *Families of Handicapped Children: Needs and Supports across the Life Span.* Austin, TX: Pro-Ed.

Levy, J, and Levy, P. (1986) 'Issues and Models in the Delivery of Respite Services.' In C. Salisbury and J. Intagliata (eds) *Respite Care: Support for Persons with a Developmental Disability and their Families.* London: Paul H. Brookes.

Mahoney, G., Boyce, G., Fewell, R., Spiker, D. and Wheeden, C.A. (1998) 'The relationship of parent–child interaction to the effectiveness of early intervention services for at-risk children and children with disabilities.' *Topics in Early Childhood Special Education 18,* 5–17.

Mallory, M.L. (1986) 'Interactions between Community Agencies and Families over the Life Cycle.' In R. Fewell and P. Vadasy (eds) *Families of Handicapped Children: Needs and Supports across the Life Span.* Austin, TX: Pro-Ed.

Meyer, D.J. (1986) 'Fathers of Handicapped Children.' In R. Fewell and P Vadasy (eds) *Families of Handicapped Children: Needs and Supports across the Life Span.* Austin, TX: Pro-Ed.

O'Brien, S. (2005) 'Parents dump disabled.' *Herald Sun,* 28 March, p.9.

Owen, L., Gordon, M., Frederico, M. and Cooper, B. (2002) *Listen to Us: Supporting Families with Children with Disabilities – Identifying Service Responses that Impact on the Risk of Family Breakdown.* Melbourne: School of Social Work and Social Policy, La Trobe University.

5

Case management in a rights-based environment: structure, context and roles

Tim Stainton

Since the early 1980s, case management has become a dominant aspect of the social service landscape in most western jurisdictions for almost all user groups – those who struggle with addiction and mental health problems, older people, and people with disabilities, including intellectual disabilities. There is, of course, huge variation across jurisdictions and user groups.

Mental health and addiction services tend to use a more directed, clinical approach and are increasingly favouring an in-house approach to case management, with a strong and active treatment component (Bedell, Cohen and Sullivan 2000; Rutter *et al.* 2004; Ziguras, Stuart and Jackson 2002). Historically, supports for older people and people with intellectual disabilities and their families tend to use a more managerial approach, emphasising service and resource coordination rather than treatment. They are moving towards a more externalised model – that is, outside of the service provider system – and more user-directed approaches (Eustis 2000; Payne 2002). Furthermore, different jurisdictions have evolved in different ways, with significant difference seen in the degree of state support and control.

There are also myriad different motivations for the introduction of case management and the particular style adopted for a given population or jurisdiction. Cost containment, deinstitutionalisation and the move to community living, fragmentation and complexity of the service and support system, and the introduction of managed care in the USA are all commonly cited reasons for the rise of case management. Certainly all of these have played a part with regard to intellectual disability practice. Payne (2002) suggests that the forms of case management adopted have more to do with the political interaction of stakeholders than the professional possibility offered by case management itself and that four factors need to be considered when trying to understand any service innovation: (i) the character of the innovation itself; (ii) the economic, political and social contexts; (iii) the political and social interests of the stakeholders; and (iv) the political and social processes that take place during introduction.

In the field of intellectual disability, and disability generally, the political and social factors that shape the nature of the system in general, and the case management or related systems in particular, have always been influenced strongly by a set of values-based principles. These in turn have articulated the political struggles of the disability movement and its interaction with other key stakeholders. This chapter somewhat turns around Payne's four factors and begins by looking at the principles that have articulated the rights movement and the interests of the primary stakeholder, the citizen with a disability. From this, one can determine a positive sense of what kinds of structure and contexts for practice can best hope to address those interests. This then provides a basis for evaluating current case management structures and practice against this 'ideal' framework. In doing so, the author draws on practice examples from both traditional models and current innovations. The focus is primarily on structure and context rather than practice per se, but in doing so it is hoped that it will be obvious how structure and context can both limit and enhance practice and that 'good practice' cannot be evaluated outside the structural context within which it exists.

Rights and structure

Since the 1970s, there has been a steadily growing focus in the disability movement on rights as the basis for supports and services. In the intellectual disability arena, rights and citizenship have gradually come to replace normalisation as the dominant idea shaping both the movement for community inclusion and, to a lesser extent, the nature of the service and support systems. Consider the 2005 English Green Paper on social care:

> Our starting point is the principle that everyone in society has a positive contribution to make and that they should have the right to control their own lives. (Department of Health 2005)

Similarly, the current English strategy for people with intellectual disabilities, *Valuing People*, is based on four related principles: rights, independence, choice, and inclusion (Department of Health 2001). In the USA, these approaches have coalesced around the rubric of 'self-determination' (see Nerney 2003) or, more broadly, 'consumer direction' (see Scala and Nerney 2000; Velgouse and Dize 2000). Similar initiatives and direction can be found in almost all western jurisdictions (Dowson and Salisbury 2001; Ministry of Children and Family Development (MCFD) 2002; Steering Committee for the Review of Common-wealth/State Service Provision 1998).

Initially, the emphasis was on eliminating barriers to participation and providing some broad legal protection to citizens with intellectual and other disabilities. By the 1980s, explicit protection for people with intellectual disabilities became apparent in a range of legal instruments. Examples include the inclusion of 'mental disability' within the Canadian Charter of Rights and Freedoms in 1982, which afforded equal protection against discrimination, and the Americans with Disabilities Act of 1990 (Stainton 1994). Similar legislation is now in place to varying degrees in numerous jurisdictions around the world. These are significant achievements and have been effective in offering protection against many things, including involuntary sterilisation, discrimination at work, denial of the right to vote, denial of medical treatment and denial of educational opportunities, although effectiveness varies across jurisdictions and for different populations of disabled people.

Although these changes have improved disabled people's access to the rights of citizenship, mainly by providing protection against discrimination, it has been less clear how policy structures and instruments needed to change in order to support individuals to proactively exercise their rights and citizenship. More recently, however, there has begun to be a convergence around what is entailed in a rights-based approach (Stainton 2005). Although the language and policy specifics vary across jurisdictions, a relatively consistent set of fundamental principles and structures is beginning to emerge. Before considering the nature of these emerging structures and their impact on case management practice, it is useful to examine the nature of rights in order to identify what makes a rights-based approach, evaluate the consistency of emerging models and understand how traditional models can adapt to this emergent rights paradigm.

A key starting point for a discussion of rights and disability is to state that the goal of a rights-based approach is not to find a way to compensate for 'natural disadvantage' but to determine how society can accommodate a range of differences that, from a justice- or rights-based perspective, are neutral. The challenge, then, 'is to take account of variations in function without treating them as inherently disadvantageous' (Silvers, Wasserman and Mahowald 1998, p.190). This implies that rights-based approaches are concerned not with 'special rights' for disabled people, as some have charged, but with developing structures and instruments that recognise and allow for the accommodation of differences in physical and mental functioning. It is plausible to consider disability policy, structures and practices such as case management as one means by which society can accommodate such variations in ways that are consistent with a justice- or rights-based approach.

A further point on the nature of rights in western democratic states is that rights are founded in notions of freedom, autonomy and self-determination. The concept of autonomy – that is, the individual's capacity to formulate and act on plans and purposes that are self-determined (Stainton 1994) – is central to both rights theory and the emerging rights-based models of practice. There is not space for a detailed examination of the concept here (see instead Stainton 1994, 2002), but one can begin to see from the above what the elements of a rights-based structure might look like and how case management fits into the mix. Two key principles form the basis of both the development and the evaluation of such models:

- The concern is with capacity not outcome. That is, a rights-based approach is concerned with how choices are made, not with what choice is made. In service terms, this is why many current initiatives focus not on programmes, such as vocational and residential services, but on ways of supporting choice-making, such as advocacy and independent planning.

- A rights-based approach is concerned with not only the act of deciding what a person wants to do but also with the person's ability to act on that choice. Telling an individual that he or she is free to decide to go to a mainstream school, but not providing the means for the individual to act on that choice, is no choice at all.

The issue of equality requires some mention and clarification here. As the comments of Silvers *et al.* (1998) suggest, a rights-based approach is concerned with addressing the variation or differences between people but at the same time ensuring some fairness and equity of outcomes. In rights terms, this outcome is a relatively equal capacity to formulate and pursue whatever plans, dreams and purposes any individual may have, but consistent with a similar right for all. If equal means simply getting the same as everyone else, then it readily becomes the basis for 'dumping' or a lowest-common-denominator approach to support. A more common practice is the categorising of people on a 1, 2, or 3 level of disability, or severe, moderate or mild, or any variation on this theme, and then assigning resources, whether in volume or nature, to individuals based not on their own choices but on their general category, implicitly assuming that what is important is not *who* they are but *what* they are – a direct rejection of their autonomy.

This problem is sometimes described as the 'difference dilemma', which refers to the problem that what people require in order to achieve an equal capacity for making and acting on life plans differs between individuals. In other words, equal treatment does not equate with equal citizenship, since different people require different types of treatment in order to achieve the same basic capacity for participation. For example, a person who has difficulty communicating formally requires different means in order to achieve a basic level of communication compared with a fully articulate person. Being concerned with equal capacity requires differential treatment based on differential needs to achieve the same relative capacity for autonomous citizenship.

Although the example above may be relatively easy to deal with, this dilemma becomes more acute as the nature and complexity of needs increase. This complexity makes it impossible to establish general universal provisions that satisfy all needs. The challenge then for social policy is not to find better services but to create a structure in which individuals can articulate their needs, wants and dreams directly and that allows the state to adjudicate and meet legitimate claims in a manner that does not in itself infringe the potential participation or autonomy of the person. In essence, what is required is a structure within which an ongoing dialogue can occur between the individual and the state, as the representative of the collective. Further, once claims are established, there must be a means to help people satisfy those claims consistent with the principles of self-determination and equity.

For policy and practice structures, this implies a need to focus not on what services a person needs, wants or will get put into place but on helping them to determine what they want and the means to move towards those self-determined goals. Through this discussion, one may begin to see the key elements of what such a structure might entail. They include three key elements:

- supporting people to articulate their wants, needs and dreams

- supporting people to identify, obtain and manage supports necessary to move towards meeting those needs and striving for their dreams

- providing control over resources.

An emerging fourth structural element is concerned with governance, or questions of who controls the above systems and elements. We touch on this briefly below.

In the first element, the concern is with issues of decision-making and advocacy and also with giving people information to make informed decisions – a key aspect of case management type services. For many people with intellectual disabilities, the simple act of articulating what they want and then having that recognised by the system can be problematic. This may be because the person does not use formal communication methods or because the person's right to express preferences and have them respected is suppressed through laws that declare the person incapable. A good example of this is the 'willing and able' requirement in the UK Community Care (Direct Payment) Act 1996, which has been a major stumbling block for people with intellectual disabilities who wish to access direct payments.

If a person is unable to articulate his or her wishes directly, then the question becomes: Who is best placed to interpret and convey that person's wishes? Although governments have increasingly been recognising and supporting advocacy, including self-advocacy (see Department of Health 2001), they have been less keen to recognise the rights of advocates to the tools needed to effectively represent the interests of those for whom they advocate (Stainton 2005). On the more formal side, many jurisdictions have been concerned with reforming their guardianship and related laws to provide options that do not involve an automatic loss of rights.

One of the most progressive pieces of legislation in this area is British Columbia's Representation Agreement Act 1996, which provides a simple, inexpensive means for individuals to formally recognise one or more people as their representatives for routine health, personal care, financial decision-making and legal affairs. The real innovation in this Act is its change to the way capacity is viewed and understood. Rather than a simple common law test of capacity to determine whether one can formally express an understanding of the meaning and consequences of a given decision, the Act relies on expanding the traditional concepts around communication and the nature and quality of the relationship. Section 3(2) notes: 'An adult's way of communicating with others is not grounds for deciding that he or she is incapable of understanding anything referred to in Sub-section (1).' Section 8 further states that taken into account in determining capacity should be whether the adult demonstrates choices and preferences and can express feelings of approval or disapproval of others and whether the adult has a relationship with the representative that is characterised by trust. Section 8 states:

> (1) An adult may make a representation agreement…even though the adult is incapable of a) making a contract, or b) managing his or her health care, personal care, legal matters, financial affairs, business or assets. (Representation Agreement Act 1996)

The first of the three key shifts that are required is an expanded notion of communication, with an emphasis on the quality of the relationship (trust) between people, so that when people may not be able to traditionally communicate their choices those best placed to interpret for them (i.e. those who know them best) are empowered to represent them, and recognition that incapacity is often a function of lack of support rather than inherent in the person. This is essential for individuals who cannot directly articulate their wants and needs if they are to avoid having their needs determined solely by professionals and legal guardians who have little knowledge of who they are as individuals and whose interest in them is structurally professional rather than personal. For case managers, the challenge is to recognise the legitimacy of personal networks and to support their development and effectiveness as key to a rights-based system.

In the second of the key shifts – supporting people to identify, obtain and manage supports necessary to move towards desired outcomes – one can see much similarity with case management, in that identifying, accessing and coordinating supports are fairly standard elements of case management practice. 'Brokerage-type' supports and person-centred planning are two common expressions of these elements.

The third element is concerned with how the person's control over resources can be increased. The key emerging strategy here is through the use of direct or individualised funding. Although this may not be case management per se, the utilisation of individualised funding increases the need in many cases for the supports identified above with regards to decision-making and planning support. Hence, many of the traditional functions of case management may be involved here, although it may change to some degree the nature of the job from one of simply linking to existing services to one of supporting people to directly hire and manage supports or directly enter into contracts. A related point is that in most emergent rights-based models, there is an emphasis on moving away from an exclusive dependence on services and more utilisation of naturally occurring supports in the community.

Later this chapter considers how case-management-related functions might work in a rights-based system and, more importantly, where the various roles and functions are located, but first the chapter looks briefly at traditional approaches to case management and where a rights-based approach might differ or modify certain functions, structures and context.

Case management

As noted above, there is wide variation in case management models and approaches, but most share the same basic characteristics. Case management generally refers to a mediating structure that provides a variety of planning, assessment, service linkage, coordination and monitoring functions. Other, less common features include evaluation, advocacy, case-finding and, in some cases, direct service (Hall *et al.* 2002; Payne 2002). As its name suggests, case manage-ment was in part intended to be a model for more efficient management and coordination of existing resources and traditionally has more to do with the drive for efficiency of the 1980s than the current demands of consumers for a more rights-based approach.

A second feature of traditional case management is that it was generally located within 'the system'. It was structurally connected to the funders or pro-viders of services, rather than having a neutral position or being allied to those who used the supports (Stainton 1998). This lack of separation, and the inherent conflict of interest that it creates, between the funders, services and those who provide support for planning, choice-making and implementation is seen as a key problem of traditional case management; conversely, the separation of such powers is critical to a rights-based approach (Dowson and Salisbury 2001; Stainton 1994). The case manager certainly has an ethical obligation to respect the client's self-determination, but the case manager also has a legal obligation to his or her employer (the local authority, state or agency) and a personal interest in maintaining his or her work and career prospects. So long as the individual's interest and those of the authority coincide, there is no difficulty; most practising case managers, however, would probably agree that this is not always or even normally the case. From a purely structural perspective, the case manager is in a clear position of conflict of interest if he or she is responsible for both planning and accessing services and has, for example, an obligation to stay within a given budget for the caseload or to use services with which the authority contracts. This circumscribes both the self-determination and the rights of the person with whom the case manager is working. As Dowson (1990) notes, there is a conflict of roles and a high degree of professional control inherent in the case management model (see also Peck and Smith 1989).

The traditional assessment processes associated with case management have also reinforced this conflict, where the person doing the assessment is linked directly to the funders and/or providers of service. This provides not only a structural incentive to understand need but also a tendency towards assessing need in line with available services – what has been termed 'service-led assessment' (Stainton 1998). The move towards more broadly based planning approaches, such as person-centred planning, reflects the recognition that if one is concerned not simply with service identification and linkage but rather with broader life plans and goals, then it is crucial to engage in a process that is grounded not in needs and services but in the person. Further, the ways and means of addressing the elements of the plan must view the broader community, and not the service system, as the primary and appropriate source of support. This is not to suggest that services and supports will not have a role to play but that these are means to a much broader end rather than ends in themselves.

The problem of conflict noted above has led gradually to a separation of purely technical assessments concerned with eligibility or establishing of specific volumes of resources to which an individual is entitled from the more person-focused, broadly based planning supports that have emerged with the advent of person-centred models of planning in the 1990s. In the first instance, the determination of eligibility is a legitimate role of the state or other authority responsible for the equitable and efficient dispersal of taxpayers' money, ideally on a clear and transparent policy basis. In the latter case, the focus is on helping individuals and their networks to articulate their life goals and dreams and the best means to move towards those goals; it is inappropriate for the agent who may be responsible for the provision of some or all of the needed resources to lead that process, as the agent has an inherent conflict of interest as both a budget-holder/manager and a planner.

Another area where one can begin to see some differences between traditional and rights-based case management is related to the role of advocacy; again, the issue is one of role conflict and the need for appropriate balance and separation. Advocacy is often cited as one of the roles fulfilled by case managers, and indeed practitioners often cite this as a key aspect of the role. The problem is that given that case managers are embedded in the system and have the kinds of conflict over resource allocation noted above, they can rarely be truly independent advocates. For instance, a person is not likely to want, nor would it be legal in most instances, for his or her interests to be represented by a lawyer who also worked for the adversary in a legal action or even a lawyer who stood to benefit materially from the outcome of the person's case beyond agreed-upon fees. Nor would a person likely want a financial adviser who worked for a company in which he or she was recommending the person's investment – at the least, the person would probably question the financial adviser's ability to represent their interests objectively and without conflict. So why would an individual ask the case manager responsible for assessing their eligibility for resources to also be their advocate?

This role conflict is being recognised increasingly in the literature (Forbat and Atkinson 2005; Kane 2004), and the need for independent advocacy is gradually being recognised in policy and law (Stainton 2005). The advocacy commitment and investment in the UK learning disability strategy *Valuing People* (Department of Health 2001) is a good example. This is not to suggest that case managers should not advocate for their clients with regards to securing or enhancing quality supports or to ensure their rights are protected. What is critical, though, is that the case manager is not the lead advocate for that person and, in a rights-based system, needs to be free of conflict and, ideally, acting not out of a paid or professional obligation but out of a personal bond and commitment to the specific individual. Put another way, the case manager may advocate (verb) for the person, but the case manager cannot, due to conflicting interests, be the person's advocate (noun).

Before leaving the discussion of traditional case management, it is interesting to note that self-determination has not consistently been a key outcome of traditional case management models. Challis and Davies (1986, p.157), in their influential study on a much replicated 'enhanced case management model', note that 'there were significant positive changes in favour of the community care scheme'; there were, however, three exceptions: diet, anxiety and felt degree of control over the client's own life. More recent studies note vast differences in the degree of client self-direction in case management models (Rapp 1998). This is not to suggest that self-determination and choice have not been goals of traditional models or that there cannot be positive outcomes with a traditional model; rather, it is simply to argue that the structure militates against the maximisation of self-determination and choice.

A rights-based system predicated on self-determination and choice can provide greater structural safeguards to protect the potential autonomy of the person. In part, this is done by increasing the balance of power and reducing the conflicts of interest and abuse of power that exist sometimes in traditional service provision. To some degree, many systems have recognised this problem of conflict, although often because of concern with efficiency rather than with self-determination or rights. A variety of models have been discussed, such as the budget-holding case manager and the splitting of purchaser, commissioner and provider roles (Department of Health 1991). This budget devolution, however, stopped at the case manager rather than devolving down to the individual. Many authorities now have some form of purchaser/provider split; in some cases this means the case manager as purchaser of contracts with a specific provider, and in others the purchase is made en bloc and the case manager simply negotiates for a 'space'. Although these approaches recognise the need for a separation of powers and seek to facilitate consumer choice, the user often remains a marginalised actor with no real power or control.

Rights-based structures for practice

So what does a rights-based structure and practice look like? Above, the three key elements of such a structure were noted: supporting people to articulate their wants, needs and dreams; supporting people to identify, obtain and manage supports necessary to move towards meeting those needs and striving for their dreams; and providing control over resources. Also noted were some other features of a rights-based system, such as a broader-based independent planning system. The critical importance of maintaining a balance of power through ensuring a strict separation of elements in order to avoid conflict of interests between planners, assessors, advocates, funders and providers has also been noted. Therefore, when analysing and designing such a structure, one needs to look at:

- the nature (or absence) of the three key elements noted above
- the relationship between system functions (planning, eligibility assessment, funding, service provision, advocacy, etc.)
- the degree to which the system allows the user control over resources (either directly or controlling allocation)
- the overall governance of the system(s) and supports.

In order to illustrate how different jurisdictions are moving toward this, this chapter looks at two examples of new and emerging structures that encompass, modify or replace the traditional functions of and structures associated with case management.

The Hampshire Direct Payments Scheme

The UK Community Care (Direct Payments) Act 1996 came into force in 1997 and gives local authorities the power to offer a direct cash payment in lieu of services to adults under the age of 65 years[3] assessed as needing community care services under Section 47 of the NHS and Community Care Act 1990. Initially, the implementation of direct payments was discretionary, but as of April 2002 in England, local authorities are required to offer direct payments and the government has indicated its desire to see the payments massively expanded over the coming years (Department of Health 2005). The recipient must be 'willing and able' to consent to and manage his or her direct payments alone or with assistance. The recipient of direct payments then becomes an employer/contractor, in most cases using the direct payments to recruit and hire personal assistants to provide the required support. Direct payments can be used for all eligible community care services, except long-term residential care and local-authority-run services.

Although much of the initial uptake of direct payments was by people with physical and sensory disabilities, there is a concerted effort to increase its use by people with intellectual disabilities (Department of Health 2004). One feature on most direct payment schemes in the UK is the independent support schemes that help users to access and manage their direct payments. Hampshire offers an interesting case study on how a more rights-based structure can be implemented in conjunction with a traditional case management model.

In Hampshire, as in all UK local authorities, the potential user of direct payments has to be assessed under existing policy and guidelines in order to establish eligibility for community care services. This is carried out by the local authority social worker or case manager, who determines the community care services, and at what level, to which the individual is entitled. Subsequent to this, the user is offered the option of direct payments in lieu of authority or contracted services. In order to assist the individual to decide on whether direct payments are appropriate for them, to understand the responsibilities and, ultimately, to implement and manage their direct payments, Hampshire offers the support of independent direct payments support workers, who can provide a range of supports and services, including:

- provide advice and support to disabled people who are already using Direct Payments or thinking about using the scheme

- assist the user in determining what hours of support they would need

- advise on how to recruit the personal assistant(s), i.e. drafting a job advert, supporting the individuals to interview possible personal assistants, and drawing up contracts

- support to deal with tax and national insurance for personal assistants and advice on any insurance that may be required

- advise on how to fill in the record keeping sheets.

(Hampshire County Council 2005)

A key point is that these workers are employed by voluntary organisations and so are independent of social services. Perhaps more critically, they are all disabled people who have experience with employing personal assistants. Information shared with these workers is confidential and is not shared with the local authority unless the person requests them to do so.

A further feature of the Hampshire scheme is that two options are now offered. Option A is the traditional direct payments approach, with a fairly simple transfer of funds to the individual, who then employs workers directly. Option B is designed for people who do not want the complexities of employing their own staff but wish to choose which agency will provide them with the support they need (Hampshire County Council 2005). This is a key development in opening up direct payment options to people with intellectual disabilities and increases the role and range of options for case managers and related professionals.

If one considers the scheme in light of the issues noted above, it can be seen that this arrangement has separated out the functions of case management so that conflicts of interest are minimised. There is a reasonably clear separation of eligibility, funding and assessment from the broader functions of advice, planning and implementation, and both sets of functions are separated from the direct service and support functions. The use of disabled people's organisations to house the support workers is typical of UK schemes, although in many cases the role delineation is not as clear as in Hampshire. Although a certain conflict remains, in that the local authority continues to fund the support worker through the agencies, the practice remains fairly insulated from direct conflict. Advocacy does not enter formally into the scheme, but there is nothing that precludes independent advocacy, and it is interesting to note that the support workers do not identify advocacy as a key aspect of their job. There are two aspects of this model that may limit its utility for people with intellectual disabilities. First is the lack of ongoing monitoring, although the local authority social worker remains responsible for ensuring that assessed needs are met; this is, potentially, an important gap for people with intellectual disabilities. The second aspect is the lack of a robust planning support role, which is often critical to success for people with intellectual disabilities.

The next example looks at how a Canadian jurisdiction is attempting to bring to the fore planning support in its model of support for people with intellectual disabilities.

Community Living British Columbia

In 2001, the British Columbia government indicated its intention to devolve service to individuals with developmental disabilities and their families to an independent authority known as Community Living British Columbia (CLBC). In response, the community indicated it would also like to see a radical change in the model of service delivery and support. To this end, the British Columbia government formed a transition steering committee composed of families, self-advocates, service providers and government workers to recommend to the minister what the new model should look like (Ministry of Children and Family Development 2002). Subsequently, a board for the new authority was appointed by the minister, and services were transferred on 1 July 2005, with a mandate to implement the new service model.

The existing service model was a fairly traditional case management model, where ministry social workers acted as both gatekeepers and support workers to families, helping them to access a range of direct government services and contracted agency services. As with many jurisdictions, high caseloads and resource scarcity had placed many case managers in the position of being largely gatekeepers for the system, with little time or support to assist people with planning and accessing supports beyond those provided or funded by the ministry. This model is of interest here because it is one of the few attempts to alter the entire system towards a more rights-based system rather than simply adding a service feature (as with the UK direct payments approach) or introducing pilot or one-off programmes as adjuncts to the mainstream system.

The key to the British Columbia model is the separation of the planning support[4] functions from eligibility and funding determination, along with a broad-based introduction of individualised funding and changes to the community governance of the system. The key point is the separation of the planning support and the gatekeeping/funding functions. In order to achieve this within a single entity, the structure divides these roles under two vice presidents, each reporting directly to the chief executive officer, hence providing some degree of autonomy for each arm of the organisation but ensuring a shared policy framework and a reasonable degree of cooperation within the organisation as a whole. Under the vice president for planning and community development will be the majority of the former case managers, who will be designated as facilitators and whose role will encompass:

- providing information and referral support

- providing help developing and implementing a plan and developing community capacity for informal and unfunded supports

- assisting with access to non-CLBC supports

- involvement as needed in crisis situations

- coordinating supports with MCFD and other children and family supports outside of CLBC

- providing support with life transitions for children, youth, individuals and families including assisting people with changes in existing supports

- ensuring people are linked to personal support networks.

(CLBC 2005, p.3)

The support is intended to be available as required, including ongoing monitoring if required. The operations analysts, who will report to the vice president of quality services, will have the following responsibilities:

- determining eligibility within policy guidelines

- evaluating and approving funding request based on individual plans and within policy and fiscal parameters. Request may come directly from individuals or via a facilitator-supported plan

- assisting coordination with other funded supports outside CLBC where required

- purchasing and monitoring service deliverables and accountabilities pursuant to contractual agreements and approved funded supports in individual plans (both individualized and block funding)

- ensuring community capacity is developed for emergency/crisis response and monitoring the contract related to this work.

(CLBC 2005, pp.2–3)

One can see from the job description that the two roles collectively encompass the majority of traditional case management functions but, by separating the roles, reduce the conflict of interest inherent in many models. It is also clear from the role description that the planning function is much broader than that described in the Hampshire scheme, closer to a person-centred planning approach that is now becoming best practice in many jurisdictions (Holburn and Vietze 2002). This planning support role is intended to be broader than simply accessing services, and includes assisting individuals and families to access generic community supports and network development. This latter point speaks to the discussion above regarding advocacy in rights-based systems. Note that the role is not to be the advocate but to support the development of independent personal networks that can take on this role without conflict. The fundamental role of families and networks to act as advocates is also recognised formally in the CLBC model (CLBC 2005).

A final point concerns the governance of the model. The board, by legislation, must have a majority of people who are either intellectually disabled or a family member or other person with a 'significant connection' to someone with an intellectual disability (Community Living Authority Act, 2004, Part 1, Section 5). In addition, the board must constitute an advisory body composed exclusively of people with intellectual disabilities.

One can see, then, how the key elements of a rights-based system are in place in this model and how the case management role is restructured in order to minimise the conflict of interest and maximise the case manager's autonomy to work solely for the support of the individual and the family. Although it is not perfect (the cohabitation of the two roles within one organisation being the most obvious flaw), the CLBC model does demonstrate how a large system can be restructured, and along with it the case management functions, into a more rights-based framework.[5]

Conclusion

Although there are many other examples illustrating the way in which case management structures and context need to be realigned in order to conform to a rights-based framework, these two examples provide a good insight into how this might be accomplished. This chapter has tried to illustrate both what is meant by a rights-based approach and what this means for case management practice. In many ways, a rights-based approach frees up the practitioner to do what most social workers entered the field to do: to defend the rights and support the self-determination of vulnerable people in society. Indeed, research has shown that social workers respond well to the challenge of these new roles and value the ability to work without conflicts between their employer and the people that they are there to serve (Stainton 2002).

References

Bedell, J.R., Cohen, N.L. and Sullivan, A. (2000) 'Case management: the current best practices and the next generation of innovation.' *Community Mental Health Journal 36*, 179–94.

Challis, D. and Davies, B. (1986) *Case Management in Community Care*. Aldershot: Gower.

CLBC (2005) *Transforming Community Living Services in British Columbia*. Vancouver: Community Living British Columbia.

Department of Health (1991) *Implementing Community Care: Purchaser, Commissioner and Provider Roles*. London: HMSO.

Department of Health (2001) *Valuing People: A New Strategy for Learning Disability for the 21st Century*. London: HMSO.

Department of Health (2004) *Direct Choices: What Councils Need to Make Direct Payments Happen for People with Learning Disabilities*. London: HMSO.

Department of Health (2005) *Independence, Well-Being and Choice: Our Vision for the Future of Social Care for Adults in England*. Green Paper. London: Department of Health.

Dowson, S. (1990) *Who Does What? The Process of Enabling People with Learning Difficulties to Achieve What They Need and Want*. London: VIA.

Dowson, S. and Salisbury, B. (2001) *Foundations for Freedom: International Perspectives on Self-Determination and Individualized Funding*. Baltimore, MD: TASH.

Eustis, N.N. (2000) 'Consumer-directed long-term-care services: evolving perspectives and alliances.' *Generations 28*, 10–15.

Forbat, L. and Atkinson, D. (2005) 'Advocacy in practice: the troubled position of advocates in adult services.' *British Journal of Social Work 35*, 321–35.

Hall, J., Carswell, C., Walsh, E., Huber, D. and Jampoler, J. (2002) 'An Iowa case management: innovative social casework.' *Social Work 47*, 132–41.

Hampshire County Council (2005) 'Direct payments.' Accessed 1 March 2007 at www3.hants.gov.uk/direct-payments.htm

Holburn, S. and Vietze, P. (2002) *Person-Centred Planning: Research, Practice and Future Directions*. Baltimore, MD: Brookes.

Kane, R.A. (2004) 'The circumscribed sometimes-advocacy of the case manager and the care provider.' *Generations 28*, 70–74.

Ministry of Children and Family Development (2002) *A New Vision of Community Living: A Vision of Choice and Change*. Report of the Community Living Transition Steering Committee, Province of British Columbia.

Nerney, T. (2003) 'Self-determination: a transfer of power, the realization of freedom.' Presented on 22 January 2003. RIIL WEBCAST. Accessed 1 March 2007 at www.ilru.org/html/training/webcasts/archive/2003/01-22-TN.html

Payne, M. (2002) 'The politics of case management and social work.' *International Journal of Social Welfare 9*, 82–91.

Peck, E. and Smith, H. (1989) 'Safeguarding service users.' *Health Service Journal*, 7 December.

Rapp, C.A. (1998) 'The active ingredients of effective case management: a research synthesis.' *Community Mental Health Journal 34*, 363–80.

Rutter, D., Tyrer, P., Emmanuel, J., Weaver, T., *et al.* (2004) 'Internal vs. external care management in severe mental illness: randomized controlled trial and qualitative study.' *Journal of Mental Health 13*, 453–66.

Scala, M.A. and Nerney, T. (2000) 'People first: the consumers in consumer direction.' *Generations 24*, 55–9.

Silvers, A., Wasserman, D. and Mahowald, M.B. (1998) *Disability, Difference, Discrimination: Perspectives in Bioethics and Public Policy.* New York: Rowman & Littlefield.

Stainton, T. (1994) *Autonomy and Social Policy: Rights, Mental Handicap and Community Care.* Aldershot: Avebury.

Stainton, T. (1998) 'Rights and Rhetoric in Practice: Contradictions for Practitioners.' In A. Symonds and A. Kelly (eds) *The Social Construction of Community Care.* London: Macmillan.

Stainton, T. (2002) 'Taking rights structurally: rights, disability and social worker responses to direct payments.' *British Journal of Social Work 32*, 751–76.

Stainton, T. (2005) 'Empowerment and the architecture of rights based social policy.' *Journal of Intellectual Disabilities 9*, 287–96.

Steering Committee for the Review of Commonwealth/State Service Provision (1998) *Implementing Reforms in Government Services 1998.* Canberra: AusInfo.

Velgouse, L. and Dize, V. (2000) 'A review of state initiatives in consumer directed long-term care.' *Generations 24*, 28–33.

Ziguras, S.J., Stuart, G.W. and Jackson, A.C. (2002) 'Assessing the evidence on case management.' *British Journal of Psychiatry 181*, 17–21.

6

Working with other organisations and other service sectors

Estelle Fyffe

Case managers do not operate in isolation: they work within and across organisations. The policies, practices and culture of their own organisation as well as those of the external organisations with whom they seek partnerships influence how case management is understood and implemented. Case managers can play an important role in challenging organisational processes and decisions that are not consistent with case management principles and create new organisational affiliations to attain the types of support required by the people for whom they work. The case manager who attempts to operate as a 'lone ranger' may achieve some individual successes but will not contribute to change in organisational policies and systems that can thereby safeguard case management standards into the future.

This chapter outlines the organisational contexts of case management practice, describes organisational processes that support or obstruct case management practice, proposes a framework for identifying and addressing barriers to effective case management, and provides practical ideas for tackling these common obstacles and dilemmas.

Organisation-wide values

An organisation-wide approach to case management ensures that all staff, including accountants, receptionists, case managers and managers, have the same sense of priorities and that the values, policies and customs across all parts of the organisation are coherent and consistently reinforce case management goals. A focus on organisational culture extends consideration of the patterns of inter-action between individuals, images and symbols, language, routines, rituals and attitudes that affect decision-making and practice (Morgan 1997). Organisations may appear to champion values, such as a commitment to improving quality of life for people with intellectual disabilities, but their day-to-day operations may fail to match these stated values. Values may be readily espoused in organisational documents but in the absence of awareness, competencies or commitment to how this can be reflected in policies or allocation of resources. For example, the active involvement for people with intellectual disabilities in the organisation may be a stated value. An invitation for people to participate at meetings may be judged unsuccessful; without time, altered processes or resources to make participation a reality, however, the genuineness of the organisational initiative is called into question. Such discrepancies between espoused values and actions can be overcome by examining forces that drive action contrary to the stated values (Argyris 1999).

Discrepancies between espoused organisational values and the practice of individual case managers can have potentially serious consequences. The first of the following examples illustrates an organisation that espouses family-centred practice but has no means to ensure its values are reflected in case management practice. The result is a narrowing of the issues and solutions discussed with the family by the case manager. The second example demonstrates how the case man-ager's family-centred approach in action, and supported within the organisation, attends to a wide range of issues relevant to the family.

> A case manager working with a preschool child with developmental delay limits interventions to organising respite for the child away from home and early intervention developmental activities. She does not intervene when the parents' relationship shows signs of stress and deterioration or when there are requests for information about permanent out-of-home placement as she has been told by her supervisor that it is 'not her job'.

> Another case manager, in similar circumstances, explores the stress on the child's parents with them, resulting in referral for marriage counselling and parent education. Subsequently, the parents' relationship and extended family support improves, and changes are made to the ongoing support for the child and family, including ideas about behaviour support within the family setting, in-home staff for family activities, and opportunities for the

parents to have a holiday and to meet another parent with an older child in order to swap experiences.

The importance of organisational coherency is illustrated further in the following contrasting examples. Case study 6.1 illustrates an organisation supporting case management, while Case study 6.2 reveals conflicting pressures within the organisation that limit the role of the case manager and, inevitably, the result for the individual.

Case study 6.1

Lisa graduates from the local country town school, which she has attended with integration assistance, at the end of the school year. Lisa and her family are unsure of what lies ahead, but because there is no apparent crisis they are reluctant to ask for extra assistance. Mike is her case manager and works for an organisation that has a policy of proactively contacting individuals at points of major life transitions, such as leaving school, leaving home and starting work, to offer assistance rather than reactively waiting until families make contact or a referral is made by another agency indicating that circumstances have deteriorated for the individual and family. Mike is encouraged through his organisation's policies to work with Lisa, her family and the school, so that Lisa has specialist assistance to undertake a further education course that leads to ongoing employment, increasing her financial independence and opportunities to meet people and make friends in the workplace. Mike also continues to work with Lisa and her family towards the goal of her living in her own flat with a friend.

Differences between stated values and practice can lead to confused and inconsistent service models, with the same words being used by different organisations for quite different things. For example, if the espoused policy is a move to flexible, individualised, community living but the bulk of available funding is allocated to group-based approaches, then the service system is likely to remain locked into approaches at odds with the policy. Case managers need to be able to disentangle these inconsistencies, because otherwise they risk confusing and distressing individuals, families and themselves.

For example, four organisations may say that they are 'doing' person-centred planning through their case management activities. What they actually do and

---

Case study 6.2

Jenny, who works with another organisation, is the case manager for Stephanie, a young woman in similar circumstances to Lisa. The organisation with which Jenny is working takes the view that Stephanie and her family have done well to have been given integration assistance at school, and extra assistance is not justified as there are no problems at this stage, despite the stressors known to be associated with leaving school for parents and school-leavers. Stephanie leaves school and remains at home. Her skills and behaviour deteriorate, and only then, in response to a telephone call from her mother, is the case manager able to become involved. Stephanie and her family have no expectations of the future, and Stephanie now becomes distressed quickly in new situations. Eventually she is placed in a group home for people with behavioural disturbances.

---

what is happening in the lives of the people with whom they are working, however, differ greatly. One organisation uses the language of person-centred approaches in policy documents and promotional reports, but without changed expectations of what the staff members are doing. The result is that well-established organisational habits determine what is available for families and individuals, rather than ideas arising from each individual planning process.

Another organisation has adopted a policy that individuals being supported in their own or shared homes are to have complete choice of activities and staff, apparently without any restrictions, but without information being provided on the choice of activities, non-discriminatory staffing practices or processes for dispute resolution. The result is the individual has a limited choice of activities as the staff members lack sufficient information and there is difficulty in retaining workers, who are not satisfied with their role.

Case managers in a third organisation invest considerable time and effort in determining and acquiring material items that individuals cannot otherwise afford, such as furniture, household goods and long journeys to visit relatives. Although beneficial and individualised, the responses are shortsighted. The provision of these items does not have a fundamental or lasting effect on the person's current and future life experiences.

The fourth organisation has adopted formal approaches to case management planning, such as personal futures planning (Mount and Zwernik 1988), Planning Alternative Tomorrows with Hope (PATH) (Pearpoint, O'Brien and

Forest 1993), the McGill Action Planning System (MAPS) (Vandercook, York and Forest 1989) and Essential Life Style Planning (Smull and Burke Harrison 1992), for implementation across the agency. The result is comprehensive and long-term life changes for individuals due to the efforts of all departments in the organisation, which have a shared understanding of the priorities arising from individualised planning and notice when pre-existing organisational practices in relation to staff recruitment, rosters and roles, accounting practices and building requirements jeopardise these directions.

Case management within organisations

Organisations providing case management services are also likely to be involved in other types of service provision. The roles and orientation of staff, such as direct care staff and employment counsellors, in other programmes are often essential for implementation of case plans, in supporting volunteer resources and in working with different communities such that people with disabilities can participate and be welcomed. The orientation of staff in roles not involved directly in service delivery, such as human resources, recruitment, training and financial management, are critical to ensure that corporate processes support case management practice. For example, implementation of case plans may require different and flexible approaches from the organisation, such as involving a person with intellectual disabilities in the management of funds or selection, training and supervision of staff, and participation of family members in the design of housing. The accounts department may need to set up new and devolved procedures in order for an individual to manage and account for his or her own budget. The human resources department may need to develop new procedures for staff selection and training that involve people who use the organisation's services. Staff involved in design and commissioning of housing may need to develop new skills to involve people with intellectual disabilities, or their families and friends, in the planning process.

Senior management and boards of non-government organisations influence case management practice through broad strategy, policy, resource allocation and risk management. New approaches may be needed to assess and manage adherence to legislative and regulatory requirements for occupational health and safety, while ensuring that they do not restrict the lives of the people they support. An underdeveloped aspect of risk management is organisational attention to the risks faced by each person with an intellectual disability, where case management planning and implementation have been inadequate (Sellars 2003). Paying greater attention to these risks would provide a balance to the emphasis on the risk to organisations. The board or senior managers may need to accept reports that give equal or more attention to outcomes for individuals being supported by the organisation as they do to organisational financial considerations. Such changes will happen only if the values that underpin case management are shared by all other parts of the organisation and discrepancies are identified, raised and acted upon.

Case management across organisations

The broad scope of case management with people with intellectual disabilities means that case managers will work with staff across a range of organisations – different levels of government, non-government organisations in sectors such as health, aged care, employment and education, as well as the disability sector and more informal community groups, such as sporting clubs and societies. The case manager must juxtapose an individual's formal support system made up of such organisations with their informal support system comprised of relatives, friends, neighbours and acquaintances.

The concept of the task environment (Hasenfield 1983) external to the case manager's organisation identifies the nature and functions of various external organisations. Of most interest to case managers are those organisations that provide funding and complementary services and supports.

Providers of funding and other resources for the organisation include national and local government, philanthropic trusts, business sponsors, community groups, private donors, fee-paying individuals and volunteers. Funding is generally accompanied by conditions that specify its uses and impose requirements for quality assurance, evaluation and reporting. When an organisation has dual roles, as both the provider of resources and the source of legitimacy, then a confusion of roles may occur.

Organisations that provide related services are often those whose services are essential to the implementation of case management plans. These might span various government departments, such as housing and social security; for-profit and not-for-profit organisations that provide in-home attendant care services; the municipal garden that provides work or volunteer time for a person with intellectual disabilities with an interest in gardening; an occupational therapist who provides advice so that a young child can attend the local preschool; and a community leisure centre that ensures people with intellectual disabilities can be part of its fitness classes.

Common barriers to cross-organisational working

The case manager will encounter barriers to effective working across organisations. The most common of these are competency-, attitude- and systems-based. If they can be identified, then it may be possible to negotiate reductions or solutions (Rothman and Sager 1998).

Competency barriers

Providers of complementary services and supports may or may not have a good understanding of people with intellectual disabilities, the role and practice of case management and its underpinning values. The case manager has an important role in informing, educating and monitoring providers of complementary services and supports. In many instances, this information role extends to friends, family and community members.

Competency barriers arise from lack of information or skill. Comments such as 'We've tried that, and it didn't work' and 'There is no point planning – there has been a lot of planning before, but not much happens' may indicate lack of competency in implementation or planning, or both. For example, see Case study 6.3, which highlights the consequences of limited vision and limited information available to staff, and the importance of complementary services and the behaviour support specialist in assisting case management processes.

Case study 6.3

Kevin is 17 years old. He is very strong and has difficulty expressing himself with words. He moved in to a group home six months ago after repeatedly injuring his mother. In the absence of an overall plan for Kevin, staff support is focused on managing the immediate circumstances. He is kept isolated from other residents and is constantly supervised by large male staff. Kevin isn't part of any activities outside of the house, as his behaviour is considered unsafe. Ellie, a new case manager, questions this short-term approach but is told that she isn't being practical and doesn't understand and that someone will get hurt without the current practices. Ellie persists despite resistance and arranges a detailed behavioural and educational programme, which results in specialist training for staff and gradual transformation of Kevin's daily life as he learns to be part of social situations in the home and the local community.

Attitudinal barriers

Stereotypes can be embedded deeply in organisational culture and affect, and indeed determine, what is expected of and for an individual. Poor competency may reinforce such attitudes. For example, a stereotype that people with intellectual disabilities are like children promotes childish behaviour by adults, overprotection and overdependence. Whether based on negative or positive stereotypes, ideology can be blinding and lead to a failure to recognise, for example, that not all families are well intentioned, not all communities are welcoming and some individuals, if unsupported, make very poor or dangerous choices.

Attitudes that specialist knowledge about intellectual disability and targeted specialist services are irrelevant create barriers. While acknowledging that, historically, many 'special' interventions and service models were exclusionary, there are many circumstances when inclusion is impossible without specialist knowledge and intervention. For example, the health of individuals can be neglected due to an attitude that people with intellectual disabilities should be using generic or mainstream health services. There can be a failure to diagnose the mental illness of a person with an intellectual disability or failure to obtain information about the health or behavioural impact of a syndrome, failure to undertake a behavioural analysis or specialist communication assessment or failure to deploy appropriate educational strategies. If the case manager is unaware of these attitudes, often within complementary services, then the result is that the person with intellectual disabilities is denied skilled and relevant specialist knowledge to make living and participating in the local community a meaningful reality.

Systemic barriers

Policies, procedures and role expectations at various levels of an organisation can create barriers to effective practice. Indeed, competency and attitude barriers often lead to fragmentation of the service system and difficulties in accessing services and supports. Systemic barriers mean it can be exceedingly difficult to arrange transition between services in the event that an individual's needs change, such as due to age, starting a training course or moving house. Eligibility requirements for the new services may differ, the person may be asked to go on a waiting list, or what is wanted may simply not exist. A change of case manager may result in breakdown of supports and services that were being maintained by the skills of the particular worker, as Case study 6.4 demonstrates.

Case study 6.4

Lynda is a middle-aged woman with varied personal support needs and strong family relationships. She has been supported to live in the local community with her family since childhood. Sudden and serious illness of her elderly mother results in Lynda being abruptly moved to a group home 30 kilometres from her home of many years, which results in loss of daily contact with her friends and family and disrupted involvement with her local community and her usual activities. Despite several approaches by the case manager and an advocate, no serious effort is made by the authority controlling supported housing to arrange accommodation in Lynda's local area. Lynda and her mother are distraught but are told that they must accept this place permanently, as no other assistance will be available. Meanwhile, a vacancy in a house close to Lynda's mother is being filled by another representative of the authority, who is placing someone from the area to where Lynda is moving.

Case managers may be involved in brokerage through authorising and facilitating the purchase of services from other organisations. Ideally, the individual chooses from a range of providers, resulting in flexible, personalised services, empowered decision-making and self-management. In practice, brokerage can increase the administration and other costs of services and create systemic barriers. The paradigm of planner–purchaser–provider split can decrease collaboration between organisations to innovate and fail to build opportunities for more people to be part of community activities, settings and situations. The case manager who operates solely on a brokerage model, in the absence of a robust service system that can cater for all needs, is likely to find his or her role restricted to that of a gatekeeper of access to limited resources.

Individualised planning of support that takes into account the unique characteristics and informal supports of the individual needs to be done one person at a time. Individual stories are an important way of communicating real experiences, but policy and planning for unmet and future populations must be informed by aggregated data across individuals and the service system. Without a link between individual plans and forward projections for policy and planning, the service system will be increasingly fractured, inadequate and inequitable.

Despite major advances in countering institutionalisation and routine exclusion of people with intellectual disabilities from the broader community and society, disability service provision has remained apart from much of the rest of the human service system, whether this be accommodation, employment, health, education, arts or sport. There is a tendency for workers within the disability sector to operate in isolation rather than to seek expertise outside the sector, which works against inclusion of the broader service system, community and society (Hirschhorn 1990; Morgan 1997; Obholzer and Roberts 1994). The case manager must constantly challenge and ask what would be available, and what processes would apply, for someone who is not regarded as having a disability and who is a valued citizen and member of their family and community. Inevitably, this means asking more of the community and public sector, the professions and business and expecting more variation from staff members in how and where they undertake their support roles.

Addressing barriers to working within and across organisations

Effective cooperation is more likely between organisations that have negotiated domain consensus – that is, agreed on their respective missions, target populations and programmes and, where these are distinct, where they intersect and where they differ (Levine and White 1974). Analysis of the organisational environment will identify relevant complementary agencies and the potential resources they can offer, identify optimum forms of influence (such as financial incentives, discretionary funds, sanctions, political support, training, liaising, networking and advocacy), and identify where relationships and means for coordination need to be initiated if they do not exist already (Rothman and Sager 1998). Relationships can be negotiated at various levels of the organisation. Partnerships can be built through cross-sector work groups that jointly promote ideas to management. Change management plans and processes can be developed with cross-sector teams, and formal partnerships can be created between organisations.

Possible coordination mechanisms include joint funding, combined information management and public relations programmes, joint surveys, accountability audits, staff secondments, demonstration projects, sharing of facilities, and partnership projects such as joint targeting of difficult-to-serve client groups. Systems integration (Leutz 1999) can occur at the three levels of linkage, coordination and integration.

Work with other case managers

A person with intellectual disabilities may have multiple case managers, as each organisation may assign a case manager. A core task for case managers in such situations is to reach agreement about their respective roles and responsibilities in order to minimise confusion for people with disabilities and to maximise coordination of effort by professionals. Obstacles to such negotiations can be the differing legal and accountability requirements of organisations, differing understandings of case management, and conflicting approaches. For example, the case manager who is working towards inclusion may be attempting to work with a case manager from another organisation who is expected to limit access to resources perceived as scarce, to respond only in a crisis or to respond only to a narrowly defined range of 'core business'. Such obstacles can arise between case managers employed in the same organisation but in different programmes if the organisation does not adopt an integrated organisation-wide approach, for example as shown in Case study 6.5.

Case study 6.5

Kylie, the case manager, establishes that Tim will be able to communicate more effectively with a certain communication aid and that this would increase his prospects of obtaining ongoing part-time employment on either a paid or voluntary basis. Neither Tim nor Irene, his mother, can afford to purchase this aid, and Kylie does not have access to sufficient funds through the agency with which she is working. Kylie applies to a government-subsidised scheme for funds towards the purchase of the equipment. A case manager administering the subsidy scheme refuses the application, saying that equity means the same services for everyone and that there should be no 'double-dipping' and that Tim is already receiving services through the agency with which Kylie is working.

Review decision-making

Person-centred approaches all emphasise the central importance of the individual, and those who care about the person, being able to make informed decisions. The case manager and service-delivery organisation need to be vigilant in monitoring and, if necessary, changing decision-making practices and procedures. Important review questions include:

- Which types of decision are taking the most time and effort? Are those about the eligibility for allocation of limited resources taking more time than those about meeting needs?

- Are family and friends involved in decision-making? Do the location and timing of meetings and decisions support the involvement of informal and natural supports?

- Are the difficult and long-term decisions explored and made? Too often, decision-making emphasises comparatively easy decisions or is reactive to immediate crisis situations.

Review roles and relationships

Given the variability of case management models, it will be important that within the case manager's own organisation, clarity exists about the case manager's roles and relationships to other workers. Important review questions include:

- What is the relationship between the roles of the case manager in this organisation and service delivery staff such as the supervisor of a group home or direct support staff working in a person's home or community? How does this change of service delivery staff impact on other complementary agencies? What about community groups?

- Does each case manager in the organisation relate to other organisations and sectors collaboratively or as a competitor? What can be done to reduce division between services?

Conclusion

An effective case manager works across the boundaries of organisations and sectors, and across the boundaries of formal services and informal supports and networks. Effective case management in the intellectual disability sector is distinct from direct service delivery because it involves holistic planning, a present and long-term futures orientation, and collaborative work across other organisations, sectors and with community groups in order to locate a range of services and supports. The case manager and his or her employing organisation has a role to play in aggregating information about group needs as a basis for planning, innovation and building the capacity of the community and sector in order to provide what is needed by individuals and groups of people with intellectual disabilities. The case manager may also have a role in coaching, educating and consulting with other staff and community groups. Organisations employing case managers have a responsibility to assist this to happen through organisation-wide, consistent approaches to case management.

The case manager needs to work with a broad range of organisations if inclusion of people with intellectual disabilities is to be achieved. Likely obstacles, and strategies for addressing these, have been outlined. Understanding the contribution required at all levels and from all departments at the organisation in which the case manager is working is necessary in order to enable and maintain effective case management and to avoid other departments unwittingly undermining the intent and possibilities of case management.

References

Argyris, C. (1999) *On Organisational Learning.* Oxford: Blackwell.

Hasenfeld, Y. (1983) *Human Service Organisations.* Englewood Cliffs, NJ: Prentice Hall.

Hirschhorn, L. (1990) *The Workplace Within: Psychodynamics of Organisational Life.* Cambridge, MA: MIT Press.

Leutz, W. (1999) 'Five laws for integrating medical and social services: lessons from the United States and United Kingdom.' *Millbank Quarterly 77,* 77–110.

Levine, S. and White, P.E. (1974) 'Exchange as a Conceptual Framework for the Study of Inter-organisational Relationships.' In Y. Hasenfeld and R.A. English (eds) *Human Service Organisations: A Book of Readings.* Ann Arbor, MI: University of Michigan Press.

Morgan, G. (1997) *Images of Organization.* Thousand Oaks, CA: Sage.

Mount, B. and Zwernik, K. (1988) *It's Never too Early, It's Never too Late: A Booklet about Personal Futures Planning.* Publication No. 421-88-109. St Paul, MN: Metropolitan Council.

Obholzer, A. and Roberts, V. (1994) *The Unconscious at Work: Individual and Organisational Stress in the Human Services.* London: Routledge.

Pearpoint, J., O'Brien, J. and Forest, M. (1993) *PATH (Planning Alternative Tomorrows with Hope): A Workbook for Planning Positive Futures.* Toronto: Inclusion Press.

Rothman, J. and Sager, J.S. (1998) *Case Management: Integrating Individual and Community Practices.* Needham Heights, MA: Allyn & Bacon.

Sellars, C. (2003) *Risk Assessment in People with Learning Disabilities.* Oxford: Blackwell.

Smull, M. and Burke Harrison, S. (1992) *Supporting People with Severe Reputations in the Community.* Alexandria, VA: National Association of State Mental Retardation Program Directors.

Vandercook, T., York, J. and Forest, M. (1989) 'The McGill Action Planning System (MAPS): a strategy for building the vision.' *Journal of the Association for Persons with Severe Handicaps 14,* 205–15.

7

Working to empower families: perspectives of care managers

Gordon Grant and Paul Ramcharan

The primary aim of this chapter is to sketch out issues faced by care managers in their work with families who have children or adult relatives with intellectual disabilities. The chapter shows that when coupled with person-centred or family-centred ideals, care management practice can be very challenging to implement. The first part of the chapter problematises the implementation issues based on the experiences of care managers. The second part of the chapter argues that there have been tensions and ambiguities in deciding what constitutes 'proper' support for families and that these have pulled care managers in different directions. It is suggested that, ultimately, these tensions need to be resolved in favour of a model that empowers rather than just supports families.

The studies

The case data presented in this chapter are drawn from two studies in which the authors have been involved. The studies are believed to have a relevance to contemporary practice in that they provide glimpses of how care managers were striving in their brokerage, support and coordination roles to enable people to achieve their goals and aspirations. Both studies were completed in Wales following the All Wales Strategy (Welsh Office 1983) that gave a strong push to the inclusion of people with intellectual disabilities and their families in the planning, management and delivery of needs-led services.

The first study, completed in 1995 (Felce *et al.* 1998; Grant, McGrath and Ramcharan 1995), involved examining how care managers sought to package support in ways that allowed person-centred goals to be met; the details described here have not been reported before. The second study examined coping strategies in families and how care managers assessed and supported them (Grant and Whittell 2001).

In the first study, interviews were held with 47 care managers who were part of community learning disability teams (CLDTs) (25 social workers, 18 community nurses, 4 health visitors) and 14 members of staff working in specialist intellectual disability services about putting person-centred individualised work into practice. Interviews were structured loosely around an aide-memoire. The findings demonstrate some of the complexities of the triadic relationships between care managers, the family and the person with intellectual disabilities.

In the second study, 100 families were interviewed about their coping strategies, following which their care managers were interviewed about how they attempted to reinforce family coping.

Study 1: enabling person-centred individualised work

Labour intensity

In effecting a shift from a service-led to a user-led system where support is determined by the articulations, hopes and dreams of individuals and families, it quickly became apparent how labour-intensive care management needed to be. Individualised packages of support had to be created and negotiated in consultation with service users and families rather than simply being handed down by professionals. It was to be a time-consuming process. In attempting to get closer to hear and understand the voices of people with intellectual disabilities, care managers were spending lots of time observing and talking to individuals directly as well as generating second-order accounts from their advocates, allies and families.

In engaging people in creative ways to find more personalised solutions to their needs and problems, care managers had to face the inevitable contradictions and fallibilities that define us all as human beings – for example, individuals were sometimes prone to change their minds about things for no apparent reason, they forgot they already had information about things but had misplaced the details, and they wanted more time to mull things over. Such things operate at a mundane level in everyday life, but they multiplied the demands on care managers and emphasised the importance of pacing decision-making in line with what individuals could cope with. This required of care managers patience, persistence and preparedness for an intensity of involvement with both the people with intellectual disabilities and their families.

Reconciling different voices

Care managers were exercised by the active listening requirements of their role when working with people with limited verbal articulacy. There was often insufficient time, however, to assimilate the personalised verbal and non-verbal vocabularies of every person with intellectual disabilities, and so there was a high dependence on being informed by the perspectives of advocates, allies and family members who knew the person more intimately. Third parties such as these had established relationships with individuals; care managers, by virtue of their role, were constantly developing and abrogating relationships with individuals. There is then a tension between accepting a family member's interpretation of an individual's needs and establishing an independent dialogue with that family member when coming to a determination of what is in the person's best interests.

Kate, a social worker, sums up the dilemma well:

> Susan's speech has actually been very difficult to understand, and her mother and her close family are the only ones who can really understand everything she is saying. I find it very difficult because I think you have to have a lot of contact with Susan over a long period of time to be able to understand her speech. Obviously I don't have that extent, although I can pick up a fair bit after a while. So a lot of what I do tends to be through the mother.

Families as gatekeepers

Care managers reported struggles with parents who firmly policed access to their children and relatives. There were many reasons for this – some families had had poor previous experiences with services, and so care managers had to earn their trust as representatives of the service system; other families had acquired considerable expertise in managing things effectively, and so care managers often had to prove themselves in being 'up to the job' by demonstrating their intimate knowledge of the client; some families simply did not want change or challenge, especially if this meant being prepared to allow risks to be a part of the person's everyday life; in other cases, there were interdependent needs and circumstances between client and family that the family was keen to protect.

Typical examples

Case studies 7.1 and 7.2 show some typical examples.

Case study 7.1

Freda, a social worker, was seeking to persuade David's 78-year-old mother, Ethel, from carrying on with her caregiving responsibilities because of her failing physical capacity and health and David's need for a more permanent housing solution:

> We don't tend to engage in confrontations with Ethel because she will just stop the conversation dead. She's well aware of what we'd like to do and how we would like to work with David and encourage him to develop, but she just puts a wall up. Not an impression. It's what she's stated. She doesn't want change. The potential conflict is always there. One would think that she needed respite and time for herself and trying to maintain her own interests, but she doesn't see it that way. David is the main interest in her life. Our concerns are about her health. She doesn't really want to recognise that.

Case study 7.2

A social worker, Carly, had been working for some time with June, a 30-year-old woman with severe intellectual disabilities who had been showing too much affection with boys and men in inappropriate situations. Carly had consulted the clinical psychologist in the team with a view to putting in place an educational programme for June, but Carly was forced to report a failed attempt to move on this front:

> Whenever you see things that are very obvious for June's development, you are just stopped. You start the ball rolling, you set up the work and all the rest of it, and Mum or Dad halts it.

Questioning the accepted family norms

Despite the 'brick walls' that families could erect to keep professionals at bay, there were success stories. Sometimes, where there seemed to be intransigence on the part of the family, care managers had to wait until a crisis occurred that legitimated their involvement. On other occasions, the maturation of the person with intellectual disabilities meant that families were forced to accept the need to change the accepted ground rules. See Case study 7.3 for an example.

Case study 7.3

Glenys, a social worker, had been working with Steve, a 20-year-old man with severe physical disabilities and very limited speech and who had been living a restricted social life because of the protective stance taken by his mother, Connie. Efforts had been made to inform Steve about community living options, since this was an age-appropriate thing for him to do. Steve had been persuaded to give this a try, but Connie was prepared to view this only as a consequence of her coping problems with Steve. In this particular case, it hinged on an acceptance that Steve was still growing and maturing and that his mother was not coping:

> On an afternoon, he has a sleep from 1.30 to 2 p.m. Mum thinks he needs a sleep and he's in bed by 6 or 7 p.m., whereas for an adolescent what we are trying to do is for him to go out of an evening. It's about power imbalance, shifting the power to the service user, and Mum's finding this difficult because it's acceptance that Steve is maturing. Her language is changing gradually – how she actually addresses Steve – so there's optimism there.

Caught in the middle: responsibility without power

Much of the work of care managers is without statutory power, and so the capacity to influence change is dependent on professional skill and expertise and the capacity to influence third parties. Individual plans, shared action plans and person-centred plans, while being the basis for action between user, family and support team, are not necessarily the same as an executive authority to act.

Kay, a social worker, reflecting on creating a personalised support package for Frank, summed up the dilemma succinctly:

> Individual plans can't be a contract. If we identify Frank's need, say for music therapy, I can't make that happen. All I can do is ask for it. I've got no clout. I've got no clout at all to make that happen, particularly if those services lie outside my own department because not only do I not have any clout, but I might not have the necessary knowledge of that department. At least in my

own department I know how to make waves. We're kind of middle people without any real power, so it's quite difficult.

The separation of professional from executive authority to act is a generic problem in health and social care services, and one that is being addressed through a variety of micro-budgeting and direct payments systems, but it remains an example of how 'system architecture' (Emerson and Stancliffe 2004) can constrain or liberate action in the frontline.

Study 2: assessing coping strategies in families
Invisible care

It was found that care managers did not realise the full extent of the coping repertoires of families. This was especially true for cognitive coping strategies, suggesting that families are much more adept at reframing the meaning of their circumstances than care managers believe. The same underlying pattern was in evidence for problem-solving and stress-alleviation strategies used by families, but to a lesser extent.

Reasons as to why this may be so remain speculative, but two plausible propositions emerged from the data. The first concerns the 'invisibility' of caregiving: families often seek to render caregiving invisible from relatives and third parties in order to maintain privacy and to protect the integrity of the person they are supporting. The person's 'best interests' are thought to be protected if they are not reminded of their dependency on others at every turn. It is easy to see how this concealment of care can lead to a perception by care managers that families might be overprotecting their relative.

The second reason is tied more to the nature of cognitive coping itself, this involving a range of dispositions, analytical capacities and frames of reference that individuals bring to their everyday caregiving. By their very nature, these are internal devices that are not always articulated. Unless care managers have particularly close working relationships with families or use assessment frameworks that map cognitive coping styles, they are unlikely to be acknowledged or reinforced.

The persistence of stereotype

We found that care managers significantly overstated the value to families of maintaining interests outside caring. They were of the view that paid work or engagement in voluntary organised activity provided families with a means of respite, escape or identity affirmation. This did appear to be the case for a few, but not for the majority and clearly not to the extent that care managers supposed. Interview narratives suggested that these 'interests outside caring' could for many be taxing and without a guarantee of psychological reward. Further, they took time, effort and a long-term commitment that had to be engineered around finely balanced family routines.

The focus of assessment

In relation to assessment and review, care managers were engaged mostly with the primary carer, typically the mother. The focus, or perspective, was therefore maternal care rather than the family system. Care managers admitted that knowledge of spouses or partners was very sketchy; information about them and about siblings and other relatives was filtered largely through the lens of the mothers. The pressures on care managers were immense, and there were both logistical and workload difficulties in engaging other family informants or in bringing together everyone for family group conferences.

Much of the time and energy of care managers was taken up in working directly with the person with intellectual disabilities, listening to the person, seeking to understand his or her views and aspirations, exploring ways of addressing these with the person, testing out possible solutions and then consulting the family in order to arrive at an agreed plan. Care managers were therefore occupied for only a small part of their time in working directly with families, as they generally gave priority to one-to-one work with their primary clients. Their knowledge, therefore, about expertise in families and about what coping strategies work was not particularly strong.

Structural issues

At the time of the research, care managers were working to an administrative model of care management that involved lots of paperwork, assessment for charging for services, and brokerage work with other agencies. This was often cited as eclipsing opportunities for the development of empathic, therapeutic relationships with families. It also required care managers to be very selective in their work and to concentrate on problem-solving and crisis work with urgent cases. Large caseloads, staff turnover and consequent discontinuities in staff covering arrangements added to these difficulties, making the coordination of continuous, seamless support to families all but impossible.

Summarising the issues

Findings from these studies suggest that there are both structural and process problems in making care management work with families. Problems relating to process issues appear to be tied to:

- the intensity of work necessary to achieve person-centred ideals
- the reconciliation of different voices
- gatekeeping roles played by families
- breaching of family norms
- recognition of invisible care in families
- stereotyping of families.

Structural factors added a further layer of complexities to these problems, especially:

- individual case working as the predominant model and lack of focus on the family as the unit of assessment and provision
- responsibility without the authority to command and control resources within an interagency system
- an administrative model of care management
- caseload size
- staff turnover.

Contemporary thinking and policy have emphasised the need to ensure that families are integral to person-centred planning (Department of Health 2001; Scottish Executive 2000; Welsh Assembly 2002) and, therefore, implicitly to care management. It is suggested, however, that there has been a lack of clarity about requirements for working in partnership with families, and that this turns on deciding whether to retain a support model or one that seeks more explicitly to empower families.

Towards a more explicit model of empowerment in working with families?

In looking at the data from the two studies outlined above, a number of features of professional interventions might be identified. For example, it remains clear that professional work including both assessment and provision is guided by a focus on the individual. Couching professional work in these terms, it is more likely that the nature of personal conflicts between members of the family will be high-lighted, as was identified in the case material presented earlier.

The direction of input structured around professionally assessed needs is also an area in which the sources of service provision are likely to be less oriented around the family and more in terms of available formal services. In this sense, bureaucracy and structure may themselves dictate how the service input is designed and delivered. This was evident in some of the data presented earlier. To understand these data further, and to mark up future prospects for engaging families more fully as partners, Table 7.1 presents a comparison of overt features of the data and sets these against what we term an empowerment-led approach. The challenges involved in effecting this implied shift towards a more empower-ment-led approach are discussed.

Professional orientation

It has been argued that families want to be free of the culture of paternalism that can still pervade services and to be liberated to direct professional attention to goals and circumstances that the family consider important (Barnes 1997; Case 2000; Clarke 2001; Murray 2000). This means shifting the focus from indi-vidualised casework to family systems models and to the systemic features of empowerment.

Family systems frameworks (Dunst, Trivette and Deal 1994; Dunst *et al.* 1993) can be a powerful device for nurturing ways of empowering families. This is essentially because the focus of attention is the family unit as a whole, how it defines itself, its membership, its boundaries of responsibility and its values and ethics. Family systems' thinking not only recognises the needs and contributions of individual family members but also draws attention to the way in which the family organises itself and how it functions as an organic unit.

Labonté (1996, p.53) has suggested that empowerment operates simulta-neously at three connected levels:

1. At the intrapersonal level it is the experience of a potent sense of self... It is power within, the experience of choice.

2. At the interpersonal level, it is power with, the experience of interdependency.

3. At the intergroup level, it is the cultivation of resources and strategies for personal and socio-political gains, enhancing advocacy and participatory democracy, creating greater social equity: it is power between, the experience of generosity.

Table 7.1 Models of family support

Parameter	Traditional support	Empowerment-led
Professional orientation	Individualised casework	Family systems models
View of family as resource	Autonomy of individual members	Appreciation of individual autonomy and reciprocities
		Support for (i) circle of support, (ii) roles beyond family caregiving
Authority base	Professional as expert	Family as expert
	Professional as case manager	Family as case manager
Predominating view of the family	Pathological	Optimistic and hopeful
	Stereotypical	(Salutogenic)
Assessment	Needs-driven	Outcome-focused and process-oriented
	Process-oriented	
Source of solution	Services	Family and community resources supported by services
		Emphasis on linkages between personal, interpersonal and intergroup levels
Perspective	Crisis management	Emphasis on temporal factors in care management
	Short-term imperatives	
Decision-making	Zero-sum game	Non-zero-sum game
Pacing	Dictated by services	Dictated by family
Organisational	Formal/bureaucratic	Organic/network driven
Knowledge base	Case knowledge	Case knowledge
	System knowledge	System knowledge
		Biographic knowledge
		Communicative knowledge
		Community knowledge

Adapted from Grant (2003), p.110

Labonté stresses the interdependencies between these three levels, and it is easy to see why. The exercise of voice (the intrapersonal level) is a prerequisite, but alone it will not necessarily change relations of power. This is why some strategies of user or family involvement fail – empowering one stakeholder does not guarantee change or transformation in others, which may be necessary in order to achieve desired outcomes. Individuals are connected to the wider world through other people and through organisations, networks and collectives – hence the need for transformations to take place at the interpersonal and intergroup levels too.

The ascendancy of thinking about person-centred planning has emphasised the importance of circles of support (family, friends, allies) as the vehicle for effecting change. In this, it does so by bringing into play power through supportive interdependent relationships (Clark, Garland and Williams 2005). It is predicated on a shared community of interest alongside the individualisation of care in the hope of bolstering the prospects of change at the intergroup level. Mechanisms for connecting circles of support to the third, intergroup, level appear to be less well articulated. It has been suggested, however, that intergroup change is possible through the careful application of evidence-based family systems-based approaches or through integrating community work into frontline practice (Ramcharan and Richardson 2005).

The dilemma for care managers is that they are still dealing with families that do not necessarily want empowerment at all three levels. From the case material presented earlier, we can see more easily the exercise of power at the intrapersonal and interpersonal levels. Aspirations implied by intergroup empowerment, although desirable, may suit the circumstances of only a minority of families.

View of family as a resource

With regard to the family as a resource, the more traditional support model would tend to emphasise the autonomy of individual members, while an understanding and reinforcement of reciprocities and exchanges between family members and with others lies at the heart of an empowerment-led approach.

It leads more naturally to recognition of factors such as mutual support and associated rewards that foster and sustain a commitment to continued care. Viewing the family as a resource, family systems thinking helps to elucidate the contributions and responsibilities of individual family members, bringing with it sensitivity to the many roles that families play and the interdependent relations between these. For example, continued caregiving may be dependent upon sustaining a work–life balance, obligations towards other family members, including children, and renegotiation of family member roles. Acknowledging and reinforcing these commitments will require care managers to be sensitive to the more invisible aspects of family care work described earlier.

Authority base

From the case material, we can see that care managers were very much aware that different families were at different points in their caregiving careers or 'journeys'. Engaging families, however, was not always straightforward, because of their stances as gatekeepers or because there were issues about reconciling the different perspectives of family members and the person with intellectual disabilities.

Although families may begin as relative novices in the business of caregiving, there is compelling evidence that over time their expertise, authority and insight into providing ethical and tailored care and in doing their own care management is beyond doubt (Nolan, Grant and Keady 1996). In such a 'carers as experts' model, the temporal dimension is important, as changing demands and circumstances provide fresh opportunities for new learning and adaptation. Hence, within an empowerment-led model, care managers need to know when to acknowledge or to nurture expertise in families.

Predominating view of the family

Within the case material, there was some evidence that families were indulging in protecting and insulating their relative, fuelling stereotypes about family pathology. Growing evidence demonstrates that despite adversity and oppression, people with intellectual disabilities and families can surface and maintain a buoyancy or resilience over time (Clarke and Clarke 2003; Grant, Ramcharan and Goward 2003; Hawley and DeHaan 1996). This requires not only a long-term, but also an optimistic, view about what individuals and families can accomplish, and to pay attention to person–environment interactions and how these are mediated. It does not mean that families will be immune to problems and difficulties; rather, contemporary thinking about this suggests that there are frameworks that may help us to understand how it is that people can cope well over time (Antonovsky 1987; Folkman 1997; Larson 1998). The evidence suggests that reward mechanisms and attachments built into family caregiving can have lasting and, to a degree, stress-insulating effects.

Assessment

In relation to assessment work with families, an approach based on empowerment principles is more likely to identify important self-determined strengths, wishes and dreams. The building blocks to potential solutions to problems will not necessarily be services; rather, what will count are how families come to define the problem themselves and how they appraise natural resources available to them. Implicit within family discourses are references to the motivational factors in care work and parenting, and from these we get a sense of what purposes and outcomes are important to families. Elsewhere (Grant *et al.* 1998) it has been suggested that this requires an appreciation of perceived gains for (i) the person with intellectual disabilities, (ii) individual family members and (iii) the family as a whole.

Source of solution

In such a model, the task for the care manager will be to identify with the family their support network and local communities of interest, for example, other families, self-help groups and community agencies, in order to help the family develop competencies and self-confidence to seek help from these sources, to problem-solve for themselves and thereby to maintain a strong sense of control. Services may well have a support role, but it may not necessarily always be as provider – it may be as coordinator, enabler, guide or information provider. The work itself may be more indirect than direct, emphasising the care management role. It is in this connection that one can begin to see the connections between the intrapersonal, interpersonal and intragroup levels that Labonté (1996) talked about as being essential to empowerment practice.

Perspective

Despite being premised on a proactive approach to planning at the individual case level, care management can itself be propelled by crisis management and short-term imperatives, but families also need to be able to take a longer-term view. They need to be able to plan for the future, to make contingency plans in the face of any sudden changes in circumstances and, in concert with this, to achieve a sense of certainty and security from the situation. This once again emphasises the importance of a temporal perspective undergirding action (Grant, Nolan and Keady 2003).

Decision-making

There are those who remain sceptical about the capacity of services to accomplish empowerment (Dowson 1997). Others, like Labonté (1996), are more optimistic. Labonté suggests that empowerment can exist in two forms – either as a zero-sum game in which the empowerment of one partner implies an opportunity cost or sacrifice to the other, or as a non-zero-sum game involving the wider transformation of partnership practice, where individuals, families and other stakeholders all participate and derive benefits. More evidence in support of either position would be very helpful, although the case for the second of these positions seems quite compelling.

For example, by working to increase a family carer's control over assessment and care management processes, it is possible that this will in turn lead to improved outcomes for carers (self-esteem, experience, self-efficacy), the family as a whole (family cohesion), the disabled child (personal development, family integration) and the care manager (subsequent reduction in the need for direct work with the family). There is something, then, about the nature of what might be termed 'contributions' that, given the 'right conditions', can have a multiplier effect.

Pacing

From the case material presented earlier, it is clear that one of the variables that families wanted to be able to control was the pace at which things happened. For care managers, this required a balancing act – if they forced things too much, families could easily withdraw and 'shut the door'; if they backed off too much, families could begin to feel excluded. Low-cost, low-profile strategies could, however, be very effective and empowering for families. Receiving unsolicited phone calls from care managers to check on things could have identity-affirming and long-lasting effects and could avoid the view that contacts with professionals were always associated with crises.

Organisational arrangements

The arrangements needed to deliver the above are unlikely to be found in a single organisational model, especially bureaucracies. The history of care management in the UK tells us that there are many organisational models, both multiagency and multiprofessional, that require consideration here and that the relationships between care management and person-centred planning still need to be worked through (Cambridge and Carnaby 2005). The creation of alliances between indi-

viduals, families, support networks, community agencies and provider organisation (statutory, not-for-profit and for-profit) with respect to issues such as
decision-making authority, control of resources, ethics and accountability
suggests the need for a set of more organic arrangements that respects the importance of organisational networking. How this is best addressed remains an open
question.

Knowledge base

These considerations pose challenges for the types of knowledge involved in
getting closer to families in professional practice. Drawing on the work of
Liaschenko (1997) and Mead and Bower (2000), these can be summarised
briefly:

- *Case knowledge* refers to disembodied biomedical knowledge, i.e.
  knowledge of aetiology, clinical symptoms and prognoses. It is this
  knowledge that most clearly differentiates professional and clinical
  workers as people with authority and power from patients, families
  and others.

- *System knowledge* concerns knowledge of the structure and functioning
  of health and personal social services relevant to a person's
  circumstances.

- *Biographic knowledge* refers to personal histories and circumstances and
  how life patterns are governed by developmental, social and cultural
  clocks. To some extent, care managers had access to such knowledge
  through case files. Care managers, however, were typically dependent
  on mothers as informants, and their direct knowledge of other family
  members was often scant or, at best, second-hand.

- *Communicative knowledge* is concerned with agency – that is, how
  people convey intent, meaning and understanding. This is especially
  important for people with high support needs, as for many such
  people their verbal competencies are severely impaired, making
  non-verbal communication, assistive communication technologies,
  allies and advocates important. In the use of these complementary
  communication systems with their own children, families are often
  more expert than the professionals.

- *Community knowledge* refers to how individuals relate to physical, social
  and political environments.

In the present policy climate, where such a great emphasis is placed on the forging of partnerships between care managers, other professionals, families and individuals, all of these types of knowledge have to be brought into the equation. A dependency on case or system knowledge is not going to work, as this reinforces traditional power relations and fails to capture other types of knowledge that are central to understanding and empowering people. Acknowledging this will itself be an act of professional humility; acting on it will require a more serious investment in getting to know people, which, although costly of time and resources in the short term, is likely to be empowering and with long-term benefits.

Conclusion

The rhetoric of empowerment has been around for some time. In this chapter, an attempt has been made to problematise the challenges and opportunities care managers face when working with families, and to locate these within a context that is increasingly emphasising empowerment practice. Although the implied shift from a support to an empowerment-led approach might be desirable, there are significant challenges to be addressed.

Process factors continued to dog progress – accomplishing the intensity of work involved; brokering the needs and contributions of different stakeholders; achieving a family systems focus; attending to the 'pacing' requirements of decision-making; unearthing and reinforcing important 'invisible' contributions of family members; and the diverse knowledge requirements of empowerment practice.

Structural problems were a continual thorn in the side – responsibility without the authority to act; workloads; discontinuous relationships with families; system architecture issues with varieties of emergent practices, such as direct payments systems (Dowson 2000) and micro-budgeting models (Cambridge and Carnaby 2005); and a lack of impetus for empowerment practice at an intergroup level.

At the time of writing, hard evidence for the kind of empowerment practice described above is not easy to find. It is once again a field in which values lead practice. It would be a pity if care managers were to be left as scapegoats for an evolving system that has devoted too little of its resources to an evaluation of what works, for whom, and under what circumstances. These core questions need to be asked now if care managers are to be helped to address the challenges of the present policy agenda in working with families.

References

Antonovsky, A. (1987) *Unraveling the Mystery of Health*. San Francisco, CA: Jossey Bass.

Barnes, M. (1997) 'Families and Empowerment.' In P. Ramcharan, G. Roberts, G. Grant and J. Borland (eds) *Empowerment in Everyday Life: Learning Disability*. London: Jessica Kingsley Publishers.

Cambridge, P. and Carnaby, S. (eds) (2005) *Person-Centred Planning and Care Management with People with Learning Disabilities*. London: Jessica Kingsley Publishers.

Case, S. (2000) 'Refocusing on the parent: what are the social issues of concern for parents of disabled children?' *Disability and Society 15*, 271–92.

Clark, D., Garland, R. and Williams, V. (2005) 'Promoting Empowerment: Your Life can Change if You Want it to.' In P. Cambridge and S. Carnaby (eds) *Person-Centred Planning and Care Management with People with Learning Disabilities*. London: Jessica Kingsley Publishers.

Clarke, A. and Clarke, A. (2003) *Human Resilience: A Fifty Year Quest*. London: Jessica Kingsley Publishers.

Clarke, N. (2001) 'Training as a vehicle to empower carers in the community: more than a question of information sharing.' *Health and Social Care in the Community 9*, 79–88.

Department of Health (2001) *Valuing People: A New Strategy for Learning Disability for the 21st Century*. London: HMSO.

Dowson, C. (2000) *Independent Successes: Implementing Direct Payments*. New York: York Publishing Services.

Dowson, S. (1997) 'Empowerment within Services: A Comfortable Delusion.' In P. Ramcharan, G. Roberts, G. Grant and J. Borland (eds) *Empowerment in Everyday Life: Learning Disability*. London: Jessica Kingsley Publishers.

Dunst, C.J., Trivette, C.M. and Deal, A.G. (1994) *Supporting and Strengthening Families*, Vol. 1. Cambridge, MA: Brookline Books.

Dunst, C.J., Trivette, C.M., Starnes, A.L., Hamby, D.W. and Gordon, N.J. (1993) *Building and Evaluating Family Support Initiatives*. Baltimore, MD: Paul H. Brookes.

Emerson, E. and Stancliffe, R. (2004) 'Planning and action: comments on Mansell and Beadle-Brown.' *Journal of Applied Research in Intellectual Disabilities 17*, 23–6.

Felce, D., Grant, G., Todd, S., Ramcharan, P., *et al.* (1998) *Towards a Full Life: Researching Policy Innovation for People with Learning Disabilities*. Oxford: Butterworth Heinemann.

Folkman, S. (1997) 'Positive psychological states and coping with severe stress.' *Social Science and Medicine 45*, 1207–21.

Grant, G. (2003) 'Caring Families: Their Support or Empowerment?' In K. Stalker (ed.) *Reconceptualising Work with Carers: New Directions for Policy and Practice*. London: Jessica Kingsley Publishers.

Grant, G. and Whittell, B. (2001) 'Do families and care managers have a similar view of family coping?' *Journal of Learning Disabilities 5*, 111–20.

Grant, G., McGrath, M. and Ramcharan, P. (1995) 'Community inclusion of older people with learning disabilities.' *Care in Place 2*, 29–44.

Grant, G., Nolan, M. and Keady, J. (2003) 'Supporting families over the life course: mapping temporality.' *Journal of Intellectual Disability Research 47*, 342–51.

Grant, G, Ramcharan, P. and Goward, P. (2003) 'Resilience, family care and people with intellectual disabilities.' *International Review of Research in Mental Retardation 26*, 135–73.

Grant, G., Ramcharan, P., McGrath, M., Nolan, M. and Keady, J. (1998) 'Rewards and gratifications among family caregivers: towards a refined model of caring and coping.' *Journal of Intellectual Disability Research 42*, 58–71.

Hawley, D. and DeHaan, L. (1996) 'Towards a definition of family resilience: Integrating life-span and family perspectives.' *Family Process 35*, 283–98.

Labonté, R. (1996) 'Measurement and Practice: Power Issues in Quality of Life, Health Promotion and Empowerment.' In R. Renwick, I. Brown and M. Nagler (eds) *Quality of Life in Health Promotion and Rehabilitation: Conceptual Approaches, Issues and Applications.* Thousand Oaks, CA: Sage.

Larson, E. (1998) 'Reframing the meaning of disability to families: the embrace of paradox.' *Social Science and Medicine 47*, 865–75.

Liaschenko, J. (1997) 'Knowing the Patient.' In S.E. Thorne and V.E. Harp (eds) *Nursing Praxis: Knowledge and Action.* Thousand Oaks, CA: Sage.

Mead, N. and Bower, P. (2000) 'Patient-centredness: a conceptual framework and review of literature.' *Social Science and Medicine 51*, 1087–110.

Murray, P. (2000) 'Disabled children, parents and professionals: partnership on whose terms?' *Disability and Society 15*, 683–98.

Nolan, M., Grant, G. and Keady, J. (1996) *Understanding Family Care: A Multidimensional Model of Caring and Coping.* Buckingham: Open University Press.

Ramcharan, P. and Richardson, M. (2005) 'Engaging Communities of Interest.' In G. Grant, P. Goward, M. Richardson and P. Ramcharan (eds) *Learning Disability: A Life Cycle Approach to Valuing People.* Maidenhead: Open University Press/McGraw-Hill Education.

Scottish Executive (2000) *The Same as You: A Review of Services for People with Learning Disabilities.* Edinburgh: Scottish Executive.

Welsh Assembly (2002) *Fulfilling the Promises: Proposals for a Framework for Services for People with Learning Disabilities.* Cardiff: Welsh Assembly.

Welsh Office (1983) *All Wales Strategy for the Development of Services for Mentally Handicapped People.* Cardiff: Welsh Office.

8

A life managed or a life lived?
A parental view on case management

Marie Knox

Case management is a prevalent and constructive set of practices used in services for people with disabilities to enable these individuals not only to more readily lead satisfying and productive lives but also to take their place in their community as valued and respected citizens. My son, Graham (where relevant, pseudonyms have been used), is one such person. Graham is a young man in his early thirties who has a significant disability. He shares his group home with four other people, also with significant disabilities. Graham also takes part in a community access programme. Both of these services use case management as a means to support him and his peers to take their part as young adults in the community and to exercise and enjoy their rights as citizens.

Case management has brought significant advantages for many people with disabilities similar to Graham. Among other things, case management, as writers such as Derezotes (2000) and Woodside and McClam (1998) have pointed out, offers a means of personalising support for the person with disabilities, a far cry from the depersonalisation of support systems for people with disabilities where exclusion and segregation were the predominant paradigms and in which the person's rights were all too often compromised.

I would like here to share some reflections, as a parent, on experiences around case management. These reflections not only come from my parental experiences with Graham but also draw on my learning from the case management experiences of many other families whose family members use a disability support service with a similar case management arrangement. I hope that these reflections may help to shed light on a different perspective on case management and its impact – a perspective that, in my view, has to date received scant attention. To do this, it is necessary to first describe the case management structure operating in the service systems with which Graham and his peers are involved.

Model of case management

Within the service sectors with which Graham and his peers are involved, the case manager (often referred to as the key worker) is not a distinctive role position. Rather, the case management duties are incorporated into the support worker's regular role. In this model, case management is a set of duties to be performed in addition to or as an integral part of support worker duties. Such an approach is akin to the 'organisational' case management model identified by Woodside and McClam (1998). As these authors further point out, this approach to case management is a common arrangement, whereby the person with a disability, particularly in adulthood, is living away from their family and the case management process is seen as ongoing rather than of a short-term nature. In this situation, the responsibilities of case managers include organising and conducting the individual planning process, monitoring the implementation and evaluation of goals set within this process, ensuring medical and health needs are met, maintaining contact with the family, and in general ensuring the lifestyle quality of the person with disabilities. The role is rotated regularly (usually annually) among the various support workers in order to ensure all relevant support-worker personnel become familiar with the particular disabled individual. The individual and his or her family have very little, if any, say either in the appointment of the case manager or in the changes to this appointment that are made. Individuals occupying this case management role vary in their competence, their commitment and their ability to carry out the role effectively within an organisational framework. Thus, these changes, while valuable to staff, can be destabilising to the person if they are not carried out in a timely and sensitive manner – a process that can, at times, be difficult in a bureaucratic or organisational setting.

Within this context, I would like to offer my observations on case management around the following issues:

- the nature of the family–case manager relationship in adulthood – the balancing act

- the balancing act in case management efforts

- significant issues impacting on case management effectiveness in the balancing act.

Nature of family–case manager relationship in adulthood: the balancing act

Effective working relationships between the key worker, family members and the person with a disability have been recognised widely as essential for ensuring the wellbeing of the person with disabilities (e.g. Dunst, Trivette and Deal 1994; Garbarino and Abramowitz 1992; Turnbull and Turnbull 2001, 2006). Indeed, effective and collaborative partnerships with families are a fundamental tenet of most services for people with disabilities. Moreover, the criticality of this relationship is entrenched in both national and international legislative and policy initiatives. The inclusion of fostering and maintaining this relationship in the service standards underpinning quality service provision in all Australian states and territories is an example of the keen attention paid to this relationship.

If the family member with a disability is an adult, however, the role of the family and the accompanying collegial relationship takes on a different perspective. The emphasis shifts from empowerment of the family to empowerment of the young adult. Dilemmas are faced by case manager and family members alike, as each attempts to encourage the adult's exercise of autonomy and control over his or her life, while at the same time making sure that essential needs are met and rights upheld. This becomes particularly evident in the case management experience when the person with a disability is an adult who needs additional support in making decisions in his or her life. The literature, however, is largely silent on this aspect of family involvement or family partnerships. With the exception of the valuable research conducted around families with ageing/older sons and daughters with disabilities (e.g. Bigby 2004; Grant and Whittell 2003; Llewellyn 2003), the majority of research in this area has been conducted around younger families with children with disabilities and, in the main, living with the parents or other family members. How such collaboration operates within the context where the person is an adult remains unanswered.

In essence, I see the case management relationship where the adult with a disability requires assistance to make decisions about his or her life as a three-way relationship. Both the case manager and I, as Graham's parent, are working to achieve the goals that Graham has set for himself. In this vein, I see the parental experiences around the case management process as a balancing act – a balancing act that revolves around balancing encouragement of Graham's autonomy in making decisions about his own lifestyle and yet at the same time, cognisant of his vulnerability, ensuring that his rights are upheld and his needs and wishes met. In effect, I am balancing Graham's very real vulnerability with his right, as an adult, to autonomy and his right to have control over his life.

The balancing act in case management efforts
More rather than less involvement

As Graham and many other people with significant disabilities become adults, the cultural norms of less family involvement, depicted by, among others, Cooney (2000), Nolan, Grant and Keady (1996), and Thorin and Irvin (1992), does not eventuate. An initial feature of the balancing act has involved my balancing of these normative feelings or expectations of less involvement, or at least non-interfering involvement, with the very real need for not only continuing involvement but much greater involvement. Services and supports that are relatively readily available in childhood seem to disappear with adulthood, and the demand for services far outweighs the supply. The rhetoric of rights becomes very confused with the reality of scrounging what you can get. The professional gift model of service provision and support outlined by Duffy (1996, 2003) becomes all too evident. Support is seen as a gift rather than a right. This greater involvement is very much experienced in the case management experience, for example individual programme- and goal-setting procedures, where a great deal of time and energy are spent in collaborating with case managers to ensure that Graham's interests and wellbeing are at the forefront. This exercise is not commonly experienced by parents of young adults without disabilities, who are not involved in case management processes.

Advocating with as well as advocating for

I have found that with Graham's adulthood, my role as an advocate has also changed. In some instances within case management arenas, I advocate for Graham, but increasingly I find that I advocate with him. I advocate with him to ensure that his wishes and choices are upheld.

In this respect, I find that my major role is to ensure that Graham's views are listened to. Often, this role then extends to working within the system and with the case manager or key worker in order to ensure that Graham's wishes are acted upon. For example, at a previous workplace, Graham wished to purchase his lunch from the local shop rather than taking sandwiches from home. Graham had the skills to speak up for himself and to say what he wanted but not the negotiation skills to ensure that it happened. This is where my advocacy was necessary – to work with the case manager in order to negotiate how this different lunch arrangement could happen, given staff working conditions, lunch-money arrangements and the like. My role in this regard is a very biased, very vested-interest one. I am there for one person and one person only – Graham. Case managers, as Hall *et al.* (2003) and Woodside and McClam (1998) inter alia argue, must consider the requirements of all the people and the circumstances with whom they are involved. A parental consideration is with one person only.

On the other hand, in case management circumstances, I sometimes find myself advocating for matters in which Graham has had very little input. In these instances, I find myself taking on what I feel is the non-adult role of advocating for Graham – advocating for him to be given the opportunity to be involved in activities I think would be 'good for him'. For example, I have advocated for Graham to participate in literacy classes at his local community college. Without such an advocacy role, these opportunities might not be open to Graham. I have found that without drawing such matters to the attention of the case manager, their importance to people such as Graham is often overlooked.

I find in these instances, however, as with many other situations, that I am representing Graham but I feel unsure whether I am representing his views on the matter in hand at all. Am I advocating for things that he truly wants or needs? When does advocacy become interference in his life? Could Graham do much of this himself? These are questions with which I continually wrestle. But underlying such wrestling is the more than niggling suspicion that if I or somebody else were not to carry out this advocacy in the case management situation, then Graham's voice would not be heard at all; or if it were heard, then his voice would be ignored and in the end would get lost in the system. Case management is located within a bureaucratic system that does not always guarantee that the person's voice will be heard or that his or her requirements or wishes will be met. At times, the barriers can seem insurmountable for case managers and families alike.

The decision-maker in case management

Increasingly, Graham is able to make decisions in many areas of his life – some of which I agree with and some of which I don't. In many case management situations, I must balance his right to make lifestyle decisions (including wrong decisions) with my role, as his legally appointed guardian, of being responsible for the making of major decisions in his life. Parents or other close family members often have the dual role of parent or family member and legal guardian under the various guardianship legislative conditions. It is often decisions surrounding these issues that arise in case management situations. The decisions I need to make have a major impact on Graham's life. I must have a majority role in decisions about where Graham is to live, where he is to work, what healthcare initiatives need to be taken for him, and many more important decisions impacting on his life. It is with such decisions, often made with case managers, that I feel the tremendous responsibility of making extremely important choices that impact on Graham. These responsibilities can weigh heavily on family members. For example, weighing the benefits of various recommended medications against their often substantial and risky side effects may be a traumatic experience for a parent. Which way is best for the person for whom you hold a deep affection? Is medication the only way? Is it the environmental circumstances that need to change? Is there another way besides these potent medications?

It is in adulthood too that the permanence or the chronicity of the disability is felt most intensely. Case management is not only a long-term organisational issue, as outlined above, but also a long-term issue for families. This permanency brings to light the need to consider the long-term future in case management situations. What decisions can I make in order to ensure that Graham's wellbeing and safety will be guaranteed when I am no longer alive? While other young adults eventually are able to make their own significant lifestyle decisions, the permanence of the decision-making role by others for people such as Graham persists. How can I minimise his vulnerability? Who will continue the case management balancing act when I am no longer able to? Will Graham's voice be increasingly lost?

Issues impacting on case management effectiveness in the balancing act

Getting things done: sometimes you've just got to do it yourself

As indicated above, the model of case management with which Graham and many of his peers are involved is one where case management is not a single role carried out by a particular staff member. The case management role is part of the support worker's role and is in addition to the many and varied other duties inherent in this role. Thus, the case management function often takes second place to the more immediate and more pressing support worker duties. Often, there is little or no time allocation to support workers to undertake case management effectively, despite the recognition and acknowledgement of the critical importance of this role. Thus, it is often family members who carry out these roles to address the particular issue of concern.

Peter's wish to vote is a telling example of such a dilemma. Peter, a young adult who uses a disability service, indicated that he wished to vote in an upcoming election, but he was not enrolled on the relevant electoral roll. To vote in the election, Peter would need to enrol within the following week. Crises occurring within the service setting (not involving Peter), however, prevented the case manager from ensuring that Peter was on the electoral roll in time to vote. It was Peter's father who stepped in to ensure Peter was registered in time and thus could cast his vote at the forthcoming election. What might have happened to Peter's right to vote if his father had not intervened and had not carried out what was perceived by the service to be a case management function?

Changing faces and continual relationship building

As indicated above, the case management role in relation to Graham and many of his peers is not a consistent one but rather a role that is rotated regularly among the support worker team. Thus, each case management relationship is different, and each needs to be built and fostered. It often seems that just when the relationship is firmly established and working effectively, the case manager changes, and there is yet another relationship to be fostered and worked on. Moreover, some case managers are more competent and more creative than others – and more compatible with Graham. Graham and I have no input into which particular staff member takes on the role of key worker or case manager. We are simply informed who the person will be, which is a very disempowering experience. Although this case management strategy may well be an effective way of ensuring all staff members gain case management skills and get to know Graham well, it also results in instability and inconsistency for Graham. Additionally, the inevitable repetitive familiarisation of new case managers with background material and understandings becomes frustrating.

Confronting reputation

Over time, Graham and many of his peers have established reputations with services – reputations that are pervasive and that in many instances precede them. As Peter (2000) notes, it is a reputation that usually emphasises the less desirable aspects of the person; indeed, rarely are the positive attributes of the person included. Many parents continually endeavour to present the more positive characteristics of their son or daughter. Nonetheless, it can often take new case managers some time to see that there are other aspects to the person in addition to those in the file or consistent with the reputation.

For example, Paula has a reputation of non-compliance. It seems that at times, refusing or declining to take part in an activity or to 'do as she is told' is pathologised as non-compliance rather than as a means used by Paula to assert her right to say no or to have an opinion differing from those supporting her. Her father needed to explain to a case manager, newly appointed to the role, that when Paula says plainly 'No, I want to be on my own' when asked to come to the dinner table, she is simply expressing a wish to eat her meal away from the hurly-burly of the common dining table – a more than reasonable request. Non-compliance was not the issue; rather, the issue was Paula exercising her right to eat her meal where she wished.

In turn, as parents, in these instances, we are likely also to have our behaviours or actions pathologised. We gain reputations as being 'in denial' or 'emotional' or 'just like a mother'. Just as often, we are seen simply as being 'difficult'.

Pushing the system

Because the case management process is located within a bureaucratic structure, case management issues such as planning a holiday, arranging support for participation in leisure activities, and arranging for opportunities for part-time employment can take a disproportionate amount of time. Approvals need to be gained, signatures are required, personnel need to be consulted – and the list goes on. This can be a frustrating experience for all concerned. Often, it is in these situations that parents need to 'push the system' in order to make sure that these particular concerns of their son or daughter are addressed. But how far can a parent push the system? The vulnerability of their adult son or daughter can put them at risk of retribution by some less competent, less ethical staff. Fortunately, these instances are very few; nonetheless, this fear of retribution is felt strongly by many families. How far do we push the system or advocate for a better life for our sons and daughters without incurring the payback? These people who provide a service and support our family members are, in the main, competent and professional people, but they are also powerful agents in our adult children's lives – and the fear is always present that that power might be abused.

The rise and rise of the risk-management culture

Increasingly, as Alaszewski and Alaszewski (2002) have indicated, risk management has become a significant feature of service provision for people with disabilities. Although nobody would like to see support workers and people who use a service injured or placed at risk of injury, the risk-management culture has imposed additional barriers to Graham and his peers enjoying their lives and taking part in ordinary community life. Currently, risk-management profiles need to be carried out by case managers on seemingly ordinary activities. For example, a case manager was required to carry out a risk-management assessment before a young woman, Tracey, could be assisted to meet a friend for a cup of coffee after work. This risk-management process was complicated, took some weeks to carry out and imposed restrictions on the way the activity could take place. In some circumstances, the risk-management issues may well have resulted in the organising of this activity simply becoming too difficult. If this were the case, then Tracey may well have been denied the opportunity to enjoy the very ordinary pleasure of having a coffee with a friend. On this basis, the risk-management process itself posed the significant risk to Tracey's wellbeing in that the activity would not take place at all. Because risk management is essentially an occupational health and safety concern, parents often have very little input into this process. They may feel disempowered, alienated and frustrated by the all too often excessive attention given to minimising risk, where a common-sense approach may well be more appropriate and productive.

Conclusion

In all, case management has been a significant force in personalising support and in supporting a positive lifestyle for individuals with disabilities. It represents a significant shift from the warehousing focus of service provision that, unfortunately, characterised many previous service provision efforts. Graham and his peers have drawn many benefits from case management. For people such as Graham, however, who need support in several aspects of their lives in order to ensure that their views are respected and upheld and their wellbeing assured, it is the structural or systemic aspects of service provision such as those identified above that present major barriers to the effectiveness of case management initiatives. It is this lack of attention to the structural aspects that maintain and entrench the vulnerability and marginalisation of Graham and his peers. Additionally, balancing the person's right as an adult with a disability to autonomy in his or her life with his or her very real, ever-present vulnerability highlights an added complexity in the family–case management relationship. This is an area that is in critical need of further exploration and would be a welcome addition to the family-professional literature.

As Fook (1993), among others, points out, there is a need for a more outward-focused approach to case management work so that regular community opportunities and resources routinely available to other community citizens might be opened up to Graham and his peers. A more person-centred approach to case management, such as that suggested by Cambridge and Carnaby (2005) and O'Brien and O'Brien (2002), with its emphasis on informal networks and circles of support and community networking and capacity-building is worthy of consideration. As O'Brien and O'Brien (2002) have argued so convincingly, it is only by embedding the person in a network of personal and caring relationships that vulnerability will be addressed adequately. Current case management practices, located in a bureaucratic system, are restricted in their capacity to ensure this happens. With a broader community focus, the range of resources available is expanded and a more creative approach to finding solutions is fostered (Duffy 2003). Moreover, as Duffy (2003) argues, the greater involvement of informal and community members in the person's life can lead more readily to the development of community networks for the person rather than his or her networks being, in the main, restricted to the service sector. Perhaps with this approach to case management, Graham and his peers may well be able to live their lives as citizens rather than have their lives managed as clients or service users.

References

Alaszewski, A. and Alaszewski, H. (2002) 'Towards the creative management of risk: perceptions, practices and policies.' *British Journal of Learning Disabilities 30*, 56–62.

Bigby, C. (2004) *Ageing with A Lifelong Disability: A Guide to Practice, Program, and Policy Issues for Human Services Professionals.* London: Jessica Kingsley Publishers.

Cambridge, S. and Carnaby, S. (eds) (2005) *Person-Centred Planning and Care Management with People with Learning Disabilities.* London: Jessica Kingsley Publishers.

Cooney, T.M. (2000) 'Parent–Child Relations across Adulthood.' In R.M. Milardo and S. Duck (eds) *Families as Relationships.* Chichester: John Wiley & Sons.

Derezotes, D.S. (2000) *Advanced Generalist Social Work Practice.* Thousand Oaks, CA: Sage.

Duffy, S. (1996) *Unlocking the Imagination: Strategies for Purchasing Services for People with Learning Difficulties.* London: Choice Press.

Duffy, S. (2003) *Keys to Citizenship: A Guide to Getting Good Support Services for People with Learning Difficulties.* London: Paradign Consultancy & Development Agency Ltd.

Dunst, C.J., Trivette, C.M. and Deal, A.G. (eds) (1994) *Supporting and Strengthening Families*, Vol. 1. Cambridge, MA: Brookline Books.

Fook, J. (1993) *Radical Casework: A Theory of Practice.* St Leonards, Australia: Allen & Unwin.

Garbarino, J. and Abramowitz, R.H. (1992) 'The Family as a Social System.' In J. Garbarino (ed.) *Children and Families in the Social Environment.* New York: Aldine de Gruyter.

Grant, G. and Whittell, B. (2003) 'Partnerships with Families over the Life Course.' In M. Nolan, U. Lundh, G. Grant and J. Keedy (eds) *Partnerships in Family Care: Understanding the Caregiving Career*. Maidenhead: Open University Press.

Hall, C., Jubila, K., Parton, N. and Poso, T. (2003) *Constructing Clienthood in Social Work and Human Services*. London: Jessica Kingsley Publishers.

Llewellyn, G. (2003) 'Family Care Decision-Making in Later Life: The Future is Now!' In M. Nolan, U. Lundh, G. Grant and J. Keedy (eds) *Partnerships in Family Care: Understanding the Caregiving Career*. Maidenhead: Open University Press.

Nolan, M., Grant, G. and Keady, J. (eds) (1996) *Understanding Family Care*. Buckingham: Open University Press.

O'Brien, C.L. and O'Brien, J. (2002) 'The Origins of Person-Centred Planning: A Community of Practice Perspective.' In J. O'Brien and C.L. O'Brien (eds) *Implementing Person-Centred Planning: The Voices of Experience*. Toronto: Inclusion Press.

Peter, D. (2000) 'Dynamics of discourse: a case study illuminating power relations in mental retardation.' *Mental Retardation 38*, 354–62.

Thorin, E.J. and Irvin, L.K. (1992) 'Family stress associated with transition to adulthood of young people with severe disabilities.' *Journal of the Association for Persons with Severe Handicaps 17*, 31–9.

Turnbull, A. and Turnbull, H.R. (2001) *Families, Professionals, and Exceptionality: Collaborating for Empowerment*. Upper Saddle River, NJ: Merrill/Prentice Hall.

Turnbull, A.P. and Turnbull, R. (2006) 'Fostering Family–Professional Partnership.' In M.E. Snell and F. Brown (eds) *Instruction of Students with Severe Disabilities*. Upper Saddle River, NJ: Pearson/Merrill/Prentice Hall.

Woodside, M. and McClam, T. (1998) *Generalist Case Management: A Method of Human Services Delivery*. Pacific Grove, CA: Brooks/Cole Publishing Company.

9

Taking it personally: challenging poor and abusive care management practice

Margaret Flynn and Peter Flynn

In the UK in December 2003, an undercover documentary was shown on Channel 5 entitled 'Who cares for Gary?' The documentary exposed practices within two abusive units, one of which had unwittingly become part of our lives. Fundamentally flawed decisions by a care manager who barely knew my brother Peter led to Peter's placement in this unit for people with intellectual disabilities and mental health problems 'for five to seven days' in 2001; this drifted into a stay of almost 12 months.

This chapter outlines how a man who had lived in his own flat for 20 years, albeit with support from his family and a community learning disability team (CLDT), ended up in 'The Unit' – an unregistered, private, for-profit and abusive service. This chapter is written in narrative form, since the experience lies on the boundary that normally separates social science from literature (e.g. Ellis and Bochner 2000). Peter's words are in italicised script.

The chapter seeks to make sense of confused and confusing care management practice. As reported in a fuller account of these events (Flynn 2004), we adopt the perspective of the 'vulnerable observer' (Behar 1996), which provides an opportunity for readers to engage with the banal heartlessness of it all.

Admission to The Unit

I learned by telephone that Peter had had an accident and had been admitted to hospital via an accident and emergency department. It was too early to know the extent of the injury to his ankle or the implications for his mobility. My visit to hospital on the same day was made outside visiting hours. As I queued to introduce myself to the staff team to ask whether I might see Peter, and to offer to talk to nursing staff about his circumstances and support needs, Clare (not her real name) asked to see Peter as she was 'his main carer'. As I did not recognise her, I assumed she was one of the people who visited Peter on a weekly basis to assist with household routines and shopping. Later, I contacted his care manager, who had known Peter for three months. The emailed reply was as follows:

> I am sure you are aware that Peter is not coping very well at the moment with living on his own. Discussions have taken place with Peter and with other team members who know and work with Peter that it is apparent he would benefit from having access to a supported tenancy. Peter has been fully involved in the process and has been having respite care to monitor the situation with Clare. It is intended that this could become a more permanent arrangement if the introductions go well and it is agreeable to Peter… I hope this brings you up to date.

It is shocking to receive information with such wide-ranging implications via email. Not only did the missive sweep aside our contribution as involved and engaged family caregivers, but it also confirmed that we had no role in decision-making regarding our brother's future. The rationale was Peter's very troubling and troubled letters to his care manager. These are a long-established and familiar means used by Peter to signal distress, although never before with the result that his family's knowledge and experience of supporting him, and his community care assessment, were totally ignored. I complained to the social services department, and the complaint was upheld. It was difficult to challenge this course of action retrospectively, however, since Peter appeared to be positive about moving in with Clare and another man with moderate support needs. My two sisters shared my concern about the prospective loss of his tenancy, not least because he had always valued his personal space, privacy and inviting people to *my flat*.

It is significant that the care manager barely knew Peter before this transforming course of action was embarked upon. In response to a letter of introduction from him, I had sent some information with the expectation that we would meet in due course. This did not happen as, unlike the previous care manager, this one took the view that 'confidentiality' meant working without any reference to Peter's family. It appeared that from the perspective of this service, care managers were accountable solely to clients and that their biographies, including routine and long-standing contacts with families, and networks were incidental.

I corresponded with a senior social services manager, who apologised for the lack of communication and the care manager's and CLDT's failure to involve the family in decision-making of such a far-reaching nature. The senior social services manager reassured us that we would be involved in any hospital discharge planning 'to discuss his future placement'.

What should have been a two-month stay in hospital became six months, and the treatment spanned three hospitals, five wards and ward staff teams, and more operations than were originally envisaged. Peter has poor coordination and could not use crutches. As a result, he walked on his damaged foot and damaged it further. I attended each weekly clinical meeting as I was concerned that new teams of ward staff might be in danger of overlooking the extent of Peter's support needs and might possibly become irritated by his assertion that he could and would use crutches. One of my sisters attended two inconclusive meetings coordinated by the CLDT to discuss Peter's inability to comply with the post-operative requirement not to 'weight-bear' (having been informed only on the day on which these meetings took place, and so making it necessary for her to find last-minute cover at work).

Unknown to us, Peter was discharged to Clare's care on a Friday afternoon. I had visited the hospital that afternoon to find that Peter was gone and his care manager had arranged the discharge. I was incredulous and worried and did not ask for Clare's address. This became known to us over the weekend when Clare contacted us to ask for help in managing Peter. Having been largely immobilised for six months, Peter appeared uncooperative and had ambitious plans for his first weekend out. These included a day on public transport. Clare did not seek to restrain him but, with his brother-in-law's encouragement, Peter agreed to rest before recommencing his pre-accident enjoyment of 'travelling on the buses and trains'. Peter's agitation and distress did not diminish; within a couple of weeks, I received, first, a notification that the CLDT intended to transfer responsibility for supporting Peter to another CLDT and, second, a telephone call from a psychiatrist advising me that she was admitting Peter to 'a nursing home for five to seven days to start him on lithium'. These were shocking developments. The first appeared to reflect a wish to transfer responsibility for the care manager's/team's poor judgement elsewhere, and the second was entirely contrary to the facts – that Peter had lived alone for many years; that his mobility and, consequently, his lifestyle had been severely compromised by his accident; that he enjoyed privacy; that his hospital discharge had been botched; and that his care manager had given notice on his tenancy. Peter had lost a great deal and was hugely distressed, and the planning of his care manager had proceeded on the basis of sketchy information, and yet a psychiatrist determined that lithium was required. In Peter's words:

> *It was very hard. I got bored in hospital. There's nothing to do and I couldn't walk anywhere. I just thought I'd be moving in with Clare but they put me in The Unit and I hated it. I wrote every day to tell people I hated it. It was terrible. I shouldn't have been left in there.*

Peter moved into The Unit, and we were dismayed. It was quite unlike anywhere Peter had ever lived or stayed. Reassuring ourselves that it was for only a few days, we resumed our pattern of visits and regular phone calls, fully expecting Peter to be back at Clare's within the week. As each of us is in full-time employment, I was surprised to receive a letter from Peter's care manager inviting me to attend a meeting giving only three working days' notice. I was disconcerted too that there was no recognition of our other family commitments or any attempt to meet us during our visits to Peter. I contacted the senior manager, who agreed that it was unrealistic to expect attendance at such short notice. We realised how grave the situation had become for Peter when the minutes of this meeting were circulated via email. Peter had met with eight professionals, including staff from The Unit, and one student. The minutes made no reference to his life before the accident and his admission to hospital, or to the role of the care manager and CLDT in bringing Peter to such a bleak period of his life. They blamed him for his limited mobility, observing that 'Peter does not consider this to be a permanent placement', and described him in ways that did not reflect our knowledge of our lovely and loving brother. Extracts from the notes are reproduced here solely to illustrate this point:

> …incidents of concern…signs of paranoia, rigid in approach, argumentative and physical aggression…low concentration which may be linked to mental health issues…well developed sense of authority, can consider who he can push around physically and emotionally…general concerns around mental health and personality…will not recommend that Peter leaves The Unit until full consideration of above issues has taken place…family are not present…requesting an advocate…[date for risk assessment] been set taking into consideration the Xmas break and personal leave of the staff involved…

On the heels of this incident, I was given unreasonably short notice to empty Peter's flat; I also received a letter from a psychiatrist. The letter appeared designed to create conflict; to assert an unchallengeable, clinician-centred model of practice; to displace the experiential knowledge of family caregivers; and to posit unbelievable implications concerning the 'risk' posed by a man who had never been described as aggressive or challenging:

> There has been a suggestion that I arrange meetings according to families' availability. I would like to inform you that I don't have the time during the week when I can adjust my meetings for the families of 150–200 patients that I see... I have also been informed that Peter himself and your family have been annoyed about the meeting and also the services which our team provide. I would like to emphasise that we respect our clients and their families and we expect they respect us in return. It is difficult to work effectively under threat of complaint... [There is a risk of] Peter harming himself and harming others...

In effect, I was on the losing side in an unequal struggle. It is up to service personnel to ensure that the needs of vulnerable adults are met, and alliances with family caregivers are unnecessary.

Although astonishing in its tone and content, the letter did confirm how instrumental my upheld complaints had been in determining the response of this team. The letter closed off any possibility of the family assisting in an evaluative understanding of Peter's circumstances. We were concerned about the questionable judgements that had influenced the drafting of the letter and horrified by the 'therapeutic' implications for Peter. I wanted different psychiatric input and learned that I was expected to write to the appropriate National Health Service (NHS) trust outlining my reasons. Peter's rapid deterioration as a result of overmedication, with symptoms including facial twitching, drooling, staring, slurring of words, incontinence, physical agitation and facial expressions suggestive of extreme anguish, added urgency to our efforts to get him off medication and out of a place he disliked so much. I responded in writing to the psychiatrist, who apologised by telephone, in person and, subsequently, in writing. She explained that her team colleagues had briefed her, and such briefing became the basis for the letter. She explained too that, as the medication did not appear to have any effect on Peter, she had increased the dosage. The following day was particularly bleak for us all. Peter's deterioration was so extensive that I barely recognised him. I emailed the psychiatrist and pleaded with her to see Peter and to halt whatever therapeutic course had been embarked upon. Although it was feared that Peter might have had a 'minor stroke', I was not informed of this by the staff in The Unit. They suggested that I take Peter to accident and emergency to see 'a duty psychiatrist', but as no explanation was offered I declined to do so.

Peter recalls:

I just lay on my bed. I couldn't do anything. I remember I wanted to go out but it was hard to move. I couldn't speak or write my letters. I just wanted to get out.

We learned that Clare did not want Peter to return to his supported tenancy, so comprehensively had his reputation been destroyed at the meeting that had produced such damaging minutes. As notice had been given on his former tenancy, he was effectively stranded in The Unit. During my weekly visits and telephone calls, I learned a great deal about the place. I gained first-hand experience of their inability to monitor or communicate concerns about the toxic effects of Peter's medication. This inattention was replicated by the CLDT. What was clear was that the rationale for putting Peter into The Unit was seriously flawed. He had been prescribed increasing dosages of lithium for which no one took responsibility, for example by monitoring the effects. The resulting damage in turn led to his medication being stopped.

Subsequently, staff in The Unit omitted to inform us that Peter had accidentally scalded his foot while making a cup of tea. He went to a minor injuries unit alone. I was alerted to his fragile condition by the stench of rotting flesh as I entered his room a couple of days later. He was perspiring and in obvious discomfort. I learned later that had it not been for my non-routine, midweek visit, Peter would have lost his foot. He required bed rest, but no one in The Unit sought to contact the minor injuries unit to find this out. I had been hesitant to express anger to staff in The Unit, as I feared what might subsequently happen to Peter. On this occasion, however, I met with a manager and told her that if my brother lost his foot (a distinct possibility confirmed by the minor injuries unit), I would sue them for negligence. I got in touch with the social services department and asked how to contact the National Care Standards Commission (NCSC). It took the NCSC eight weeks to let me know that since The Unit was an unregistered unit, and therefore not a care home, they could not investigate and suggested that I use Manchester social services department's complaints procedure.

This was the first we as Peter's family knew that he was in an unregistered service. It had been described to us as a 'specialist nursing home' when he was admitted there. In the meantime, an undercover TV programme was trailed in *The Guardian* (17 December 2003): In 'There should be a law against it', Donal MacIntyre argued the case for a 'tough new approach...an urgent need for a specific law of neglect that targets care home staff and establishments' in order to remedy 'the culture of neglect at the heart of Britain's care industry'. This article prefaced the undercover TV programme, 'Who cares for Gary?', shown on 21 December

2003, which exposed seriously deficient practices in services for people with intellectual disabilities and added impetus to the debate about the adequacy of regulatory systems for scrutinising the care of vulnerable adults. It brought home to viewers the apathy, minimising and denial that are often associated with allegations of abuse.

What Macintyre and Manchester social services department omitted to do was warn former residents and their relatives that the programme would feature so-called 'homes' that had become part of our lives. The Unit was one of the two places featured in the film – and it was heart-stopping to recognise residents who had no safe way of expressing their distress, to see people blamed for their plight, and to have my knowledge of a traffic of unskilled, unsupervised and unsupported staff confirmed by the programme. The observations of two members of staff – 'I don't want to be flogging fucking dead horses all my life' and (to justify eating residents' food and using their monies to pay for meals out with residents) 'You don't come to work to be out of pocket' – underscored the consequences of a fragmented regulatory system and a private, for-profit unit that deliberately remained outside the regulatory environment. There is a great deal wrong with a service system that allowed my brother to be admitted to an unregistered unit for people with intellectual disabilities and mental health problems where there was no one qualified to administer or monitor medication, and yet the sole purpose of his admission was to establish him on medication. The programme made no reference to the personal efforts of residents and their relatives to highlight system-wide failures within and surrounding such 'homes'. Peter was writing daily to the social services department telling them of his distress at being in The Unit, but he received neither a reply nor an offer to invoke the adult protection procedure or the complaints procedure. I could not change or ameliorate Peter's situation. The professionals involved distanced us from any solving of problems in which they had been instrumental in creating and that entailed excessive harm, and yet they appeared lead-shielded from any challenge or criticism.

'Careful assessment of need, comprehensive care planning, co-ordination of services and follow-up' is how care management was initially conceived by researchers tracking the experiences of vulnerable adults as they transferred from long-stay institutions in the UK in the early 1980s (Renshaw et al. 1988). Care management had a lot in common with notions of key working and initially offered promise in terms of identifying 'systems agents' with coordinating roles. This did not characterise our experience. It was less about coordinating resources than about planning and making arrangements independently of family caregivers. Ultimately, it resulted in Peter being left in an unsuitable and abusive service for almost a year.

It is frequently observed by the relatives of vulnerable people that we are deterred from complaining because we fear the consequences that will be visited on our loved ones. Confirmatory evidence features in the 'grey' literature (e.g. Miller 2004) but remains to be credibly tackled operationally. I have first-hand experience of this, arising from the period before and during my brother's stay in The Unit.

Having been alerted to Peter's changed accommodation and support arrangements by Clare, and subsequently confirmed by email, I used the complaints procedure. I was incredulous that a community team of qualified nurses, social workers and therapists could embark on a course of action with such far-reaching consequences. During the investigation of this complaint, I learned that the team's questionable understanding of confidentiality precluded all contact with us. Further, the care manager duly visited Peter in hospital to inform him of my complaint – that is, their failure to inform his family about moving him out of his tenancy and arranging a supported tenancy for him. Peter was angry and distressed and at my next hospital visit greeted me with 'Because of you I haven't got a social worker any more.' I requested that this bizarre and needless intervention should also be investigated under the complaints procedure. The complaint was upheld, and the first round of apologies followed.

It is right that efforts are made to deal with complaints at the earliest opportunity. Indications that Manchester social services department's procedures were wanting, however, were many and compelling. It appeared that it was unnecessary for the role of the care manager to be accountable.

The relief I experienced that poor practice had been challenged was short-lived. Peter's abrupt discharge from hospital, without the promised planning and collaboration, had detrimental and far-reaching consequences. Although the decision to discharge Peter was not scrutinised by the complaints procedure, the care manager was disciplined. This combination of being challenged both externally and internally appeared to influence specific subsequent events, namely the following:

- The implacably negative and damaging discussion about Peter in The Unit by eight professionals, including a member of The Unit's staff, and a student took no account of their contributory role. Wisely, Peter covers his ears when he wants to absent himself from surrounding events and discussions. I know this is how he responded to the eight professionals united behind their particularly ungenerous and misleading view of him. (The size of the meeting was subsequently justified with the mantra 'Nothing about us without us.') On the telephone after this meeting, Peter told me '*They were cross you were not here*.'

- There was no evidence that my challenges concerning the explicit exclusion of the family, or the apologies of senior managers, had any bearing on subsequent decision-making. Their 'meeting' confirmed that they were concerned with the 'personal leave of the staff involved'. Family calendars were of no significance, irrespective of our frequent contact or even of Re (A&B) (2003).

- The promised stay of 'five to seven days' was fiction. The meeting's minutes stated that 'Peter does not consider this to be a permanent placement…will not recommend that Peter leaves The Unit until full consideration of…issues' and neatly identified a new problem requiring the attention of their skills.

- The unfeasibly short notice to empty Peter's flat and the failure to ensure that Peter's possessions were safely transferred to either the supported tenancy or The Unit meant that he lost many of these.

Such hostile service responses, in combination with the lithium solution (albeit short-lived), sidestepped my brother's known experience of loneliness, his loss of mobility and his loss of his valued identity as an independent man. They bear witness to unprofessional practice and the absence of discernible compassion. It was only when Peter was safely out of The Unit, with daily support in his own tenancy, that I invoked the complaints procedure once again. I wanted the service 'partnership' to account for their interventions. I have described elsewhere the hardship of working with an ineffectual complaints procedure (Flynn 2004).

As a result of a new care manager's intervention, Peter's life was changed beyond recognition. Peter was previously ill-served, and efforts to challenge the decision-making of the care manager exposed the limitations of a complaints procedure, which compounded our distress.

Some conclusions

It may be that this narrative conveys, to some degree, the frustration for families when care managers' practice is wanting; when abuse is continually denied; when mechanisms for review are ineffectually implemented; and when dangerous practice is challenged. It is paradoxical that during an epoch in which the values of individualism and independence are exalted, disregard for my brother's personhood and independence prevailed. Events in our lives generated a host of concerns about injurious service responses, without regard for Peter's enduring attachments. These correspond to iatrogenic conditions – that is, illnesses caused by medical treatment. Arguably, Peter's circumstances illuminate a parallel phenomenon of philanthrogenic conditions (as proposed by Gwyneth Roberts, honorary research fellow and previously senior lecturer in social policy and lecturer at the School of Social Science, University of Wales, Bangor), namely, injury or damage or deficit to individuals caused by the care system.

We have learned the hard way that unless we conceptualise problems holistically and not in relation to specialised and client-specific services, vulnerable people will be made even more vulnerable. The CLDT hit back hard when its poor practice was challenged. We, as the relatives of vulnerable people, are united in not wanting our loved ones to be harmed. This is not a confirmation of simplistic notions of overprotection; rather, it is an asset that service commissioners have been slow to realise. I would wish those who administer complaints procedures to make clear to complainants what measures they will take immediately in order to ensure the safety of vulnerable people. This narrative reveals something of what can happen if such measures are not in place.

Vulnerable adults are not renowned for bringing poor and abusive practice to the attention of senior managers, but my brother sought to do so. His letters were not seen as valuable commissioning 'intelligence', and they did not automatically trigger the attentions of adult protection or even complaints personnel when they should have done so. Instead, it took an undercover TV programme to confirm that The Unit was without merit or promise. For as long as there are ineffectual mechanisms for challenging poor care management practice and services, there will always be a need for such programmes. Unbelievably, The Unit is still in operation, continuing to offer accommodation with support on a 24-hour basis and accordingly able to evade local and national scrutiny, irrespective of the support needs of 'tenants'. This loophole must be closed and effective legislation must be introduced. My fears for the people who remain there are based on my experiential knowledge of the place.

- Care management cannot be a justification for setting aside family caregivers' knowledge and involvement in the lives of their loved ones while running for cover behind spurious claims of 'confidentiality' or 'team decision-making'. We have never sought to be immersed in the minutiae of Peter's day-to-day life, but as relatives who for many years had routinely paid bills for the upkeep of his flat, we had legitimate financial as well as overriding personal interests in decisions regarding his home and support. Peter: *'It's hard living by yourself and I wanted more help. You can get low by yourself, especially if you like being with people and friends. I didn't want to be in The Unit though. That wasn't right.'*

- Care management hinges on assessment and knowledge of a person's biographical life. This cannot be achieved by reference to narrow case records and 'case knowledge'. Unless the perspectives of loved ones are embraced, a needlessly incomplete picture of a person's needs is considered. Peter: *'I was bored in The Unit. I was missing my voluntary work, my music and videos and going out and the church...we wrote to all my friends and people at church so that they knew where I was and so that they could write to me and ring me up and take me out. I like getting letters and I like writing them.'*

- Care management has to be accountable, not least in terms of the target efficiency of the outcomes secured. Families need to be confident that the challenges they make will not trigger defensive, abusive and damaging responses. Peter: *'I've never liked meetings. They've been told they can't have meetings like the ones I had.'*

- Care management cannot assume that a vulnerable adult's 'placement' in a residential service signals the conclusion of involvement, or the withdrawal of monitoring, most particularly if a service is beyond the purview of a regulatory framework. The failure of the care manager/team to monitor Peter's medication was paralleled by the inattention of staff in The Unit. Further, information about the accidental scalding was not shared with the care manager or the family. Against such a backdrop, families have no option but to sustain their vigilance. Peter: *'I used to ring my sisters and they used to ring me and then we'd go out at the weekends. Sometimes friends came to take me out. It was hard being stuck in there when I burned my foot. The staff used to stay in the office and sometimes they'd shout.'*

- Although care management is associated with the efficient alignment of individual needs and resources, as a result of one care manager's ill-judged interventions the costs of Peter's support needs increased steeply.

Families do not regard care management as an abstraction. We connect it with our experience of assessment, reviews, minutes and correspondence and, most particularly, outcomes. Although I cannot comment on the system dynamics that influenced one care manager's imprudent judgement, the outcomes for Peter did not conform to any model of care management with which I am familiar. It would be difficult to imagine a more obstacle-strewn course than the one that we faced. We are no longer deluded by the misuse of terms such as 'homes', 'partnership', 'support', 'expertise', 'professionals', 'care management' or even 'carers'. Our recovery is ongoing. Our experience confirms that we should be cautious in our use of such terms and, hardest of all, that silence is the voice of collusion. In Peter's words:

> *I didn't like being in The Unit. It was a bloody awful place – like a jail. I was so unhappy I used to lie on my bed. I was so drugged up I couldn't do anything else. I wrote letters so that people would know how horrible The Unit was. I hope no one else has to go in there. We don't need to be in places like that. I've got my own place now, like I used to have, and I'm happy again. I was asked to help Manchester social services and so I did. They wanted me to tell them what it was like. I'm glad they asked me. I remembered it so I told them. It's important that they know how bad it is.*

Acknowledgements

Special thanks are due to Gwyneth Roberts, Hilary Brown, Mary Cornelius, Ruth Eley, Gordon Grant, Aled Griffiths, Kirsty Keywood, Paul Ramcharan and Frances Taylor, who made comments on an earlier draft of this chapter.

References

Behar, R. (1996) *The Vulnerable Observer: Anthropology that Breaks Your Heart*. Boston, MA: Beacon Press.

Ellis, C. and Bochner, A.P. (2000) 'Autoethnography, Personal Narrative, Reflexivity: Researcher as Subject.' In N. Denzin and Y. Lincoln (eds) *Handbook of Qualitative Research*. London: Sage.

Flynn, M. (2004) 'Challenging poor practice, abusive practice and inadequate complaints procedures.' *Journal of Adult Protection 6*, 34–44.

Miller, S. (2004) *The Story of My Father*. London: Bloomsbury Publishing.

Re (A&B) v East Sussex County Council (2003) [EXHC 167] Admin. 2003 [No. 6 CCLR] 194.

Renshaw, J., Hampson, R., Thomason, C., Darton, R., *et al.* (1988) *Care in the Community: The First Steps*. Aldershot: Gower.

Be there for me: case management in my life

Colin Hiscoe, with Kelley Johnson

Kelley: We have been friends and colleagues for a long time. We have worked together on a project researching leadership for people with disabilities, spent hours talking about our work, and given each other support in life crises. In this time, Colin has talked of some of the difficulties he has experienced in negotiating complex health and welfare systems, both for himself and for those who are close to him. This chapter is based on a discussion that brought together these concerns. We talked for about two hours one Saturday afternoon. Kelley taped the discussion, transcribed it and then wrote the chapter using only Colin's words. She added her own reflections to his account. Colin then read through the chapter and made changes that he thought were necessary.

Colin: Before case management

I am a 55-year-old man. I was born in Leeds, Yorkshire. Up in the north. I lived with my mother, my granddad and my grandma. My grandma basically brought me up, because Mum had to work to bring money into the house, you know, to feed us all. And every Sunday would be a roast and Yorkshire pudding. I remember in the winter we used to go up to the big hill and get on our sledges and go sliding down the hill and what not. I loved it. I absolutely loved that. It was really good. I loved the place. And my heart still belongs to England. And even though I live in Australia, I'm an English person. Not an Australian person.

And then when I was 12 Mum decided we're going to leave and come to Australia on an assisted-passage scheme. My aunty wrote to my mum saying 'Come over here and Colin and you can have a better life, better country, better scenery, better time, better weather, better everything.' Worst day of my life was that. I didn't want to leave. I wanted to stay there. I was happy there. I came out here and I wasn't happy and didn't like living with my aunty and uncle. No matter what I did, it was always wrong. We were living in this house, out in the bush.

They suggested would I like to go to a boys' home in Melbourne. So I jumped at the opportunity to get away. I lived at St John's Home for Boys and Girls in Canterbury. I absolutely loved it there. The foster parents were fantastic. I don't know why I had to live there. I have no idea. I went to Blackburn Tech. Hated it with a passion. And I ended up getting expelled when I was half way through second form, and I was rapt. Absolutely rapt.

I was still in the boys' home at that stage. And they put me on to a training farm up in Tatura. Absolutely hated it with a passion. And I knew, as soon as I set eyes on the owner, 'I hate you'. And he really did violate my rights and my privileges and my wellbeing. He really made me look like dirt and feel like dirt. And I had no respect for myself or anybody else. Once he belted me until I was black and blue from the top of my shoulders to the bottom of my legs. I rang up the boys' home and complained to the priest. I rang my mother. I rang the social worker at the boy's home. I rang every possible person I could think of. And they all called me a liar. That would not happen. I said, 'Well come up and see the bloody marks.' Nobody came. The only reason that I got out of that place was that the manager was frightened for my safety. I was a mess.

In 1969, I got into some trouble. The judge basically said, 'I'm going to recommend that you go to a psychiatric institution.' I didn't know what a psychiatric institution was. I thought it was just like a hospital. Ended up there for…I think it was about five or six months. Banged myself around a little bit in there. Smashing things. I really can't understand how it all happened. I went to occupational therapy and then to a sheltered workshop. Absolutely hated that too.

I got out of the institution because I kept pushing this nurse: 'I've had enough of this and I want to get out.' The only way the doctor would agree to let me out was to go into a hostel. So I went into a hostel for people with a disability.

And I was there for a good couple of years. And then I went and lived with Mum in a home for elderly people. She was the caretaker at night time. It was good. I liked talking to some of them elderly people. I was on a pension. Then the place where Mum worked got sold. So Mum went and moved into a flat and I moved with her. And I was living with her for a while. It was great. It was good fun.

I have been married now for six years. It was a good wedding. Down at Coburg Lakes, and then we went to the Coburg Motor Inn for our reception. And I remember saying goodnight to everybody. And that's the last thing I remember. I must have been drunk.

I have worked at Reinforce [a self-advocacy organisation in Victoria, Australia, for people with intellectual disabilities] voluntarily since about 1982. And I had some paid employment with Reinforce, where we tried to write a book on the stories of people with intellectual disability. And I have worked with the Department of Human Services going around Victoria and telling people about the standards for services for people with disabilities. It's been really interesting work. And I've done it because I'm passionate about people's lives and trying to get people to understand that they do have rights.

I don't know how I got the label of intellectual disability. I think it's just something that…because I was in the institution I've got to be disabled in some way. I don't know. Because I'm on the disability support pension, I have to have a disability. I can't access disability services though. Because when I was living here in Victoria, I managed to get somebody to come out to see if I was eligible for services through DHS. And to get a service you've got to be 70 per cent or below on an IQ test. I was 71. That 1 per cent stopped me. So, again, that creates a problem. What happens to people who are just that 1 per cent over? People like myself? It's absolutely ridiculous.

Kelley: Reflection – thinking about case management

Colin's account of his early life is one before case management became part of the service system. His account illustrates graphically some of the problems that case management is meant to address. In times of crisis, he relied on his own, very able, advocacy and that of his mother. Less often, service providers supported his case. He often felt as if things were happening to him that he did not understand and that left him feeling powerless in the face of service and justice systems. Social workers whom he encountered were attached to agencies or services and when approached did not seem to provide assistance or support. There was no independent person for whom Colin was important and whose job was to provide him with support in a crisis.

Kelley: Waiting for case management

When we began to discuss case management, Colin talked about two times in his life when he needed a case manager. He is in poor health at the moment and talked about his efforts to get a case manager to help him. And he talked about the illness and death of his mother some years ago.

Colin: Managing my health

I've never had a case manager. I'm in the process of being put on the waiting list for case management. Things are happening now within my life. My health is starting to suffer. And we've tried to apply for a case manager and we can't, we can't get it. Well, we can get one, but we can't get one for a while. It's two years now.

I thought that a case manager was somebody who was employed to do things I wanted or required or needed. So, say, like if I went to the hospital, then they would be able to come and be able to translate what was happening to me. Or what the doctor was trying to tell me. And to maybe translate what I'm trying to say back, if that needed to be done. Sometimes you go to the hospital, particularly in the emergency department. You go in. The doctor examines you. Maybe wants some tests done. The doctor does it and then disappears and you don't see that doctor again for goodness knows how long. So, hopefully, the case manager may be able to find out what the hell's going on and why you're just sitting there for the last two hours, laying on the bed and not even knowing what in the hell's going on.

I think somewhere in my file there may be something that says that I've got some kind of disability. Maybe it does say that because quite often they've talked about aggression to me and things like that. And being angry and getting really upset and worried and – so maybe that's the reason. There's something in there that says don't say anything to this person because he'll get really worried and upset and panic. I don't know. I don't know. I may be a person with a disability and I may have feelings, but don't leave me out. I may get angry. I may get upset. I may be confused. But, hey, I've got a right to know.

Having a case manager was suggested to me by somebody from the Austin Hospital and the social worker at the rehabilitation centre I go to. Rosy is my good friend. She did some leg work and what not to find out where things are and so forth. And what has to be done to get a case manager. And then all that information was passed on to the social worker, because the recommendation had to come from her. And then the social worker did all the writing and working out. I didn't have any part in putting the submission together. Don't remember what was in it. How long ago? 2003! I got told that there is a long, long, long, long,

long, long, long, long two years down the track, long, long, long waiting list. Now I haven't heard anything from the social worker. I haven't heard anything from anybody. Except Rosy saying to me 'You're on the waiting list.' Now also we tried to go through DHS in Fitzroy [a regional branch of the Victorian State Government Department of Human Services] to try and get outreach support for me. And couldn't get that either. They said there was no money.

At Moreland Health Centre [a community-based health service, usually with a range of health and medical personnel], here was some woman. I think she's a nurse or something up there. She wanted a meeting with me to talk to me about some stuff, because I was on their books. And I asked Rosy to come and be with me. And they started talking about case management. And somebody coming and being part of my life and all that sort of stuff. And immediately I thought... I started getting really angry and pissed off. And really confused. Because I thought that meant that I was going to lose Rosy completely. And that's not what I wanted. So I absolutely hit the roof. There's no way I wanted a case manager. No way on earth. And then when Rosy was talking to me about, you know, it doesn't mean that.

I think I can understand now what Rosy's saying. And that, you know, it's like a team. You know? So there's going to be the case manager. There's going to be Rosy. There might be the respiratory nurse that comes out and sees me, and there's my local doctor. And Amanda, my wife. And it's all part of that one team.

Managing my mum's illness

Then there was my mum. Mum was living in a flat through the Ministry of Housing. She started getting really sick. What I now believed to be what's called dementia, which I didn't know at that particular time. And she used to ring me up quite often, saying she can't find things. At least ten times a day. Maybe more. And she tried to make tea on the heater while the stove is cold. It was a great worry to me. And then, somehow, I don't know how, Mum ended up going into St George's Hospital in Kew. And she was having accidents and messing herself and what not. And never even known that she'd done it. She was a right mess. My mother was very angry with me. She wanted to go back home, and everyone was saying no, she can't. And I wanted to – because Mum brought me up and looked after me for 50-odd years – I wanted to do what she wanted. And I knew what she wanted. And I knew she couldn't live by herself. Which made that really hard and difficult. I didn't want to front the social worker by myself. And a couple of doctors and nurses. So that's why I asked if you'd [Kelley] come along as my support and as a friend of mine.

When we saw the social worker, they were trying to get Mum out of hospital within 24 hours. We just couldn't do that. That's when, I think, I asked Rosy, you know: 'What in the hell am I going to do?' John next door told us about the place at Bell Haven [a nursing home for older people]. So Rosy and I went up and had a look and there was a place. Rosy checked out a couple of other places. I couldn't go with her. She did that as my friend, a really good friend. And I was in control of Mum's money, and paying bills and all that sort of stuff. And things really started to get difficult and hard. When I used to go up and see Mum, Mum would accuse me of not going and seeing her and so forth – which I had been doing, but she couldn't remember. Nobody was telling me anything, and I didn't know anything. So I asked Rosy if she would talk to somebody or try to get somebody to do this stuff for me. So we decided that Rosy had to take over control of the money. Then we applied for Rosy to become Mum's guardian. And we had this meeting with this woman and I don't know who in the hell she was. We managed to get Rosy as Mum's guardian. But there was no case manager to help with these things. No one at the hospital.

It's just really hard seeing the state Mum was in when she was in the hospital. And seeing that she'd had some falls and seeing she was all bruised and everything. And the way she was bruised and the way she would have fallen would mean that the bruises were in a different place. And I was really, really angry with that. And I couldn't get Rosy to understand that I wanted something done about it. You know? I wanted some investigation, OK? Why is she falling out of bed? Why haven't they got the sides up on the bed? Why this? Why that? Why the other? There were some complaints that Rosy did make on my behalf against the hospital. Who knows what in the hell happened with that? Probably just got shoved into the 'too-hard basket'. You know?

And one Wednesday, Rosy just came knocking on the door and Mum had gone. She'd passed away. And I had nobody. No case manager. No nothing. No support. And I, I just couldn't think. I couldn't think. Who could I ring? What can I do? Who do I...what do I have to do? All I could think of was my mum's gone. I'm all alone. What's going to happen? That's all I could think of. I didn't even think about Rosy.

You asked me what do I think a case manager is, and I think it's somebody that – I know I'm totally wrong now, but when I first started thinking about it, it was somebody that was there for me and when I needed and wanted it. It's almost like somebody is on 24-hour call. You know? Provided that it's an emergency. Maybe, oh, maybe just a phone call away.

I can't see the difference between a support worker and a case manager, really can't see the difference. My understanding of the case manager is somebody there to help and support me. And be there for me. And that's what the job of a support worker is. Now Rosy's told me that's not what the case manager is. A case manager's there to help link you into services. They can't be there at the hospital explaining all these things that the doctors and nurses are saying. That's what her role is. That's Rosy's role. And that's what she wants to do. And she's prepared to do that. And she's told me that. But that's not what case manager means to me.

I've no idea how to get a case manager. I know there's Moreland Linkages [a case management programme], but that doesn't mean anything to me. Does that mean there's an organisation in Moreland called Linkages and I've got to go there? Or does that mean it's part of the council. Or is it part of Moreland Community Health? Or – I don't know if I've got the energy left to fight for a case manager. I think I'll leave that up to people like Rosy. Because Rosy's going to be getting on to that next week.

If I had a case manager in front of me, I would say: Blow what you're there to do. Blow the rules. I want you there for what I want. Part of that may include linking me into all these other things. But you say to me 'Would I like to go do a sporting thing?' So therefore you're going to link me to a sporting club. No, I don't know if I want that. No idea. OK? Do I want this, or do I want this, do I want this, this and this? I've no idea what I want. Because at the moment I'm that confused, that burnt out, I don't know what I want. You know? I might just say yes, just to shut you up. I think the case manager should be there for what I want. Stuff the system. I mean, the system might – we may be able to use the system in some ways. But also, besides that, be there for me.

Kelley: Reflection

Case management is now an important part of the service system for people with disabilities. Yet many of the issues raised by Colin in his account of his early life remain. He is still struggling to make sense of the systems in which he is involved. People still do not give him information, he believes, because of notes on his file. Or they do not give him information in ways that he can understand. He continues to struggle to advocate for himself and for those he supports. He still does not have a case manager.

His story of trying to get a case manager becomes yet another problem that he needs to solve. He now has to struggle to understand the system in order to obtain the case manager. And there is an undefined waiting list. If Colin was 'in crisis', as defined by the system, then a case manager would be found. But from Colin's perspective, he has been in crisis. So who identifies the crisis, and who, on Colin's behalf, informs the system of his needs?

Further, it is unclear to Colin what a case manager does. Over time, and with explanations from Rosy, Colin has gradually come to a view of what he wants. No one within the service system has explained this to him clearly. There are lessons here for people involved in case management practice. Telling someone they may need or should have a case manager may have little meaning to them. It may be necessary to spend time with someone so that they understand how this service may be helpful to them. More than this, it is important to understand that having a case manager may be seen by the person as a threat. For Colin, at one stage there was a fear that a stranger – a case manager – would remove a friend and supporter, Rosy, from his life. He also expresses some anxiety that a case manager may persuade or force him to agree to things he does not want to do. Appointing a case manager without discussion of these issues may be unhelpful to Colin and add to his anxieties and concerns.

When Colin talks of what he wants from a case manager, he speaks of someone to support him, someone to help him understand the system when he confronts a personal crisis. Perhaps this is not, in fact, the role of a case manager. Perhaps Colin is really expressing the need for someone who knows him and who can be an independent advocate. Yet there is not really anyone currently in the service system with this kind of role.

Currently, Rosy acts as an unofficial case manager. This may seem to be ideal. After all, we all use friends and family to support us. But it is also clear that there are problems with this arrangement if it is unsupported. If, for some reason, Rosy is unable to continue her role, then Colin is without support. There have been times when Rosy has not been able to address Colin's concerns and where she has been unable to 'work the system' for him. Further, her role as a 'voluntary' case manager inevitably changes their relationship. Rosy is a friend, but she is also responsible for dealing with the system for Colin. This can complicate their relationship. Colin does not want to lose Rosy's support, but he also recognises the need for someone else to be part of the team.

Kelley: Conclusion

Case managers can make life easier for someone experiencing difficulties in managing a range of services or life crises. As Colin says, however, it is important that the case manager 'be there' for the person with whom they are working. For Colin, at the moment the case manager is not 'there' in any sense of the word.

Endnote

Colin was allocated a case manager in May 2006. He commented that, while he was waiting, it would have been good for the organisation to have written regularly to say he had not been forgotten.

11

Working things out together: a collaborative approach to supporting parents with intellectual disabilities

Margaret Spencer and Gwynnyth Llewellyn

In this chapter, we attempt to answer the question of how to support parents with intellectual disabilities through good case management practice. The chapter begins by defining parents with intellectual disabilities and exploring some of the common problems they encounter. The second part of the chapter outlines the principles underlying a collaborative case management approach. The chapter then describes how a collaborative case management approach can be applied with parents with intellectual disabilities. This is illustrated with reflections on a case management relationship between the first author and a young single Australian woman with an intellectual disability during her first year as a mother.

Identifying parents with intellectual disabilities

Identification of parents with intellectual disabilities is not straightforward (Greenspan 1999), as the vast majority of people with intellectual disabilities who do parent have IQ scores that place them in the mild to borderline category of intellectual impairment. Known as the 'hidden majority' (Edgerton 1999), these are individuals who may have fulfilled the criteria for a diagnosis of mild mental retardation at some time in their lives, typically at school (Tymchuk, Lakin and Luckasson 2001). Their cognitive limitations place them in the borderline low average range (IQ of 70–85), and they do not meet the formal diagnostic criteria for intellectual disability (IQ less than 70). They do, however, have special learning needs, which makes it difficult for them to access the support they require, and it is only when they make the transition from being an individual in the community to becoming a parent with responsibilities that their intellectual capacity is brought into question and the intellectual disability label is reassigned. This chapter defines parents with intellectual disabilities as parents who self-identify as having intellectual disabilities or are identified by health, educational or welfare agencies as being intellectually disabled.

Common problems encountered by parents with intellectual disabilities

Deeply ingrained prejudices exist towards people with learning difficulties becoming parents, often based on a common assumption that adults with intellectual disabilities lack the capacity to learn the skills necessary to provide a safe, healthy, nurturing and stimulating environment for their children (Llewellyn and McConnell 2005). Such attitudes are encountered not only from the broader community but also from family, friends and service personnel (Llewellyn 1990). Typically, the concern is that the chances of normal development for the children of a parent with a disability will be jeopardised (McConnell and Llewellyn 2000). Over six decades of empirical evidence demonstrates that cognitive intelligence per se is a poor predictor of parenting competence and child outcomes (Dowdney and Skuse 1993; Llewellyn 1993). Contrary to popular myths, a significant number of parents with intellectual disabilities do just fine (Booth and Booth 2003; Llewellyn 1994). This is not to deny the fact that parenting poses problems for some. As most parents with intellectual disabilities are socially and economically disadvantaged, they come up against the same issues that cause other parents rearing children in disadvantaged conditions to become unstuck. These issues include poverty, inadequate housing, unemployment, relationship difficulties, unsafe neighbourhoods, social isolation and poor health (Aunos, Goupil and Feldman 2004; Llewellyn and McConnell 2002; Wilson, Oke and Vecellio 2005). Problems for parents with intellectual disabilities, however, are often exacerbated by the fact that, unlike their peers, they are more likely to come under greater external scrutiny – and when things go wrong, they are rarely given the benefit of the doubt (Hayman 1990; McConnell and Llewellyn 2002). The problems experienced by these parents are attributed solely to their intellectual disabilities, ignoring other influences in their lives (Booth and Booth 1994).

Parents with intellectual disabilities are 15–50 times more likely than other parents in Australia, the USA and the UK to have their children removed and placed in care (Llewellyn and McConnell 2005), mostly on the grounds that they are 'at risk' of harm due to neglect but rarely due to allegations of abuse.

The best predictor of 'success' by parents with intellectual disabilities is their ability to receive timely, adequate and appropriate parenting assistance, thus highlighting the importance of good case management for these families (Llewellyn, McConnell and Bye 1998). A number of common problems get in the way of parents with intellectual disabilities experiencing effective case management services.

In developed countries, it is often the case that neither disability-specific nor mainstream services are willing to take on parents with intellectual disabilities. Generic family support services contend that their support needs should be the responsibility of specialist disability services, while disability services argue that parents with intellectual disabilities have a right to utilise mainstream services and deflect responsibility back to generic services.

A common strategy adopted by case managers is a scatter-gun approach to case referral, whereby parents are referred to all and sundry, with the hope that as many service providers as possible will pick them up. As a result, service provision becomes feast or famine. It is not uncommon for a family to go from having no one in their lives to being inundated with services that do not match the parents' wants or needs. For example, the mothers in one study of parents with intellectual disabilities reported being overserviced in some areas, such as childcare training, and underserviced in support that enhanced parental wellbeing (Walton-Allen and Feldman 1999). Poor coordination of service delivery can mean service providers work at cross-purposes. This is not only a waste of precious resources but also stressful for the parents, who struggle to make sense of mixed messages and contradictory advice, and it often results in interagency conflict (Llewellyn *et al.* 1998).

Case managers can too readily attribute parenting problems solely to the parent's cognitive limitations and aim to only educate or modify parental behaviours. Environmental pressures and system failures are often overlooked or glossed over (Booth and Booth 1994; Tymchuk 1990), despite the abundant evidence of the effect of environmental pressures on parenting success and the need to explore parents' informal and formal support systems (Llewellyn, McConnell and Mayes 2003).

In Australia, case management services for parents with intellectual disabilities have fallen largely to the child protection system. This can be problematic as, by virtue of not being able to access support through other means, parents with intellectual disabilities and their children are put in a situation where they must be labelled as 'at risk' in order to receive the help they need. Understandably, many parents with intellectual disabilities are frightened by this to such an extent that they would rather go it alone than have 'the welfare' involved. This does not bode well for parents developing a constructive relationship with a case manager appointed by the local statutory child protection agency. Moreover, unwieldy caseload demands can mean child protection agencies are ill-equipped to provide the proactive, specialised and long-term case management many parents with intellectual disabilities require and are usually able to provide only short-term case management to families in crisis. High staff turnover within the child protection system also means case managers tend to come and go in the lives of these families, exacerbating mistrust within the case management relationship.

There is a risk that decisions about support provision are 'hammered out' among professionals, with little more than token gesture given to the inclusion of the parents' views. This is often most pronounced in formal case conference meetings, which are structured in ways that preclude parents with intellectual disabilities from genuine participation and leave them feeling bewildered and frustrated. For example, although parents are invited to attend such meetings, they may be given little or no say as to when or how the meeting is held, they are confronted by a range of professionals, many of whom they have never met, and they are handed an agenda that they cannot read, makes little sense or lists confronting items, such as alternative care arrangements for their children.

As Booth and Booth (2003) note, the 'professional knows best' approach sits uncomfortably alongside the fact that few professionals who take on roles as case managers for parents with intellectual disabilities have any training in this area. As a consequence, their evaluation of what these parents need can be ill-informed. For example, child protection case managers may assume that parents with intellectual disabilities require no less than 24-hour supervision based on the misconception that people with intellectual disabilities are likely to be forgetful, erratic and predisposed to aggressive outbursts. In contrast, case managers may set unrealistic goals, such as expecting that, after participating in a parenting programme typically designed for parents without disabilities, a mother with intellectual disabilities will be able to parent independently without any further support. As well as having limited knowledge about working with people with intellectual disabilities and parenting with intellectual disabilities, many case managers have limited knowledge of resources outside their own sector or those in the parent's local community. Effective case management with parents with intellectual disabilities requires a case manager to have cross-sector knowledge and the aptitude to create cross-sector partnerships.

Principles and practices of effective case management with parents with intellectual disabilities

The following section is based on the authors' extensive clinical experience in supporting professionals and parents with intellectual disabilities who are endeavouring to forge effective case management partnerships and practices. We advocate a collaborative case management approach, underpinned by a commitment to collaboration, critical reflection and strengths-based practice. It is informed by the work of Anderson (1997), de Shazer (1988) and White and Epston (1990), who apply social constructionist and postmodern theory to therapeutic practice (see Paré and Larner 2004, www.taosinstitute.net and www.dulwichcentre.com.au).

Collaboration

The first principle in a collaborative case management approach is a commitment to collaboration that is not only about people working cooperatively and in a coordinated manner but also working as a process. Collaboration involves taking a particular epistemological stance that views the process through which we come to know support needs as co-constructed in and through a dialogical process. Accordingly, collaboration is not confined only to bringing all with an interest in affecting change to share ideas in order to foster cooperation but is based on a philosophical belief that it is in the sharing of knowledge through just and constructive conversation that knowledge of what is required (i.e. support) can be ascertained. It requires an acknowledgement and appreciation of the knowledge, ideas and expertise that all stakeholders bring to the case management process. Most importantly, collaboration in this sense means working with, rather than for, parents with intellectual disabilities and respecting the local knowledge and expertise they bring to the case management conversation. To do so means that case managers may need to add to their typical primary practice of talking and include other media such as pictures, observation and demonstration to facilitate understanding of the parents' situation, their concerns and their need for support.

Critical reflection

The second principle in a collaborative case management approach is critical reflection – a process that involves people examining the assumptions and values within which they operate. Put simply, it means thinking about why they believe and act as they do (Taylor and White 2000). Critical reflection has two steps when working with parents with intellectual disabilities. The first is to allow the professionals, the parents and their supporters to examine tacit and pejorative assumptions held about parenting and, more specifically, parenting with intellectual disabilities. The second step is for the case manager to work with all involved to foster attitudinal change and ownership of decision-making and particularly to support the parents to take control of the decisions that most affect their lives.

Strengths-based practice

The third principle in collaborative case management is a commitment to strengths-based practice (Elliott 2000). Strengths-based practice is based on an understanding that all people are capable of positive change and that change is incremental and builds on existing strengths and resources. As the name implies, strengths-based practice concentrates and capitalises on the capacities and abilities of participants, including the parents and their informal and formal supports, and invites lateral and innovative thinking to occur.

Putting a collaborative case management approach into practice

In this section, we describe how these principles that underpin a collaborative case management approach can be put into practice when working with parents with intellectual disabilities. The discussion is illustrated by reflections drawn from the first author's collaborative case management relationship with a 22-year-old woman with intellectual disabilities, whom we shall call Fiona, as she makes the life-changing transition from being a young woman to being a single mother of twins in a large Australian city. I invited Fiona to reflect on her personal experiences of collaborative case management for this study, because she was eager to share her experiences with others. Fiona's reflections were collected through a series of conversations with me. We also worked together on later versions of this chapter, so that writing up her experiences was a collaborative process in which her knowledge, ideas and expertise were as valuable as mine. Excerpts of our reflections are interspersed throughout the following discussion, beginning with the following, which provides some background to the case management relationship.

Margaret: My formal case management relationship with Fiona began around the time her babies were born, although I have known Fiona and her extended family for many years in my clinical position as a community health and family worker in an Australian inner-city suburb. Despite our best efforts, Fiona and her two younger sisters were placed in foster care when Fiona was seven years old. During her time in care, Fiona moved between 12 foster placements. I kept in touch with Fiona and her sisters during their time in care, out of personal interest rather than professional duty.

On leaving care, Fiona was referred to the service where I work for community support. My colleagues and I provided her with practical aid, advocacy assistance and living-skills training. From a service outcome perspective, Fiona was doing well, living in the community, maintaining a rented property and working part-time in open employment. Fiona wanted what other girls her age had, however – a boyfriend.

One day Fiona left her job and gave up her flat to move in with a man she met through her birth mother. The man was older and exploitative, but Fiona was just happy to have a boyfriend. Within a short period of time, Fiona fell pregnant to him. When she told him, he abandoned her. Having lost her own housing and afraid that I and my co-workers would be angry with her, Fiona kept her distance from formal supports. As the birth of her twins became imminent, numerous prenatal reports were made to the child protection authorities. Fiona realised that if she was to have any hope of being allowed to keep her babies, she needed to seek support outside her birth family. She approached one of her ex-foster carers, Joy, to ask whether our service would assist her. I was appointed Fiona's case manager.

Building trust

Given that the parents have the most at stake and have good reason to be mistrustful of professionals who want to 'help', the first requirement is to gain their trust. This means taking time to get to know the parents beyond the problems they bring with them to the case management situation. As parents with intellectual disabilities are more likely to disclose in less formal settings, perhaps in their own home or on neutral territory, a simple act such as driving or accompanying a parent to an appointment can be a good opportunity to start up a conversation, which in turn may lead to a closer, more trusting, collaborative relationship.

Margaret: Before I could meet with Fiona to discuss her support needs, she gave birth prematurely to very small but healthy babies. When I visited her in the maternity ward, she was distracted and focused on the babies' birth registration forms, finding them hard to follow.

Fiona: I was a bit scared about seeing Margaret at the hospital. I wanted to see her, but I was scared she might be angry with me for giving up my flat and job and stuff. But she just acted normal.

Margaret: Before meeting with her, I needed to be attentive to my feelings about working with Fiona and her family again. I found it helpful to talk about my case management role with a clinical supervisor. I also kept a critical reflective journal to help me be aware of the stance I was taking and decisions I was making in my case management relationship with Fiona.

Fiona: Margaret brought a present for me and the babies, which was really nice, and she just wanted me to tell her all about the girls and the birth and stuff… I remember her saying that she would help me and we could start again. She didn't go cranky at me or nothing.

It is also important to build trust with a parent's partner, children and other family members. The person's partner may resent professional intrusion. Older children may be worried or confused by professional involvement, especially if they perceive professionals to be threatening family integrity. Grandparents may hold fears that professional case management may misconstrue, usurp or place additional demands on their involvement in their adult son's or daughter's life and the lives of their grandchild(ren) (Llewellyn *et al.* 1999).

Genuine respect for and interest in the parent

In addition to building trust, it is vital that the case manager brings to the case management relationship genuine respect and interest in the other person.

Margaret: One day, I commented on how well Fiona appeared to be getting on with the other mothers and workers at the refuge where she was living. She said: 'Yeah, I get on with everyone here, but I know they are only nice to me because they like my babies. If it was just me, they wouldn't be interested.' She was right: the babies were very cute and, being identical twins, attracted a lot of attention. I realised I was also culpable of asking Fiona about the babies and spending time playing with them on my visits. Fiona's comment alerted me to the fact that she needed to know that we were interested in her, not just her as 'the twins' mother'. From that day, I have made a conscious effort when I ring or visit to ask about Fiona first before talking with her about her 'angels', as she calls them. As her case manager, I also talk to Fiona about things she may like to do for herself and build that into our support plan. For example, Fiona indicated recently that she would like to do a dressmaking course run by a local community adult education programme. When this was raised at a support planning meeting, some workers suggested to Fiona she may have enough to occupy her looking after the babies. I supported Fiona with her enquiries, however, realising that within her support plan she needed activities that replenished and nurtured her as a 22-year-old woman, not just as a mother.

Actively listening

In order to communicate effectively, the collaborative case manager needs to refine his or her skills of actively listening. This is particularly important when working with people whose expertise and experience are obscured by diagnostic labelling and entrenched assumptions. In collaborative practice, this way of listening is referred to as taking a 'not-knowing' stance (Anderson 1997). This does not mean 'playing dumb', as case managers bring experience and expertise to the relationship; rather, it involves shifting one's knowledge and experience from centre-stage in order to entertain other perspectives and possibilities, being genuinely curious, and asking questions to clarify and learn more about what is being said.

Margaret: Fiona tends to communicate her ideas in a convoluted and detailed form. I admit that sometimes I am not very patient with her long-winded explanations about how she has or is proposing to resolve an issue, particularly when she is talking to me on my mobile phone or when I am in a rush to get somewhere. As a consequence, I am at times guilty of jumping in and giving her solutions, when in fact she has already worked out or is capable of working out what it is that she needs to do. Fiona is actually very good at solving problems if given the chance and not stressed. I learn a lot about how she solves problems by being curious with her.

Fiona: One day I rang Margaret to tell her how hot it had been and how I needed to save up to buy another fan because the girls' room gets really hot. I wanted to let her know how I could buy the fans out of my savings because I saw one for sale for $40. I told her how yesterday I had dampened two cloths in cool water and lay one on each girl's forehead while they had their afternoon sleep. Margaret laughed and said she was going to tell me to do just that. But, see, I already knew this was a good thing to do when babies are hot. Margaret asked me how I knew to do this and I said, 'Because that is what I do when the girls have fevers and being hot is like having a fever…also I saw [Joy] do it with her son.'

Negotiating a language for shared enquiry

The role of the case manager in the collaborative case management approach is to foster shared enquiry and to help develop possibilities into realities. Fostering shared enquiry demands more than setting up a meeting with everyone with an interest in how the job of parenting is being done. It involves facilitating dialogue by creating a 'conversational space' in which those interested in making the parenting role work can share and reflect on experiences, feelings, beliefs, opinion, observation and ideas, with the intent of co-constructing solutions that may previously have been unimagined, overlooked or obscure (Anderson 1997).

This requires a willingness to learn the parent's language and to find communication formats that foster dialogue. The best way to do this is for the case manager to invite the parent to help him or her understand what works for the parent when it comes to taking on board new information or saying what they think (Booth and Booth 2003; Llewellyn and McConnell 2005). Visual tools (see www.innovativeresources.com.au), such as picture prompts and feeling and metaphor cards, have been found to be effective in fostering dialogue and learning with parents with intellectual disabilities (Llewellyn et al. 2002; Tymchuk et al. 2003). Mapping and drawing are also helpful in facilitating conversation about past experiences, current concerns, needs and aspirations. Another useful visual tool is the Support Interview Guide (Llewellyn and McConnell 2002; see www.afdsrc.org), designed specifically for practitioners working with parents with intellectual disabilities in order to identify the diversity of supports in the parents' lives.

Using alternative communication forms requires the case manager to give additional time to the process and to be willing to be creative in how they communicate. It can be helpful if the case manager works from the position that it is his or her responsibility to get the message across in a way that is comprehensible to the parent – that is, to see oneself, rather than the parent with intellectual disabilities, as having the communication difficulty.

Margaret: While in the hospital, Fiona's biggest concern was not being allowed to bring her babies home. She explained to me that the child protection authority did not think it was safe for her and the babies to live with her mum. I decided to adopt Fiona's use of the word 'safe' to explore what she thought she may need in order to feel safe herself and to provide safety for her babies. To assist our dialogue, I explained how, with some other mothers, I had found it helpful to work things out through drawing. I took my sketchbook and coloured pens and drew stick figures depicting Fiona and the babies. I then suggested we draw what made her feel safe and what made her babies safe. Her first suggestion was having safe and secure housing, and so I drew a house around her and the babies. Then I asked her to tell me what that house might be like. Fiona said it needed to be in a neighbourhood that was OK, near her foster mother and affordable. We then talked about safe and unsafe people in her life; Fiona defined these, respectively, as people she could trust and not trust.

Fiona: I like it when we draw things, so we can talk about them. When workers talk about lots of things one after the other, I get confused. When important things are written down in an order like in point form and like pictures, I can concentrate and understand it better. When we have to make decisions, Margaret will draw different possibilities – options – on a sheet of paper. Sometimes we need a big piece of paper to fit all our ideas and thinking. On the paper we write down the fors and againsts beside different options. I keep these pages in [a cupboard] away from the babies... With important decisions, Margaret will leave the options with me and say 'Think about it overnight' or 'Talk to Joy about it.' She does this because she says I have to be happy with the decision or it's no good. When I am having trouble saying what I think, Margaret will give me the pens and say 'Draw it for me.'

Viewing the problem as the problem, not the person as the problem

The collaborative case manager also builds trust by externalising problems or, as the narrative dictum states, '(viewing) the problem as the problem, not the person as the problem' (Monk *et al.* 1997). Separating problems from people avoids energies being sidetracked or diminished in blame games or other damaging practices (Chalmers 2001). By keeping the focus on the problem, participants are enabled to work together against the problem rather than against each other.

Margaret: After leaving hospital, I secured for Fiona and the babies a self-contained flat that was part of a supported accommodation unit. One of the rules of the facility was that mothers and children were to be home after dark. After a few months, I received a call from the coordinator of the service saying, 'We have a problem. Staff have seen Fiona taking the babies out in the evening and hanging around the local shopping mall chatting with locals and workers.' The coordinator said she had confronted Fiona about her behaviour, but Fiona denied doing anything of the sort. As it was winter, and considering the babies' prematurity, the coordinator said she had a duty of care to report Fiona's action to the child protection authority. I arranged to meet with Fiona to discuss the issue. At first, Fiona was withdrawn. I sensed she was afraid of getting into trouble and her fear was getting in the way of us treating the problem as the problem. To get around this, I reassured her that I wasn't angry with her but that together we need to work out a solution. To help Fiona enter into a constructive conversation with me, I presented her with a set of feeling cards.

Fiona: Margaret has these feeling cards she uses when we have to talk about some things, like when people found out me and the girls were going up to the shops in the evenings. The feeling cards helped me talk about all this stuff. Margaret calls this 'laying the cards on the table'…this means we get things out into the open.

Margaret: The feeling cards are just a simple set of ten cards, each with a face depicting a feeling, for example happy, sad, scared, confused, angry and guilty. I designed these for my own use, but similar visual cards are available at www.innovativeresources.com.au. They are especially useful in helping individuals with poor communication and/or conflict-resolution skills to give expression to feelings they are unable to articulate.

As Fiona began to express her feelings, we were able to move on to the issue at hand. The stance I took was one of curiosity. I worked from the premise that Fiona had a reason for going to the trouble of leaving her flat at night with two small babies to sit in the mall, and I wanted her to help me to understand what it was. She explained how, after the staff left for the day, she often felt very lonely and scared about being alone all night. Her solution was to go up to the mall, where it was warm and people were nice to her. It was a solution, however, that had a number of drawbacks, such as breaking the rules of her accommodation contract, how hanging around the mall with two small babies would be perceived by others, and the risk factors for herself and the babies. The challenge we faced was finding a new solution to the problem of loneliness at night that was safer and socially acceptable. Fiona and the babies ended up moving from the supported accommodation unit into a shared household with two young mothers awaiting public housing. Here, Fiona had the company of the other women in the evenings.

Building trust with and between service providers

Although trust between service providers should underpin all successful collaborative case-work scenarios, it is particularly pertinent when it comes to collaborations built around supporting parents with intellectual disabilities. Case managers are commonly faced with the challenge of bringing together services that may not be used to working with each other, for example disability-specific services working alongside family support services. This requires the case manager to help cross-sector services to understand each other's aims and objectives, protocols and restraints. One practical strategy we have found to be effective is to bring them together for joint learning in the form of a workshop regarding parenting with intellectual disabilities. In addition, it is important that the case manager clarifies with each service provider who will be providing what services to the parent, in order to avoid duplication, demarcation disputes and confusion. Having done this, a helpful exercise is to road-test the roles and responsibilities through hypothetical scenarios. Finally, keeping all stakeholders within the communication loop is vital. One practical and efficient way the collaborative case manager can do this is by establishing an email listserv, so that all stakeholders can be kept informed on emerging issues, changes to plans, new ideas and critical events.

Margaret: When the twins were a year old, Fiona sought treatment from her local doctor for anxiety and depression. She was still waiting to be given a public housing flat and, because her current accommodation had expired, she had to move into a family refuge. Because of Fiona's intellectual disability and the fact that she had twins, the refuge was at first unwilling to accept the family. I negotiated with the child protection worker that individual support funds would be provided to the refuge to cover any additional staffing hours that may be necessary to meet the needs of Fiona and the girls. I also provided some in-service training to the staff about working with parents with intellectual disabilities and, in particular, helping them to understand Fiona's special learning needs and communication style.

Fiona and the babies now had a number of professionals involved in their lives. These included the early childhood nurse, a child protection case worker, staff at the day-care centre where the babies were now attending two days a week, her local doctor, a counsellor, an after-care worker (a worker appointed to assist young adults in the years following leaving foster care), a financial manager and the staff at the refuge into which she was moving. One of the biggest challenges was keeping the lines of communication clear.

Fiona: Often, I was unsure who I was supposed to be talking to about what. I would ring Margaret a lot and then sometimes I would get into trouble from staff at the refuge because they would say I should be going to them for help and I would just not know.

Margaret: As case manager, I called a meeting so all those involved in Fiona's life could explain their involvement. Those who could not attend were invited to send a short description of their roles. I collated this information and drew up a colour-coded diagram for Fiona, explaining to whom she talked about what issues. This diagram was also sent to all the professionals involved. To assist us in keeping up our communication with one another, I set up an email listserv. This enabled me to keep abreast of what was happening, to field questions, to pass on information regularly and efficiently and to avoid the frustration of me and others playing 'telephone tag'.

Helping possibilities become realities

In addition to fostering shared enquiry, the collaborative case manager helps to turn possibilities into practical and achievable plans by seeking out strengths and resources and looking for ways in which these may be harnessed in order to bring about change.

Fiona: Margaret says that me and her have 'different abilities'. Sometimes I can do things much better than her...like, I am much better at being on time and she knows nothing about public transport. My job is to remind her of things.

A lot of what I know about being a mum comes from watching my foster mum, [Joy], look after [her son]... [Joy] is a great mum and I want to be just like her. Margaret says to me sometimes, 'What would [Joy] do in such-and-such situation?' This gets me thinking... I use this strategy when the girls are unsettled and I am a bit stressed.

I am also good at finding out information – I like to find things out on the
Internet at my local library. I also borrow books and videos about parenting.
When we were buying a new pram, Margaret got me to find out what was available by visiting the baby stores and collecting information. We then sat down and
made a decision.

If the girls are not eating or got a temperature or something like that, I ring
Tresillian [a mother and child 24-hour helpline] because they are the experts on
babies. If I ring Margaret, she says, 'What did Tresillian say?' See – they have different abilities too.

The collaborative case manager does not assume to have the answers or solutions
or accept responsibility for every problem. As strengths and resources are identified and possibilities also emerge, the collaborative case manager highlights these
as propositions for further exploration, trusting that the best and most achievable
solutions emerge as participants take ownership and are willing to act.

One way to achieve this is to work with participants to devise a staged
approach, breaking down desired goals into sequenced, achievable steps. This
may require coming up with temporary solutions while resources are sought to
enable a more permanent solution or preferable possibilities.

Margaret: Ideally, Fiona wanted to get a public housing unit near Joy. Joy and I
agreed this was ideal but may not be realistic and feasible in terms of Fiona's
immediate accommodation needs and the length of time it may take to be
accepted for public housing. The child protection worker was not so sure. She
said that because Fiona has intellectual disability, she may require more supported
accommodation – in her view, 24 hours a day, seven days a week was ideal. I was
able to contribute from my experience of working with other parents with intellectual disabilities and knowledge of the local supported accommodation unit to
suggest that this may be neither necessary nor possible. Joy pointed out that Fiona
had good independent living skills and had managed her own flat previously.
Learning this allowed the child protection worker to consider Fiona's competencies, rather than only her deficits, and to entertain the possibility that Fiona may
be able to manage in a less supervised environment.

Another way of finding the best solution is to trial new strategies. This requires
the case manager to work in a more hands-on way with parents, for example by
undertaking new activities with parents until they feel comfortable or confident
to attempt the activity independently.

Margaret: Rather than simply referring Fiona to a service, I will organise to partner her until she feels comfortable about going herself. In the early stages, Fiona would ask about things such as local playgroups and mothers' groups; I would get her the information but she wouldn't follow through. When I asked her to help me understand why she was not following through, she told me she felt shy and nervous that people would ask her things she did not understand and then misjudge her. That made sense. So now I factor in time so that I or one of Fiona's other support workers can accompany her to activities and appointments at least until she feels confident.

In supporting Fiona to do new things, I also believe it is important that she is the one who decides what is and what is not supportive. This can be hard at times, especially when it is counter to my professional opinion.

Fiona: The playgroup was OK, but after trying it out I decided maybe the playgroup wasn't any good for me. There were too many mothers and a lot of them were different from me.

Margaret: I really hoped that Fiona would continue to attend the local playgroup run by a colleague of mine, but after attending a few times she decided it wasn't appropriate. I respected her reasons and left it at that. Some of the workers said she should continue for the sake of the girls, but on reflection I didn't think that at this stage it was going to jeopardise the girls' development if they didn't go.

Just as it is beneficial for the case manager to provide hands-on support to the parent when trialling a new strategy, so workers may also feel more confident in providing a service if the case manager is prepared to work alongside them. One way in which the case manager may do this is by undertaking joint home visits with a worker initially and then on an intermittent basis. This gives the collaborative case manager the opportunity to model collaborative practice and to better understand day-to-day case management issues.

Margaret: After moving into her own flat, the community support worker who took Fiona shopping fortnightly was concerned that Fiona had difficulty with housework. The worker reported that simply talking about the issue and providing strategies was not improving the situation. One day, I spent time working alongside Fiona to clean up the flat. This gave me invaluable insight into why getting the housework done was problematic. It also enabled me and Fiona to talk about the problems openly without blame being laid or taken. I now understood that it wasn't that she didn't know how to do the tasks required, but it was more the difficulty of balancing the demands of supervising two active toddlers while trying to complete daily routines such as emptying the bins, hanging out washing and sweeping the floor. What we came to see together was that she needed an occasional extra pair of hands. I made a referral to a home-help service for people with disabilities. A worker was allocated; Fiona and I then met with the worker and her supervisor to negotiate the service that would best meet Fiona's needs.

Conclusions

This chapter highlights the particular aspects of the collaborative case management model that makes this approach beneficial for parents with intellectual disabilities. The most critical aspect of collaborative case management is that all of the people involved, and in particular the case manager, need to approach case management as dynamic and flexible. This is very different from the more traditional approach in which the case manager assesses the case, implements some type of intervention, evaluates the case and then monitors the situation through regular check-up telephone calls. In conventional case management, a division is drawn between case planning and implementation, and it is not uncommon for detailed support plans to be devised only to be filed and then resurrected before a case review meeting.

In contrast, in collaborative case management, shared enquiry and turning possibilities into reality occur in tandem. Part of the flexibility of a collaborative approach is being prepared to try another way. People with intellectual disabilities may communicate better and learn more when offered alternative ways of communication, whether pictorial, in plain English, modelling, demonstrating or providing plenty of opportunities for practice. In this way, more is understood by parents and, in turn, case managers come to have a better understanding of the parent's situation. Approaching case management as a flexible work in progress also allows solutions to be tweaked along the way and uncertainties to be accommodated. What may have been considered possible in earlier dialogue may no longer be achievable, for a host of reasons, such as relationship breakdown, ill-health, staff turnover and family relocation.

The collaborative approach also allows for the unpredictability of parenting demands to be responded to rather than waiting for festering issues to reach crisis point. It allows for new horizons to be spotted early; for example, a transition in a child's development, such as becoming mobile, may alter parenting support needs.

Key to this approach is the case manager's commitment to collaboration. The role of the case manager is to work with, rather than on behalf of, the parent with a disability and by continually planning, acting and reflecting on the case together. To achieve this, the case manager takes responsibility for managing the process, rather than the person, resulting in a more egalitarian distribution of power between the case manager and their 'client'.

This collaborative relationship extends to others, such as other professionals, family members and friends, who have an interest in the parent succeeding in their role. The collaborative case manager does this by keeping the conversational space alive, thus enabling interested parties to re-evaluate possibilities, directions and resources. This is particularly valuable when working with parents with intellectual disabilities, where solutions may be obscure, change may be slow and fear and pessimism lurk in the background.

It has been our experience that when service providers have had the opportunity to participate in this approach to case management and to see that it works, particularly for a family for whom they believed there were no solutions, it serves as a catalyst for reappraising and improving their work practices with their other clients.

Undoubtedly, the collaborative case management approach is, in the short term, more labour-intensive than many other approaches to case management. More reflective planning, however, means that in the longer term, labour and resources are used more efficiently and effectively and the likelihood of service duplication is reduced greatly. Most importantly, the supports put in place mean that more widespread use of the case management approach may contribute to fewer children being removed unnecessarily from their parents with intellectual disabilities.

Acknowledgements

The authors are very grateful to Fiona for her time and candour and for generously allowing her case management experiences to be shared with others. Thanks also to Mrs Margaret Zucker and Dr Nikki Wedgwood for their comments and invaluable editing skills.

References

Anderson, H. (1997) *Conversation, Language and Possibilities: A Postmodern Approach to Therapy.* New York: Basic Books.

Aunos, M., Goupil, G. and Feldman, M. (2004) 'Influences of parenting abilities, mother's health, stress levels and social support on children's behaviours.' *Journal of Intellectual Disability Research 48*, 379.

Booth, T. and Booth, M. (1994) *Parenting Under Pressure: Mothers and Fathers with Learning Difficulties.* Buckingham: Open University Press.

Booth, T. and Booth, W. (2003) 'In the frame: photovoice and mothers with learning difficulties.' *Disability and Society 18*, 431–42.

Chalmers, B. (2001) 'Collaborative assessment: an alternative to psychological evaluation.' Accessed 1 March 2007 at www.somewareinvt.com/vcca/collab_assess_paper.pdf

De Shazer, S. (1988) *Clues: Investigating Solutions in Brief Therapy.* New York: W.W. Norton.

Dowdney, L. and Skuse, D. (1993) 'Parenting provided by adults with mental retardation.' *Journal of Child Psychology and Child Psychiatry 34*, 25–47.

Edgerton, R.B. (1999) 'The forward.' *Journal of Intellectual and Developmental Disability 24*, 1–2.

Elliott, B. (2000) *Promoting Family Change: The Optimism Factor.* Sydney: Allen & Unwin.

Greenspan, S. (1999) 'What is meant by mental retardation?' *International Review of Psychiatry 11*, 739–44.

Hayman, R.L. (1990) 'Presumptions of justice: law, politics, and the mentally retarded parent.' *Harvard Law Review 103*, 1201–71.

Llewellyn, G. (1990) 'People with intellectual disability as parents: perspectives from the professional literature.' *Australia and New Zealand Journal of Developmental Disabilities 16*, 369–80.

Llewellyn, G. (1993) 'Parents with intellectual disability: facts, fallacies and professional responsibilities.' *Community Bulletin 17*, 10–19.

Llewellyn, G. (1994) *Intellectual Disability and Parenting: A Shared Experience.* Sydney: University of Sydney.

Llewellyn, G. and McConnell, D. (2002) 'Mothers with learning difficulties and their support networks.' *Journal of Intellectual Disability Research 46*, 17–34.

Llewellyn, G. and McConnell, D. (2005) 'You Have to Prove Yourself all the Time: People with Learning Disabilities as Parents.' In P. Goward, G. Grant, P. Ramcharan and M. Richardson (eds) *Learning Disability: A Life Cycle Approach to Valuing People.* Maidenhead: Open University Press.

Llewellyn, G., McConnell, D. and Bye, R. (1998) 'Perception of service needs by parents with intellectual disability, their significant others and their service workers.' *Research in Developmental Disabilities 19*, 245–60.

Llewellyn, G., McConnell, D., Cant, R. and Westbrook, M. (1999) 'Support networks of mothers with an intellectual disability: an exploratory study.' *Journal of Intellectual and Developmental Disability 24*, 7–26.

Llewellyn, G., McConnell, D., Russo, D. and Mayes, R. (2002) 'Home-based programmes for parents with intellectual disabilities: lessons from practice.' *Journal of Applied Research in Intellectual Disabilities 15*, 341–53.

Llewellyn, G., McConnell, D. and Mayes, R. (2003) 'Health of mothers with intellectual limitations.' *Australian and New Zealand Journal of Public Health 27*, 17–19.

McConnell, D. and Llewellyn, G. (2000) 'Disability and discrimination in statutory child protection proceedings.' *Disability and Society 15*, 883–95.

McConnell, D. and Llewellyn, G. (2002) 'Stereotypes, parents with intellectual disability and child protection.' *Journal of Social Welfare and Family Law 24*, 297–317.

Monk, G., Winslade, J., Crocket, K. and Epston, D. (1997) *Narrative Therapy in Practice: The Archaeology of Hope.* San Francisco, CA: Jossey-Bass.

Paré, D.A. and Larner, G. (eds) (2004) *Collaborative Practice in Psychology and Therapy.* New York: Haworth Clinical Practice Press.

Taylor, C. and White, S. (2000) *Practising Reflexivity in Health and Welfare: Making Knowledge.* Philadelphia, PA: Open University Press.

Tymchuk, A.J. (1990) 'Parents with mental retardation: a national strategy.' *Journal of Disability Policy Studies 1*, 43–55.

Tymchuk, A.J., Lakin, K.C. and Luckasson, R. (2001) *The Forgotten Generation: The Status and Challenges of Adults with Mild Cognitive Limitations.* Baltimore, MD: Paul H. Brookes.

Tymchuk, A.J., Lang, C., Lieberman, S. and Koo, S. (2003) 'Development and validation of the illustrated version of the home inventory for dangers and safety precautions: continuing to address learning needs of parents in healthcare and safety.' *Journal of Family Violence 18*, 241–52.

Walton-Allen, N.G. and Feldman, M.A. (1999) 'Perceptions of service needs by parents who are mentally retarded and their social service workers.' *Comprehensive Mental Health Care 1*, 37–47.

White, M. and Epston, D. (1990) *Narrative Means to Therapeutic Ends.* New York: W.W. Norton.

Wilson, E., Oke, N. and Vecellio, L. (2005) '1-in-4 poll – 2005: economic hardship and social participation.' Accessed 1 March 2007 at www.scopevic.org.au/what_media_1in4021205.html

12

Intellectual disability and the complexity of challenging behaviour and mental illness: some case management suggestions

Gary W. LaVigna and Thomas J. Willis

Case management in support of people with intellectual disabilities is a challenge in and of itself. It can be more challenging, however, when those disabilities are associated with biopsychosocial issues (Sovner, Beasley and Hurley 1995), such as behavioural disorders and mental illness. Unfortunately, this scenario is not an uncommon one. The reality is that mental disorders and behavioural disorders (which may or may not be related to mental disorders) occur in the population of people with intellectual disabilities at least to the same extent, and if not more so, than they occur in the general population. Case managers today need to be able to identify the needs of these individuals as early as possible and to target the appropriate resources and services to meet those needs.

A case manager may first become aware that a person with an intellectual disability has a need as a result of a referral for (or concerns about) a 'problem' behaviour. These may include behavioural excesses (e.g. physical aggression, property destruction, self-injury and stereotypic responses) and/or behavioural deficits (e.g. lack of engagement in daily activities, refusal to respond to reasonable requests, loss of previously acquired skills and lack of self-initiated activities). When supporting a person whose behaviour is a challenge to the involved family, support staff or other informant, the initial inclination may be to seek services that focus only on contingency management to address the behaviour – that is, to take a linear approach that focuses on providing consequences and, at best, manipulates the environmental events (i.e. the antecedents) that affect the rate of occurrence of the behaviour. This may be a mistake. Such a narrow approach often misses more complex biopsychosocial dimensions of a problem requiring a non-linear approach (Goldiamond 1974, 1975). The term 'biopsychosocial' (Sovner *et al.* 1995) refers to a comprehensive picture of a person and includes information about physical, biological, psychological (mental and behavioural), social health and other factors that may contribute to the problem. There is a need, therefore, for some specific considerations in case management for people with intellectual disabilities who also manifest significant behaviour challenges.

Given the complexities of serving people with intellectual disabilities, especially those with challenging behaviours, case management needs to focus on several service-related issues. These include comprehensive functional assessment, outcome measurement, individualised multi-element support planning, monitoring and evaluation, and crisis management (when necessary) (LaVigna and Willis 2005a). As discussed later, given that the needed resources may not be available, case management may also need to address resource development. Accordingly, case management standards considered in each of these areas are described in the following sections of this chapter.

Assessment

When providing case management services to a person with an intellectual disability, there are three criteria, any one of which should prompt the need for a comprehensive functional assessment. These criteria are (i) the problem behaviours have persisted in spite of less formal and/or less time-consuming efforts; (ii) there is a risk of serious harm or injury, including risks to the person for further exclusion and devaluation; and (iii) a restrictive or intrusive (either punitive or otherwise aversive) approach is being considered. The failure to provide for a comprehensive functional assessment (CFA) where these conditions exist may result in more years of unsuccessful, one-shot behavioural treatments, continued escalation of the rate and episodic severity (LaVigna and Willis 2005b) of the person's challenges, and further erosion of the individual's quality of life. The CFA is the first step in the development of a multi-element support plan that may stop this downward spiral.

Comprehensive functional assessment aims to understand the meaning of the behaviour from the person's point of view. It looks at all possible relevant information gathered from sources such as:

- direct observations and interactions with the person

- interviews with family, support staff and others who may have relevant information, and a thorough review of available records.

The process of CFA then summarises, synthesises and analyses the gathered information into an integrated report that puts the behaviour within a coherent context from the person's perspective.

This biopsychosocial, person-centred approach to assessment addresses all of the areas shown in Box 12.1. Further, in addition to its primary purpose regarding the referral problem, a CFA may identify conflicts (mismatches) in the environment that may be contributing to the person's behaviour challenges. These mismatches may be in the form of:

- a conflict between the person's needs and characteristics and the services the person is or is not receiving

- conflicts between the person's needs and some aspect of the physical environment (e.g. crowding, noise)

- conflicts between the person's needs and the family and staff's skills, training, attitudes, expectations, styles of interaction and resources.

Box 12.1 Outline of a comprehensive functional assessment

1   Identifying information: person's name, date of birth, present address, referring agency.

2   Reason(s) for referral: source of referral, referral behaviours, key social agent's reasons for referral, possible discrepancies.

3   Data sources: methods used to collect assessment information (e.g. interviews, direct observation, records review, rating scales, inventories).

4   Background information:

- Client description: age, gender, diagnosis, appearance, ambulation, motor skills, physical disabilities, cognitive abilities, expressive and receptive language, social/emotional skills and characteristics, self-care skills, domestic skills, academic skills, leisure skills, community skills.

- Past and present living arrangements: location, relationships, type of residence, description of residence, family members.

- Past and present educational and day-service settings: location, type of service, description of service, relationships.
- Past and present health, medical and psychiatric status: general health, seizure activity, psychiatric evaluation and diagnosis, medication.
- Past and present treatment received for referral behaviour(s): description of any treatment received for currently referred (or related) behaviour problem now or in the past and the effects of those treatments.

5   Functional analysis/functional assessment:

- Operational definition of target behaviour: topography, cycle, episodic severity, course and current strength in terms of rate of occurrence and episodic severity.
- History of the problem: onset of target behaviour, duration, changes throughout history of problem and their possible relationship to life events.
- Antecedent analysis: settings, locations, people, times, activities, immediate events that make the target behaviour more or less likely.
- Consequence analysis: reactions of others to behaviour, methods used to manage the behaviour when it occurs, maintaining events, what resolves/escalates an episode.
- Ecological analysis: ecological factors impacting on behaviour (interpersonal, service, physical environment).
- Impressions and analysis of meaning: list of hypotheses regarding possible function(s) of the behaviour, i.e. its meaning from the client's perspective.

6   Motivational analysis: method of analysis, list of preferred events that could be used to improve the person's quality of life and/or used as potential incentives.

7   Mediator analysis: description of key social agents and an estimate of their abilities, expectations, styles and willingness to provide support.

For example, one common mismatch occurs when there is evidence of a mental disorder contributing to the person's behaviour and there is a need for services from a psychiatrist trained to work with and familiar with people who have a dual diagnosis, but no such psychiatrist is available. Unfortunately, the involvement, and even the availability, of professionals with these credentials is rare. This mismatch often leads to inappropriate medications being prescribed and an exacerbation of behaviour challenges. A good ecological analysis aimed at identifying such mismatches can almost serve as a case management audit.

Another mismatch might be based on the assumption that all people with mental illness require medication. Simply carrying a diagnosis within the spectrum of mental illness does not mean automatically that the person needs medication. Rather, the person's behavioural manifestation may reflect a need not for medication but for a different service altogether, such as counselling, psychotherapy or occupational therapy.

For example, in a case reported by Salt (2005), a CFA uncovered that a person's refusal to go anywhere in a car (including attempting to leave a vehicle when it was in motion) was, among other biopsychosocial factors, related functionally to the sexual abuse by her father that she experienced as a child. Neither the contribution to her 'fear of autos' of the resulting post-traumatic stress disorder nor the need for 'services of a psychologist experienced in working with victims of sexual abuse' had been recognised previously. The identification of, and arranging for the provision of, such identified services becomes an agenda item for the case manager.

Outcome measurement

The provision of such counselling and psychotherapy is only one element in an individualised plan of support. What should drive the development of the total plan, however, from a case management perspective are the desired outcomes – that is, what is to be achieved as a function of the plan. Box 12.2 shows the outcomes of a professionally driven, person-centred behavioural support plan, based on the principles of applied behaviour analysis. Case managers may want to consider incorporating these desired outcomes into their referral to the relevant specialists from whom they seek assessment and intervention services.

Multi-element support plans

With these outcomes in mind, and with the results of the CFA to inform the process, an individualised, multi-element support plan should be developed. The need for a multi-element plan of support (as opposed to tackling the problem with single behavioural techniques) should be apparent not only because of the

Box 12.2 Outcome measurement

The following represents the outcomes that are sought through a multi-element behavioural support plan based on the principles of applied behaviour analysis. For each outcome, depending on the specific circumstances surrounding the situation, an appropriate methodology for collecting data to measure success or failure in meeting these outcomes, and for assessing the reliability of the data so collected, would have to be specified.

1   *Quality of life*: The primary outcomes sought through a multi-element behavioural support plan are concerned with an improvement in the person's quality of life. Measures here might include the following:

   • amount and quality of the person's social and community integration

   • autonomy and control the person is able to exert in living his or her own life

   • extent to which the person continues to learn, grow and develop

   • relationships the person has with other people, including interdependent relationships

   • the person's productivity and ability to contribute.

2   *Behavioural improvement*: A focus of the plan is to reduce the barriers to a better quality of life caused by the referred problem behaviour. Consequently, the plan aims to reduce:

   • the occurrence of problem behaviour, as measured either by rate, percentage of opportunity or percentage of observation intervals

   • the episodic severity of the problem, such as the average duration of an outburst, or the average (and/or range of) degree of harm resulting from an episode of self-injury or aggression based on, for example, a five-point scale of outcome severity.

3   *Durability*: How long quality-of-life and behavioural improvements last, especially after treatment is terminated.

4   *Generalisation*: The extent to which improvement extends to non-treatment environments.

5   *Side effects:* The extent to which negative side effects have been avoided.

6   *Social validity:* The extent to which the person being supported, their family, support staff and the wider community agree with the goals, objectives and methods of the plan of support.

wide range of outcomes that are sought but also because of the complex biopsychosocial factors that are likely to have contributed to the problem and that need to be addressed. The multiple elements of a plan that a case manager should expect to see are shown in Box 12.3. As can be seen, this recommended support plan also represents an agenda for the case manager to pursue in finding and arranging for the provision of these services.

Box 12.3 Outline of a multi-element behavioural support plan

Support strategies

1   *Ecological strategies:* Specific recommendations regarding the person's physical, interpersonal or service environments, including recommendations for needed medical, psychiatric and psychotherapeutic services.

2   *Positive programming:* The following indicates the categories of skills that are likely to be needed to be taught. For each, a teaching strategy appropriate to the person's intellectual disability needs to be specified:

   • *General skills:* statement regarding systematic training in areas of self-care, vocational, domestic, leisure, recreational and community. Should be functional, chronologically age-appropriate and performed under natural conditions.

   • *Functionally equivalent skills:* description of specific behaviours to be taught that provide the person with a more appropriate and effective way of achieving the function served by the target behaviour.

- Functionally related skills: description of specific skills to be taught that are related to, but not functionally equivalent to, the target behaviour.
- Coping/tolerance skills: description of specific skills to be taught that help the person tolerate or cope with the natural environment. These and several of the skills referred to above might very well be taught within the context of counselling or cognitive behavioural therapy.

4. Focused support (preventive) strategies: description of strategies that are designed to produce rapid changes in the target behaviour, e.g. different schedules of reinforcement, instructional control, antecedent control and stimulus control.

5. Reactive strategies: description of specific strategies for managing the target behaviour when it occurs in order to maintain safe and rapid control of the situation, i.e. to reduce episodic severity.

6. Staff training and development: description of specific strategies used to teach key social agents how to carry out the recommended support plans and how to assure consistency.

Comments and recommendations

1. Anticipated difficulties: statement regarding level of anticipated cooperation and motivation of key social agents.

2. Additional resources and/or services requested: statement regarding any other services the client may require, e.g. medical examination, psychiatric evaluation.

3. Strategies for evaluating treatment outcomes: timeframe for evaluating treatment outcomes and the need for continuous monitoring and revision of the recommended support plans.

Monitoring and evaluation

With an individualised, multi-element behavioural support plan in place, case managers should then turn their attention to ongoing monitoring and evaluation of progress. We make the following recommendations.

- Formal monitoring by case managers should be done at least once a year on an unannounced basis, or more often depending on a variety of factors.

- Case managers should require standards for the provision of behavioural services for clients that require these in accordance with their service plans.

- Case managers should require measurable objectives addressing the person's quality of life and the other outcome areas and concrete plans for meeting those objectives as part of the person's service plan.

- Sanctions should include plans for improvement, plans for correction, follow-up surveys, provisional funding, etc., as provided for by the system.

- A quality management system based on the principles of organisational behaviour management (OBM) and total quality management (TQM), such as the periodic service review (PSR) (LaVigna *et al.* 1994), should be required by case management, as a self-monitoring system for service agencies (including the provision of regularly scheduled procedural reliability checks to assure the consistent implementation of all components of a plan), and it should be integrated to be part of the case management monitoring system. The lack of effective quality management systems is probably the single most prevalent reason why client services do not produce the desired outcomes.

- Web-based data-management systems for agency and case management monitoring should be employed to increase cost-effectiveness of the quality improvement and monitoring system, to maximise the early identification of problems, and to assure early and timely response times. (See www.epsr.com).

Crisis management

If case management practices assure the provision of behavioural services as described above, then behavioural crises that follow from limited behavioural services that do not take into account complex biopsychosocial factors may be largely avoided. The avoidance of crises is not likely in all such complex situations, however. For this reason, case management aimed at addressing crisis situations and arranging for the availability and provision of crisis management services is necessary. Further, where possible, crisis management services should be available and provided in the community in an effort to avoid inpatient placement.

Community-based crisis management

Community-based crisis management service should incorporate three different elements:

- *Training and consultation to prevent crises from occurring:* The best crisis management strategies are those that are effective in preventing the crisis in the first place. A number of training and consultation resources should be identified that are intended to enhance the service agencies' abilities to prevent crises from occurring. For each of these areas, training and consultation could include centralised sessions for multiple agencies and then further on-site training and consultation in order to maximise generalisation and follow-through. Crisis management staff could provide these training and consultation services to the extent that they are not needed to deal with a crisis in progress.

- *Crisis management:* In those situations in which it is needed, on a case-by-case basis, on-site crisis management services should be provided, with the goal of avoiding hospitalisation and institutionalisation (LaVigna and Willis 2002). These should be standardised services that include intake, rapid crisis team deployment and implementation of a standardised crisis management plan (in order to control the occurrence and severity of the crisis-generating behaviours), informed by intake information.

- *Intensive support:* In some instances, parents and care-providers may not be able to carry out an effective plan themselves. Services may need to be provided temporarily by a trained team of individuals who have the resources and training to do so. The effectiveness of this intensive support service has been reported formally in the professional literature (Donnellan *et al.* 1985). It includes the comprehensive approach described above plus the systematic transfer of responsibilities from the crisis/intensive team to the family or regularly assigned staff.

Inpatient crisis management

Not all crises can be managed in the community, but inpatient placements can be lengthy and expensive. We think case managers would find it useful to be aware of Sovner *et al.*'s (1995) thoughtful delineation of different categories and reasons for placement and listing quality-of-care functions for inpatient psychiatric units as they plan for their clients (see Box 12.4). Case managers may be better prepared in seeking appropriate placement if they have identified which facilities available to them are best able to meet the six quality-of-care functions and what category of hospitalisation they are seeking at the time.

Case management standards

Providing case management services for people with intellectual disabilities associated with complex biopsychosocial issues can be challenging. The case manager must understand the person's needs and then identify, arrange for, monitor and evaluate the services to meet those needs. Standards for the provision of such case management services have not been developed by the field, but they should be, as they have for other specialised case management services. For example, the US state of Kansas (2002) has identified 35 measurable standards for the provision of human immunodeficiency virus (HIV)/acquired immune deficiency syndrome (AIDS) case management services in its rural state. These include general agency requirements, intake, general file requirements, assessment, personal case plan development, personal case plan monitoring and evaluation, and discharge.

The need for services as described above brings a number of specific responsibilities to the case manager, especially since best practices as described in the sections above may not be available.

Resource identification

The case manager needs to have identified the resources that are available in his or her catchment area for the provision of the various services described above. Ideally, these resources should be identified before their need, in order that they can be provided in a timely manner under circumstances that are often quite serious in nature.

Resource development

The most likely reason for the above services not to be provided is that professionals trained to provide these services at the level of best practices are simply not available. Where the above resources do not exist, the case manager has the responsibility to notify the system as to their absence and to advocate for their development through training and consultation initiatives (e.g. LaVigna, Christian and Willis 2005). Failure to develop the appropriate resources may mean that the person has no choice but to live in the most restrictive settings and

Box 12.4 Reasons for placement and quality of care functions for inpatient psychiatric units

1 Proposed categories of hospitalization

- *Type I hospitalization*: the psychiatric diagnosis has been established and hospitalization is for rapidly implementing a specific treatment or the management of acute side effects. (3–5 days to 14 days)

- *Type II hospitalization*: patient is out of control. Admission is for emergency containment and a review of current psychiatric diagnosis and outpatient drug therapy is indicated. (1–3 weeks)

- *Type III hospitalization*: psychiatric diagnosis has not been established and hospitalization is for determining whether patient has a drug-responsive psychiatric disorder. (4–6 weeks)

- *Type IV hospitalization*: psychiatric diagnosis has not been established. Patient is on a complicated and ineffective drug regimen. Hospitalization is for discontinuing drug therapy, determining whether the patient has a drug-responsive disorder and implementing treatment. (4–12 weeks)

2 Six quality of care functions for inpatient psychiatric units

- *Monitoring*: the unit is able to monitor clinical course and treatment efficacy using objective measure of change 24 hours per day.

- *Crisis management*: the unit is able to use non-pharmacological interventions to manage out-of-control behaviour.

- *Formulations*: the unit creates psychiatric formulations that take into account developmental and social factors.

- *Prescribed medication*: unit psychiatrists prescribe psychotropic medication only when there is a clear formulation based upon a syndrome or symptom cluster model.

- *Activities*: the unit provides meaningful activities.

- *Circle of support*: family members, community care providers, and patient advocates are included in clinical decision-making.

Sovner et al. (1995). Reprinted by permission of Psych-Media of North Carolina, Inc., www.mhaspectsofdd.com

suffer the indignity of experiencing the most restrictive strategies, such as restraint. Albert's story in Case study 12.1 shows an alternative approach (Willis and LaVigna 2003).

Case study 12.1 Albert's story

Albert, a 20-year-old man with severe intellectual disabilities, was referred by his case manager. Albert lived at home with his mother, but because of the severity of his physical aggression and the danger he represented to his mother and the community, his mother was considering out-of-home placement in a restrictive residential setting located in an isolated part of the California desert, at a cost of more than $200,000 per year. The case manager recognised that Albert and his mother wanted to live together, but his behaviour was jeopardising this arrangement. The case manager, knowing the services provided by the Institute for Applied Behavior Analysis (IABA), requested that a comprehensive functional assessment (CFA) be conducted and asked that a plan be developed to help him remain at home. The CFA identified that Albert's brain injury was of a severity that he was unlikely to learn through the use of consequences; in fact, Albert was unlikely to learn anything new. Consequently, the plan involved eco- logical strategies designed to encourage appropriate behaviours already existent in his (long-term memory) repertoire, and antecedent control and reactive strategies designed to prevent the occurrence and minimise the episodic severity of his challenging behaviours. In his home, Albert received one-to-one services 12 hours a day by trained and supervised 'mentors'. As a result, he has been able to continue living with his mother for the past 11 years.

Records maintenance

Case managers should also maintain a central file for all clients so that the records review carried out as part of the CFA can be undertaken efficiently. Further, the case manager should make sure that certain evaluations are kept current and that they are carried out on a regular basis. These should include regular medical evaluations and, where relevant, regular psychological, psychiatric and neurological evaluations. A complete social history, with annual updates, should also be in the files, perhaps with the case manager taking this responsibility. Other historical records should also be gathered and maintained by the case manager, including, for example, school records and previous treatment records. The importance of a good records database cannot be overstated. Changes in behaviour can be a direct result of changes in psychiatric, medical, neurological and ecological events. As clients move from one service to another, and as so often happens, records are misplaced, data are lost and important details are forgotten. The records and knowledge base maintained by the case manager may be the only source of this information and may be critical to the person's wellbeing.

To help convey some of the complexities a case manager may face, we present Jayne's story in Case study 12.2.

Case study 12.2 Jayne's story

Jayne is a 45-year-old, very friendly woman with short, curly brown hair and beautiful blue eyes. Generally, she is very loving and affectionate to those around her – even people she has just met. She faces life with the dual challenges of a moderate level of learning difficulty combined with paranoid schizophrenia with command hallucinations. Her primary referral problem was physical aggression towards others, which took the form of punching, either from the shoulder or in a backhanded fashion, as well as biting, kicking, scratching, pinching and pulling the hair of another person.

Jayne was separated from her family on their initiative at age four years due to the difficulties they were having in dealing with her behaviour at home. Accordingly, she was placed in a state hospital in 1965, where, with subsequent placements in various other state hospitals, she resided until 1988. In 1988, due to the progress she had shown, she was placed in a group home in the community, with additional behavioural support being provided by the Institute for Applied Behavior Analysis (IABA). In 1990, Jayne moved into her own apartment, receiving supported living services from IABA. By all accounts, Jayne was traumatised by her early separation from her family, who by choice and circumstances discontinued any contact with her. To this day, she will say 'I wish I had my mommy' and 'I miss my mommy', often projecting her mother's identity on to the people she meets.

In its supported living service, IABA organised its support around Jayne's positive futures plan. According to this plan, her vision for her future included continuing to live in her apartment with her housemate, learning how to cross the street independently, purchasing items in the neighbourhood shop independently, taking a beauty class, taking a cooking class, taking more walks around her neighbourhood and around the park, enrolling in an exercise class, and working full-time in a hospital setting. It is also fair to say that many of her IABA staff have now worked with her for many years and have become in many ways her surrogate family, with staff members having reciprocal feelings of affection for her even as she does for them, although appropriate staff–client boundaries are maintained. This formed the basis for her positive, multi-element plan of support (LaVigna et al. 2005), which also included other ecological strategies, positive programming (instructional) strategies, preventive strategies and, when necessary, (non-restrictive) reactive strategies aimed at rapid, safe situational management (LaVigna and Willis 2002). Because of her paranoid schizophrenia, psychiatric care was provided by a university-based psychiatrist knowledgeable and experienced in treating people with dual diagnosis.

In spite of having an increasingly good quality of life, a consistently implemented multi-element positive behavioural support plan and competent psychiatric care (see Box 12.5), every five or so years Jayne experiences extreme 'decompensation of her psychotic illness and a marked increase in her psychotic symptoms…including her command hallucinations and associated physical aggression.' Although it was advised that Jayne be hospitalised while her psychiatrist attempted to stabilise her, the last time this was necessary, in 2000, IABA direct service staff resisted this option because they were not comfortable with the psychiatric care she would get in the public hospital that was available to her and the resistance from the professional staff there to any input from IABA and her university-based psychiatrist. Accordingly, with the concurrence of her case manager, a very tight approach to antecedent control and reactive strategies was necessary in order to keep staff safe, giving her psychiatrist the time he needed to once again establish psychiatric stability, while she remained in the familiar surroundings of her own apartment.

Jayne has now been stable for the past five years. She is surrounded by staff who consider her, and whom she considers, to be family. Lately, she has joined a social group that, among other things, has travelled to the Grand Canyon and Las Vegas and taken a cruise to the Mexican Riviera. Jayne lives in her own home in the community, has a life and is happy.

Box 12.5 Jayne's recommended positive multi-element behavioural support plan based on comprehensive functional assessment

Ecological strategies

- Attempted reconnection with family
- Sponsorship of a child from the developing world
- Continued supported living and supported employment services
- Daily affirmation from people in her 'circle of support' in the form of personal letters, greeting cards, flowers and gifts

Positive programming

- Learning how to independently make a purchase at a neighbourhood store
- Psychotherapy to address unresolved and underlying emotional issues concerned with rejection and abandonment
- Learning to cope with being told 'no'

Focused (preventive) support

- Continued psychiatric care by her university-based psychiatrist
- Hourly, time-based treats to 'celebrate life'
- Differential reinforcement of other behaviour with progressively increased reinforcement (DROP), which involved her earning a 'fantasy night out' (getting her hair done, fancy restaurant, movie of choice, etc.) for going specified periods of time without any aggressive behaviour
- Antecedent control, which involved giving staff training on how to respond specifically to precursor behaviour

Reactive strategies

- Stimulus change – sending an electronic signal to the office to trigger a phone call to Jayne, which is known to interrupt physical aggression, even when related to command hallucinations
- Capitulation, under specified guidelines to protect against counter-therapeutic effects, such as the unwanted reinforcement of the problem behaviour

Conclusion

To summarise, as in the general population, a proportion of people with intellectual disabilities have serious biopsychosocial problems. Case management needs to be informed by the complex biopsychosocial factors that can contribute to these problems. Accordingly, case management may need to provide for comprehensive functional assessment, outcome evaluation, multi-element support planning, crisis management, monitoring and evaluation, and the development of objective standards that define the quality provision of case management services.

References

Donnellan, A.M., LaVigna, G.W., Zambito, J. and Thvedt, J. (1985) 'A time limited intensive intervention program model to support community placement for persons with severe behavior problems.' *Journal of the Association for Persons with Severe Handicaps 10*, 123–31.

Goldiamond, I. (1974) 'Toward a constructional approach to social problems: ethical and constitutional issues raised by applied behavior analysis.' *Behaviorism 2*, 1–85.

Goldiamond, I. (1975) 'Alternative sets as a framework for behavioral formulations and research.' *Behaviorism 3*, 49–86.

LaVigna, G.W. and Willis, T.J. (2002) 'Counter-Intuitive Strategies for Crisis Management within a Non-aversive Framework.' In D. Allen (ed.) *Behaviour Management in Intellectual Disabilities: Ethical Responses to Challenging Behavior.* Kidderminster: British Institute of Learning Disabilities.

LaVigna, G.W. and Willis, T.J. (2005a) 'A positive behavioural support model for breaking the barriers to social and community inclusion.' *Learning Disability Review Positive Behaviour Support 10*, 16–23.

LaVigna, G.W. and Willis, T.J. (2005b) 'Episodic severity: an overlooked dependent variable in the application of behavior analysis to challenging behavior.' *Journal of Positive Behavior Intervention 7*, 47–54.

LaVigna, G.W., Willis, T.J., Shaull, J.F., Abedi, M. and Sweitzer, M. (1994) *The Periodic Service Review: A Total Quality Assurance System for Human Services and Education.* Baltimore, MD: Paul H. Brookes.

LaVigna, G.W., Christian, L. and Willis, T.J. (2005) 'Developing behavioural services to meet defined standards within a national system of specialist education services.' *Pediatric Rehabilitation 8*, 144–55.

Salt, A. (2005) 'Learning to fly.' Presented at the third International Conference of the Institute for Applied Behavior Analysis, Mont Clare Hotel, Dublin, Ireland, 11 April 2005.

Sovner, R., Beasley, J. and Hurley, A.D. (1995) 'How long should a psychiatric inpatient stay be for a person with developmental disabilities?' *Habilitative Mental Healthcare Newsletter 14*, 1–8.

State of Kansas (2002) *Case Management Standards of Care.* State of Kansas.

Willis, T.J. and LaVigna, G.W. (2003) 'The safe management of physical aggression using multi-element positive practices in community settings.' *Journal of Head Trauma Rehabilitation 18*, 75–87.

13

The importance of friendships for young people with intellectual disabilities

Brenda Burgen and Christine Bigby

People with intellectual disabilities have similar social and emotional needs to people in the general population, but these needs develop at a slower rate, as do the skills required to negotiate and meet them. The transition from adolescence to adulthood is a time when parents, adolescents and case managers focus on practical issues such as leaving school, employment, further education and acquiring independent living skills. Friendships and social acceptance from a wider peer group are particularly important at this time as sources of emotional support, self-worth and growth (Bukowski 2001). Such relationships provide the foundation for autonomy, self-confidence and independence from parents. Despite awareness of the importance of friendships for young people with intellectual disabilities and the emotional impact of isolation, transition plans to adulthood often neglect these social and emotional needs (Priestley 2003). Care is required with the trend to individualised planning that opportunities for friendships and social relationships are not excluded.

Young people with intellectual disabilities face significant barriers to more informal and independent socialisation, including difficulties in knowing how to initiate contact, organising where to meet and understanding how to get there. The problems are exacerbated by the often limited ability of young people with intellectual disabilities to travel independently.

The aim of this chapter is to highlight the central importance of friendships to the social and emotional development of young people with intellectual disabilities and to discuss ways to ensure that the social environment is supportive of their needs. The chapter draws primarily on the doctoral research of the first author, which explored, using a qualitative approach, the social and emotional development and relationships important to a small group of young people, aged 18–29 years, with mild to moderate intellectual disabilities (Burgen 2006).

The importance of friendships and social development

Periods of transition are marked by change both within the individual and in their social context. As young people move from adolescence to adulthood, their emotional and relational investments shift from parents to friends, and then to significant others. Young people with intellectual disabilities often have a strong desire for friendships, but they may not have adequate social skills or the experiences required to negotiate such relationships. They may regard previous friendships as though they were current and describe acquaintances, family members, paid staff and characters from television programmes as 'friends' (Jobling, Moni and Nolan 2000). These ascriptions are indicative of the desire for friendships but the absence of opportunities, skills and support for their maintenance and development. As a result, young people with intellectual disabilities are often frustrated, lonely and unhappy and may became involved in exploitative, and sometimes abusive and violent, relationships as a preferable option to remaining alone. Loneliness, experienced as emotional and social isolation, is identified as one of the major problems faced by people with intellectual disabilities (Jobling *et al.* 2000; Rickwood and d'Espaignet 1996).

Wellbeing and mental health may be seriously compromised by a lack of close friendships and positive peer relationships. Research has found that students with disabilities have significantly lower scores for satisfaction, wellbeing and social belonging than their peers without disabilities (Watson and Keith 2002). Lowered feelings of wellbeing affect the ability to make friends, which in turn reinforces poor self-image and feelings of depression. Although depression has multiple causes, such as repeated experience of failure and biological predisposition, the experiences of living with an intellectual disability, such as negative social attitudes, poor social supports and absence of close friends and partners, are all associated with poorer mental health (Reiss and Benson 1985).

Developing and supporting friendships

Social development is a complex process derived from personal attributes, close relationships, and the broader social context (Bukowski *et al.* 1996). Experience of friendships is crucial to this process and the acquisition of social skills. The young people in Burgen's (2006) study with a history of close friends during their school years had much better social skills, understanding of reciprocity and sensitivity towards others than those who had not had such friendships. Those without the experience of friendships did not lack interest in or the potential to form relationships, but they did lack the skills and experiences necessary to build them. This was illustrated when, during the study, one of the young men formed his first close friendship with another participant. After only several months, the experience of this relationship had clearly increased the young man's skills, deepened his understanding of friendships and opened up his social world. Previously, the mother of this young man had identified him as never having been sociable or interested in having friends. This suggests that a young person's social skills are more likely to reflect their experiences rather than their personality or stage of social and emotional development.

Regular, close contact with others is one of the most important factors that facilitates development and maintenance of friendships (Heslop *et al.* 2002). Key for participants in Burgen's study were the close relationships developed with others they had met in disability-specific environments, such as special school and further education courses. Although all participants strongly preferred their long-standing friends, few had the skills necessary to maintain them without the previous regular structured opportunities for contact that school had provided. One young woman, for example, was excited by a chance encounter with an old school friend while out shopping but dismayed to find she had no means of further contact as they had not exchanged telephone numbers. In another study, one young person said in relation to staying in touch by keeping telephone numbers and addresses that 'it never occurred to him that this is what friends do' (Nunkoosing and John 1997). There is a clear role here for case managers to draw attention to the importance of continued development of social skills in the post-school period. They can facilitate attendance by young people with intellectual disabilities at educational and support groups where social skills are practised and made explicit so that young people can learn the steps needed to maintain their relationships beyond day programmes if they choose.

Burgen's study identified that, regardless of their social skills, young people at different developmental stages had marked differences in their emotional investment. For those in their early to mid-twenties, the bulk of their emotional investment remained with their parents or siblings. They found discussion of intimate relationships embarrassing or viewed this type of relationship as peripheral to those with family and friends. In contrast, adults in their late twenties had a much greater investment in friends, expressed greater interest in intimate relationships and failed to mention their parents. Thus, it is in their mid- to late twenties rather than early twenties, that adults with intellectual disabilities are likely to be most concerned with intimate relationships and other independence issues.

Limits imposed on young people's life experiences, and ultimately their social development and potential to become adults, perpetuate the misperceptions that adults with intellectual disabilities remain childlike. The gradual nature of developmental shifts means that parents may fail to recognise their adult child's changing friendship needs or the importance of opportunities to see friends informally.

Friendships don't just happen

These findings mean that opportunities or facilitation may be needed for young adults with intellectual disabilities to develop friendships or to socialise. For example, encouragement and support to meet informally for a coffee or a meal, to see a movie or play sport would all assist in building independent relationships. Much can be done by formal day, employment and educational settings to support friendships, from simply encouraging after-hours interactions between people who appear to enjoy each other's company, through familiarising young people with potential venues for informal meetings, to providing assistance with the steps necessary to plan an outing.

Studies have shown, however, that the high importance placed on friendships by service providers is not translated into support. There is a pervasive belief among staff that friendships somehow just happen or are serendipitous. Although this is true for most people in the general population, who learn social skills unconsciously or by modelling others, young people with intellectual disabilities may require more planned assistance. For example, an Australian study showed that 30 per cent of day-programme staff did not see support for the development of friendships as central to their role, and less than 5 per cent of individual programme plans included attention to this issue (McLeod, Nelson, & Associates 2001). Case managers can address this by advocating that goals around friendships (as part of considering all areas of development) are included in individual plans, with clear strategies for staff and informal support. Individual planning that occurs based around young people's friendship groups is one way in which this could occur. Case managers can also act as a source of knowledge about the resources designed specifically to assist young people and adults with intellectual disabilities to be more likely to develop friendships and social skills.

Shearn and Todd (1996) suggest that supporting their young adults to find and attend activities represents a significant aspect of parental work. This was the case for some of the parents in Burgen's study, who had to prompt, organise and then drive their son or daughter to their activities. One parent said she felt like a taxi driver, driving her son several times a week to activities and then often having to wait for a couple of hours to take him home again. He could not use public transport and she felt that if she did not drive him, he would never go anywhere. She was frustrated, and felt it should not be left to parents to support the social activities of young people. Not all parents are able to assist, however, and so do not, or do not want to, see the importance of friendships. In Burgen's study, social isolation of young people was associated with the absence of practical family and other support to participate in activities. A role for case managers is to find alternatives, such as advocating for the young person's participation in travel-training programmes to develop their confidence and skills in using public transport, to advocate for formal activities to provide transport, to encourage use of community transport such as late-night courtesy buses from sports events, and to facilitate carpooling among families.

Maintaining friendships in transition

The period during the transition of young people from secondary school to further education or employment is when friendship networks are particularly likely to be disrupted (Blacher 2001). This is common with the general population, but for young people with intellectual disabilities, it is more difficult to redevelop or maintain friendships. For example, a UK study found only a few of 272 young people remained in contact with school friends after they moved to a different setting (Heslop et al. 2002). In Burgen's study, young people who sustained previous friendships did so through attendance at disability-specific activities, such as discos and clubs. They relied on parental assistance to attend, however, and some social clubs and activities were specific to local councils, so not all friends are able to attend the same activities. In Burgen's study, some young people said they did not feel safe or comfortable mixing in mainstream groups. Only one participant regularly attended a mainstream social activity, a church-run friendship group. His mother was keen for him to attend but saw that her son was isolated within the group:

...it is segregated – nobody realises this except me – I keep complaining about it. We have a cup of coffee after church. People from the friendship group hand out biscuits, say hello. They ask other people but never [her son] or others with a disability back to their place for dinner...the young people ask each other out to the pictures but never include [her son] or other disabled people...no one [from the friendship group] asks them to sit with them, no one will get up and dance with them...

Simply because they are present at a mainstream group does not mean that young people with intellectual disabilities feel comfortable or included or will build new friendships. Case managers should advocate for young people to have a range of options from which to choose, including disability-specific activities.

Conclusion

For young people with intellectual disabilities, experiences of friendship, opportunities and support for social interaction, personal attributes and the broader social context are important factors in their social emotional development. Case managers, together with the young people, have a vital role to play in raising the awareness of parents, formal programmes and other service providers about a young person's social and emotional development. Case managers can advocate for more flexible services that cater for the different timing of social developmental stages for young people and adults. Linking young people with intellectual disabilities to services and supports generally is also important. Facilitating adequate opportunities for young people to meet outside day programmes, education settings and workplaces in structured activities is important; so too is equipping them with the ongoing skills to initiate and organise meeting with friends informally so that friendships can be maintained regardless of transitions. Advocating that services implement practical responses and recognising that friendships do not 'just happen' and opportunities to interact need to be created is required. Parents' support can be vital to young people developing social and friendship skills and independent friendships. Recognition of the workload on parents and support for them and facilitation is also important. Case managers can provide invaluable support to young people and their families by giving attention to this critical importance of friendship.

References

Blacher, J. (2001) 'Transition to adulthood: mental retardation, families, and culture.' *American Journal on Mental Retardation 106*, 173–88.

Bukowski, W.M. (2001) 'Friendships and the Worlds of Childhood.' In D. Nangle and C. Erdley (eds) *The Role of Friendship in Psychological Adjustment*. San Francisco, CA: Jossey-Bass.

Bukowski, W.M., Newcomb, A.F. and Hartup, W.W. (1996) 'Friendship and its Significance in Childhood and Adolescence.' In W.M. Bukowski, A.F. Newcomb and W.W. Hartup (eds) *The Company They Keep: Friendship in Childhood and Adolescence*. Cambridge: Cambridge University Press.

Burgen, B. (2006). 'Shifting emotional investments: young adults' friendship and social emotional development.' *Journal of Applied Research in Intellectual Disabilities 19*, 240.

Heslop, P., Mallett, R., Simons, K. and Ward, L. (2002) *Bridging the Divide at Transition: What Happens for Young People with Learning Difficulties and their Families*. Kidderminster: British Institute of Learning Disabilities.

Jobling, A., Moni, K. and Nolan, A. (2000) 'Understanding friendship: young adults with Down syndrome exploring relationships.' *Journal of Intellectual and Developmental Disability 25*, 235–6.

McLeod, Nelson, & Associates (2001) *Community Inclusion: Enhancing Friendship Networks Among People with a Cognitive Impairment*. Melbourne: Department of Human Services Victoria.

Nunkoosing, K. and John, M. (1997) 'Friendships, relationships and the management of rejection and loneliness by people with learning difficulty.' *Journal of Learning Disabilities for Nursing, Health and Social Care 1*, 10–18.

Priestley, M. (2003) *Disability: A Life Course Approach*. Cambridge: Polity Press.

Reiss, S. and Benson, B.A. (1985). 'Psychosocial correlates of depression in mentally retarded adults: I. Minimal social support and stigmatization.' *American Journal on Mental Retardation 89*, 331–7.

Rickwood, D. and d'Espaignet, E.T. (1996) 'Psychological distress among older adolescents and young adults in Australia.' *Australian and New Zealand Journal of Public Health 20*, 83–6.

Shearn, J. and Todd, S. (1996) 'Identities at risk: the relationships parents and their coresident adult offspring with learning disabilities have with each other and their social world.' *European Journal on Mental Disability 3*, 47–60.

Watson, S.M. and Keith, K.D. (2002) 'Quality of life of school-age children.' *Mental Retardation 40*, 304–12.

14

Issues of middle age and beyond for people with intellectual disabilities and their families

Christine Bigby

The life expectancy of people with intellectual disability has increased significantly in the past three decades and now approximates more closely that of the general population. For example, between 1930 and 1955, less than 10 per cent of residents with intellectual disabilities in UK institutions survived to age 50 years compared with just over 50 per cent between 1955 and 1980 (Carter and Jancar 1983). The average life expectancy of people with Down syndrome was 25 years in 1983 compared with 49 years in 1997, demonstrating almost a doubling of life expectancy during this period (Yang, Rasmussen and Friedman 2002). People with intellectual disabilities now have a much increased likelihood of living with elderly parents, outliving their parents and surviving to later life. The absolute numbers of older people with intellectual disabilities are still small but increasing. For example, UK estimates suggest that 12 per cent of the population with severe intellectual disabilities are 60 years or older (Department of Health 2001); in Australia, the proportion is generally smaller, at around 6 per cent (Bigby 2004). These demographic changes are undoubtedly positive and potentially add broader and richer experiences to people's lives. Survival to an older age brings, however, some particular challenges to individuals, service systems and case managers. It demands, for example, a more finely grained understanding of adulthood than has occurred previously for people with intellectual disabilities – an understanding that includes middle age and differentiates, for example, younger fitter older people from frail aged people.

The aim of this chapter is to alert case managers to some of the issues associated with increasing life expectancy, considering in particular the transition from living with parents for adults who have remained in the family home and ways of ensuring people with intellectual disabilities can continue to experience a sense of belonging and purpose as they age. These issues in particular require an anticipatory rather than a passive stance from the service system via case managers.

Planning for the future with older families

One of the most specific and predictable contexts within which case managers are required to respond is the transition for the person with intellectual disabilities from living in the parental home. For many of the current generation of middle-aged people with intellectual disabilities who remained living at home with parents, care and support have been largely private family responsibilities. As many as half of older families are found to be out of touch with formal services (Janicki *et al.* 1998). Reasons for their limited contact with services other than day centres include a lack of perceived need by parents who have not seen caring or continued living together as a problem, a lack of trust or confidence in the service sector, previous unsatisfactory experiences with services, limited knowledge of services and fear of intrusion into their lives (Bigby 2004; Grant 2001; Llewellyn *et al.* 2004).

As it has become more likely that adults with intellectual disabilities will outlive their parents, concerns about future care, exacerbated by the shortage of accommodation support in disability services, have gained increased policy attention This has coincided with the more explicit recognition of the importance of formal support for informal carers of older and disabled people to enable continuation of caring. The particular issues faced by older carers – the inevitability of the cessation of their caring role and the impact of their own ageing on caring capacity – have been clearly recognised. Various policy and service initiatives have occurred in the UK and Australia (Foundation for People with Learning Disabilities 2002), many of which revolve around outreach to carers and encouragement of a proactive approach to planning and preparation for the future. Underpinning assumptions are that planning will avoid individual crises of care by locating other informal carers in the family system and facilitate system-level planning. It may also reduce the future need for care by fostering greater skill and independence levels among middle-aged adults. In Australia, older carers have been a priority group in federally funded carer respite initiatives. Case management roles with older carers vary from provision of community education, outreach, information provision, facilitating mutual support groups and low-intensity monitoring and support, to intensive, longer-term support that includes linkage to community care services, detailed planning and assistance with transition for the individual from the parental household.

A family-focused approach

Case management initiatives with older carers have generally focused quite narrowly on caring dyads – an elderly parent and a middle-aged person with intellectual disability. It is important to recognise, however, that older carers remain part of a broader family system, although they are more likely to be single and live in smaller households than younger parents (Hayden and Heller 1997; Janicki 1996). For example, Krauss *et al.* (1996) found that the majority of adults with intellectual disabilities living at home with older parents had siblings with whom they continued to have meaningful relationships. Adult siblings provided emotional support and companionship rather than personal care, which was sustained over many years, and had considerable knowledge about their brothers and sisters with intellectual disabilities.

Working with middle-aged adults and their families is complex and poses difficult issues of negotiation and balancing rights, needs, wishes and resources. The work of case managers must take into account the roles and the places in the family constellation of other family members and the person with intellectual disabilities. A qualitative study highlighted the way in which families regard support for the member with intellectual disabilities not as care but simply as an aspect of ordinary family life: 'Mum doesn't see it like she is caring for Claudia…it's more like they're getting on with their lives together' (Knox and Bigby 2007). This study illustrated too the importance of the interdependence of family members:

> Michael's mother Barbara McCarty commented 'Michael does his own room – everything – makes his bed, dusts etc. He also gets the evening coffee. I vacuum, wash and cook. And we both do the dishes together'. Raymond from the Bennett family spoke of the social routines that characterised their 'family business'. He said 'Everyone in the family drops in and keeps in regular contact with Mum and Claudia… I drop in when I can and the others do too. The family get together fairly regularly as well for social occasions'. Denise from the Carr family spoke of the need to ensure their

mother Margaret's well-being as a key aspect of their 'family business'. Thus she rings her mother 'everyday to see she's ok…my other sister manages the financial affairs and pays the bills because Mum sometimes forgets to pay them'. (Knox and Bigby 2007, in press)

A family-focused approach derives from practice with younger families based on recognition of the interdependence of child and family needs (Allen and Petr 1998). It suggests that decisions about needs and formal support to an individual must also take account of the needs of the family system, other family members, lifestyle and values. Work with older families, however, differs from that of family-focused practice with children, particularly with regard to decision-making and outcomes sought. For children, the active promotion of fully informed decision-making by parents is appropriate. In older families, the adult with disabilities should be supported to make his or her own choices and decisions as much as possible, and care must be taken to distinguish the person's needs from those of the wider family.

Conflicting needs and views are more likely in older families than in younger families and may stem from parental failure to recognise the right of the adult to make his or her own choices or the need to maintain a relationship of interdependence in a shared household, rather than one more characterised by independence. For example, the reduced mobility of parents or their need for the physical presence and support of their adult child can restrict the lifestyle of the adult, who may have been reliant on their parents for social outings. The inability of parents to meet inflexible pick-up times or full-time attendance requirements of day programmes may lead to some adults dropping out, thus further restricting their lifestyle. This is exemplified by comments such as 'I couldn't get out then [when I was living at home] like I do now' (Bigby 2000). Adults living with elderly parents may have had few opportunities to develop a separate life, and in some cases they may never have spent a night away from home (Bigby, Ozanne and Gordon 2002). Parents may continue to exert considerable control over key aspects of the person's life, such as finances and personal relationships (Walmsley 1996; Willams and Robinson 2001).

Conflicting needs are more likely to be perceived by outsiders such as professionals or siblings than identified by parents or adults (Bigby 2000; Williams and Robinson 2001). A central task of work with older families is negotiation and reconciliation of differing priorities, needs and perhaps aspirations. This requires an emphasis on complementarity of individual rather than whole-family outcomes. Strategies for doing this are strengthening the family's capacity to provide support, guidance and/or advocacy for the adult to make choices and express their views. Consequently, much work with older parents revolves around gaining trust, achieving change and building a greater acceptance of support services either for themselves or their adult son or daughter. Similar to earlier parts of the life course, however, tradeoffs are inevitable for adults living with older parents and gains will be balanced by losses; failure by workers to acknowledge this may lead to alienation from the parents, which is unlikely to be helpful for anyone.

Middle-aged adults anticipating ageing issues

People with intellectual disabilities have little understanding of social expectations that surround ageing or individual ageing processes (Erickson *et al.* 1989; Urlings 1992). They therefore have little forewarning or knowledge about the changes that may occur or the types of decision to be confronted. Some research also suggests they may not be consulted about parental plans for their future and that decisions embedded in plans are reached by working around rather than with the person with intellectual disabilities (Heller and Factor 1991; Knox and Bigby 2007). All of these factors militate against the person's meaningful involvement in decisions about aspects of his or her life. Mutual support and education groups can be used to enable people with intellectual disabilities to explore aspects of ageing and associated social expectations so that they are better prepared to be involved in decisions about their lives. Examples are found of specialist curricula designed to educate adults with intellectual disabilities about future planning and lifestyle options (Heller *et al.* 2000; O'Malley 1996). One unexpected outcome of such programmes, however, has been a drop in expressed satisfaction as adults became more aware of broader opportunities and the limited nature of their lives. Other examples of this kind of work are found in the development of pre-retirement and seniors' group programmes run by day centres (Laughlin and Cotton 1994).

Making plans with middle-aged adults

Planning for the future has two major functions – facilitating the transition from living with parents and disruption of an often interdependent household, and ensuring, in the longer term, an optimum quality of life and security for an ageing adult with intellectual disability (Bigby 2000). A third function may be dealing with an emergency situation, such as a fall or sudden death of an elderly parent.

Construction of a plan that involves an identified residential situation for the rest of a middle-aged person's life may not be a desirable or realistic task. Put simply, private or public resources may not be available until an urgent need arises, but the timing of transition from parental care is unpredictable, as many parents want to continue living with their son or daughter for as long as possible, or vice versa. For example, in the UK, 29 per cent of older parents were found to welcome the opportunity to relinquish their caring role, but over half assigned considerable meaning to their caring role and did not want to relinquish it (Todd and Shearn 1996). More importantly, residential plans cannot take into account later life development that is yet to be experienced by the adult with intellectual disabilities. Unless plans are flexible, they risk locking a person into an environment that he or she may not like or that may, over time, become inappropriate or more restrictive than warranted (Bigby 2000).

Most families do not make formal written plans, although many discuss the broad issues and make more informal plans, whereby a key person is identified to oversee the adult's wellbeing and negotiate access to support rather than provide hands-on care. For example:

> They asked me [a church minister] to be the executor of the will and they charged me as it were to keep a roof over Rod's head. (Bigby 2000, p.72)

> Dad certainly talked to me about that [future plans for Nora]. We [brother and sister-in-law] would be responsible for her. He never expected us to take her into our own home… It was written in the will 'your love and attention will be given to Nora during her lifetime'. (Bigby 2000, p.73)

This type of 'key person succession plan' is more likely to provide a good foundation for the future than plans of a more definite or proscriptive nature (Bigby 2000). Critical features of plans are flexibility and responsiveness, ensured by the existence of a key person or people to negotiate what the individual wants and the detailed provision of primary care and other types of support important to the person's quality of life. Although key person succession plans are unspecific and often unwritten, the relatively smooth nature of transition, where such plans exist, suggests their efficacy in this facet of planning. By mandating the intervention of a key person who is less emotionally involved than parents, these plans relieve parents from confronting the challenges of making detailed transition arrangements that may involve difficult choices and conflicting values and needs. Such plans avoid a need for more definite residential plans and perhaps also counter the conservatism of parents by involving in decision-making key people with different ideas and, perhaps, less protective attitudes. Plans such as these avoid tying adults with intellectual disabilities the visions of their parents and earlier times. Instead, they allow for new opportunities to be created and expectations about potential that parents could not have foreseen. Identified key people, with their open brief, can be responsive to unexpected changes that occur and to the preferences of the person with intellectual disabilities. These plans are not intended to guarantee stability for the person with intellectual disability, but they provide the security of an advocate to negotiate service provision and ensure that the advocate is foremost in decisions made about aspects of the person's life when their parents are no longer there.

Nominated key people are characterised by their long-term relationship with both the parent and the adult with a disability. Key people are generally siblings, but they can be other relatives and long-term family friends. Key person succession planning suggests that a major challenge for case managers is to extend discussions of the future beyond parents, reaching out to and involving others such as non-resident family members and informal network members. Important roles for case managers are extending the vision of families about the life a person wants to live, such as the type of living situation and support that might be possible for the person when they are no longer able to live with parents. This may extend to supporting creative collaboration between families to create new options that may blend private and public resources. Various guides are available that aim to assist parents, their adult child and identified key people to express their views about the future and to document information about the person's life history, support requirements and aspirations. Compilation of a life book can be a valuable way into discussion about future options and a vital means of preserving a person's personal history to inform those who may become involved with the person. See, for example, 'My Life Book', developed by the Sharing the Caring Project in Sheffield (Foundation for People with Learning Disabilities 2002).

Case management relationships

A trusting relationship is the medium for supporting effective problem-solving and experimentation with change. This type of relationship, characterised by respect, consistency, reliability and acceptance, can take many months of painstaking work to establish. Developing trust and achieving change can mean that workers must 'hang in with families' until families are ready to tackle issues or involve workers. Use of low-key practical support is one way of building up the trust and confidence to accept other types of support. Acceptance and establishing trust involves not expecting families to undertake tasks they are not yet ready to do or see as irrelevant, and not expecting them to change long-established ways of coping and behaving that have worked over many years. This means taking at face value the parents' assessment of their needs and finding creative respectful ways to respond to conflicting values and approaches. It means making a reality of phrases such as 'starting where the family is' and 'listening and responding to them'.

Acceptance involves the provision of emotional support, backup and non-judgemental understanding of each family member's perspective. Accepting and validating the past choices of older parents, their expertise about their adult child and their current fears about the future are essential supportive strategies. The generation to which a person belongs is an important indicator of the historic influences through which they have lived and the factors that shaped their opportunities and life chances. Imagine, for example, the very different experiences of a family whose adult child was born in 1945, at a time when institutionalisation was the only available form of family support, and 'retarded' was the term of common usage, and a family with a young adult born in 1980. Relatives nowadays are often acutely aware of the lost opportunities for the current generation of older people with intellectual disabilities. In Bigby's (2000, p.116) study, for example, a niece said: '…it just makes you realise that had things been available for Amy as they are now, the potential that could have been realised.'

During their extended caring career, contemporary older parents have experienced many different philosophies and practices. Many will have been devalued and disempowered by services that disregarded their expert knowledge and motivation as parents (Llewellyn *et al.* 2004). Service systems and their staff still have the potential to disempower, particularly when the values of parents and professionals are very different. Some case managers are found to judge or blame parents for their parenting styles and perceived overprotectiveness or simply disregard their different opinions about contemporary policy (McCallion and Tobin 1995). Such approaches can alienate parents and may lead to their withdrawal from services. Awareness of the different understandings of people with intellectual disabilities that families have lived through and acknowledgement of the many professionals in different guises that have passed through their lives are central in sensitising case managers to work with people with intellectual disabilities and their family members in mid- to late life-course stages. Such generational understanding may act as a brake on judgemental approaches towards older families whose stance and expectations may be out of step from, or at least suspicious of, current ideologies.

Later-life decisions

The transition from living with parents and decisions about living situations are likely to occur during middle age and may be the precursor to other significant transitions as a person with intellectual disabilities gets older. It is important that case managers have knowledge of the physiological, social and psychological aspects of ageing, both generally and for people with intellectual disabilities (e.g. Bigby 2004). This will enable case managers to anticipate and facilitate planning in a timely manner for at least some of the age-related changes likely to be experienced by people with intellectual disabilities.

Important too are awareness and preparedness to challenge ageism and stereotypical expectations that can limit opportunities and options offered. Older people with intellectual disabilities are found to have more limited access to specialist support such as day programmes, are given fewer opportunities for social activity and development, and may be expected by paid staff to do much less compared with their younger counterparts (Thompson and Wright 2001; Walker and Walker 1998; Walker, Walker and Ryan 1996). Many of these factors stem from age-related discriminatory societal attitudes rather than from their inherent characteristics or the process of ageing per se. Negative views and low expectations held by workers can become self-fulfilling prophecies and contrast sharply with evidence that older people with intellectual disabilities can adapt to community living, become more independent, learn new skills, acquire new interests and want to lead active lives (Ashman et al. 1995; Bigby et al 2001; Lifshitz 1998).

Terms such as 'the aged' convey strong and dangerous messages of difference, suggesting the acquisition of particular characteristics and fostering stereotypical views that lead to age discrimination. Countering ageism means there must be a concerted focus on the needs and aspirations of the individual rather than the individual's membership of the 'aged' group. The principles of equity and inclusion suggest that older people with intellectual disabilities should have opportunities to mix with people of all abilities and ages, to use generally available community facilities, and to be included in the broader community, groups, activities, organisations and a diverse social milieu. Such a focus does not mean that the right to age-related specialist supports or the potential legitimacy of groups or friendships based on age should be disregarded in the process of planning.

Prior consideration of issues by the individual, the family and key service providers will help combat ageism, retain a person-centred approach and reduce the likelihood of decisions being driven by crisis, resource or systems issues.

Potential decisions may include when and whether to retire or vary day activities, what physical adaptations to the home or personal aids may be necessary in order to compensate for sensory or mobility loss, what rituals should be observed for a parent's funeral, who will be involved in decision-making processes for end-of-life care, and the feasibility of remaining at home (which may be a group home) if the person becomes frail or develops Alzheimer's disease.

The particular life experiences of ageing people with intellectual disabilities limit later-life opportunities and add to the complexity of later-life decisions. For example, few will have pensions or wealth, most will not have a spouse or children, most will not have been in paid employment during their lifetime, most will have relatively poor health, and most after midlife are very likely to be living in some form of supported accommodation. Complexity may be compounded by the age-related issues unique to particular groups of people with intellectual disabilities, such as the particularly high risk of people with Down syndrome developing early-onset Alzheimer's disease. Elsewhere, I have suggested that Nolan's 'senses framework' provides a useful approach to understanding the breadth of factors that contribute to an older person's quality of life and in orienting professionals such as case managers to the outcomes their work with individuals should seek to achieve (Bigby 2004).

The framework proposes work towards achievement of six senses (Nolan, Davies and Grant 2001, p.175):

- *Sense of security:* attention to physical and psychological needs, to feel safe from pain or discomfort and receive competent sensitive care.

- *Sense of continuity:* recognition of the individual's biography and connection with his or her past.

- *Sense of belonging:* opportunities to maintain or develop meaningful relationships with family and friends and to be part of a chosen community or group.

- *Sense of purpose:* opportunities to engage in purposeful activity, identify and pursue goals and exercise choice.

- *Sense of achievement:* opportunities to meet meaningful goals and make a recognised and valued contribution.

- *Sense of significance:* to feel recognised and valued as a person of worth, that you matter as a person.

The last part of this chapter focuses in particular on some of the issues that arise in ensuring a sense of belonging, purpose and achievement for older people with intellectual disabilities.

Ensuring a sense of belonging

Many of the changes experienced in mid- to later life by people with intellectual disabilities risk disrupting their social relationships and connections to their community. Social connections may be based around a locality, a family, a day centre or a place of work. For example, the social connections of adults who have remained living with parents are often intertwined with their parents through shared family friends and relationships with extended family members. As discussed earlier, the death or incapacity of the parents will lead to a move to alternative accommodation, such as living with other family members, in a supported housing option or, in most cases, in some form of shared supported accommodation (Bigby 2000). Being no longer based in the family home will disrupt the intellectually disabled person's contact with other family members such as nieces, nephews and cousins and with family friends, and more specific effort will be required in order to involve them in family gatherings and social occasions. In addition to issues of distance and convenience, as older relatives begin to experience mobility and health problems, more effort may be needed in order to maintain family relationships. Moving away from the neighbourhood in which a person has lived for many years also threatens the person's sense of belonging and of being known by others, such as neighbours, shopkeepers and local officials, through regular contact.

Friendships of people with intellectual disabilities, particularly those with peers, are often specific to a particular context, such as a group home, employment or day centre, and friends are seldom seen away from such settings. This means that life changes such as retirement or a residential move may compromise long-term relationships. For example, one study found that none of the people with intellectual disabilities who had retired from day programmes or who had moved to aged-care accommodation retained contact with friends from their previous settings (Bigby 2000). In the past, the emphasis on valued social roles has often detracted from recognising the value of friendships between people with intellectual disabilities (Chappell 1994) – ironically, being a friend is a valued social role that has been neglected. These friendships should not be overlooked, as they can have depth, richness and longevity and be central to a person's sense of significance and belonging (Knox and Hickson 2001). It is important, however, to distinguish between friendships, acquaintances and groupings of people who are proximate to each other. An important part of a case manager's role is to ensure that all the elements of a person's informal network are identified and, when age-associated changes occur, that enthusiastic steps are taken to maintain and nurture these relationships.

Social relationships can also play a more instrumental role in ensuring a person's sense of security as the person's reliance for everyday support shifts from his or her family to formal service systems. It is particularly difficult for formal organisations and people in paid relationships to have a long-term or sole commitment to the person with intellectual disability and to adopt an advocacy stance that involves monitoring quality of care and negotiating with services. These tasks, however, are critically important for people dependent on services to meet their day-to-day needs. The inability of formal services to substitute for some of the key roles fulfilled by informal network members emphasises the vulnerability of those people who lack strong informal networks of support. The comments of a sister illustrate her role in ensuring her brother's quality of care in a nursing home: 'They weren't really listening to him. It's his condition, Down syndrome. I know Norman very well and I said there's something wrong with him. He's in pain in his tummy. I forced the issue and demanded he was treated' (Bigby 2000, p.172).

Intergenerational key person succession planning to ensure others continue to play such 'caring about' roles as negotiation with services and advocacy should not stop once such roles are relinquished by parents to siblings or another key person. This next generation will age alongside the person with intellectual disabilities and may not outlive the person. Case managers must be alert to a conscious need to involve the younger generation in the lives of older people. Relationships with nieces, nephews and cousins may be crucial to ensure advocacy roles that initially are passed from parents to siblings are then transferred again and continue to be fulfilled as people move into very old age.

Finding appropriate services and supports

Knowing the kind of formal support that might be available and gaining access to it are two core functions of case managers. Evidence suggests that older people with intellectual disabilities, particularly those in receipt of accommodation support from the disability sector, have difficulty accessing aged and community care services, such as in-home nursing and household adaptations, which are available to older people in general to enable them to remain at home as they age

(Fyffe *et al.* 2006). Evidence also suggests older people with intellectual disabilities may be 'misplaced and forgotten' in residential aged care (Thompson and Wright 2001). Inappropriate placements, difficulty accessing appropriate support, and poor-quality care stem from the lack of policy in relation to older people with lifelong disabilities and unresolved debates about the stage at which, if at all, a person with a lifelong disability simply becomes an older person and which service system – disability or aged care – should be responsible for supporting the person. Framing the issues in this way is not helpful for case managers. Rather than seeing the question as either one system or another, case managers need to consider possibilities offered by multiple systems – disability care, aged care, healthcare and social security – which will all, at different times and in different combinations, have services relevant to ageing people with intellectual disabilities.

It is indisputable, however, that some needs of older people with intellectual disabilities, particularly those related to health, are best met by professionals with expertise in aged care or specialist geriatric healthcare. For example, a whole infrastructure of specialist assessment and treatment programmes, such as memory and falls clinics, is found in the geriatric branch of medicine, and it is, for example, aged-care professionals who are most knowledgeable about adapting the environment and supporting people with Alzheimer's disease, providing palliative care, offering volunteer options for older citizens and dealing with everyday issues such as incontinence.

Evidence from both the UK and Australia suggests that staff in disability services have limited knowledge about ageing processes, and staff in the healthcare and aged-care sectors have little knowledge about people with intellectual disabilities (Bigby *et al.* 2001; Fyffe *et al.* 2006; Thompson and Wright 2001). Evidence also suggests that people with intellectual disabilities are particularly disadvantaged in terms of poor access to good-quality healthcare, untreated health conditions and lack of preventive screening, which delays early detection of acute and chronic problems (Cooper 1997; Haveman 2004). For example, Haveman (2004) cites a study that found a substantial number of older adults with intellectual disability living in the community with undiagnosed, untreated hyperlipidemia, and another study that found 40 per cent of people with intellectual disability had hearing loss, of which 85 per cent was undetected. Haveman discusses the enormous impact of such undetected and untreated loss on an individual's day-to-day quality of life and support needs. Examples are found in the international literature of strategic measures such as the use of nurse practitioners, specialist geriatric clinics, hospital liaison programmes and specialist professional training staff, and yet in Australia health-related initiatives are seldom debated or instigated as part of strategies to support ageing-in-place for people with disabilities (Janicki and Ansello 2000).

This suggests that ensuring regular timely access to quality health services should be central to case management with older people. It also points to the importance of a partnership approach between sectors and suggests that a key role for the case manager working with older people is to build their own knowledge of the health and aged care system in their locality so that its expertise can be utilised where and in whatever form is appropriate. This might be as a complement to disability support services, in place of disability services or provision of consultation, or as training or advice to staff in the disability system. Similarly, it may at times also be necessary for case managers from the disability sector to provide consultancy or training to aged-care and local general practice clinic staff.

Retirement

A role for case managers is to support a critical approach to discussion of the meaning of retirement for people with intellectual disabilities. Many people with intellectual disabilities may not be in full- or even part-time paid employment, and retirement may mean ceasing to attend a day centre or supported employment programme. Case managers must ask why the question is being raised, what purpose (and for whom) retirement will serve, whether part-time attendance is a possibility, and what the individual wants to do. Case managers must ensure that all possible options are explored in order to enable the older persons' continued engagement in purposeful activity, pursuit of their own goals and exercise of choice. This cannot be left to chance, as older people with intellectual disabilities are likely to be reliant on others to present opportunities, provide support to exercise choice and support their participation in meaningful activities.

Evidence suggests that people with intellectual disabilities do prefer their lives to be active rather than passive, express the desire to continue working, continue learning, participate in more leisure activities and place a high value on organised activities (Ashman et al. 1995; Bigby 1992, 1997; Heller 1999). Bigby's (2000) study highlighted the opportunities relished by some older people who perceived later life as a period when they were free to pursue their own interests and relationships, unrestricted by parental protectiveness. The limited data available contrast starkly with the many anecdotal stories that older people just want to 'stay at home and put their feet up' or that they are more likely to be 'observers than participants' (Bigby *et al.* 2001).

A major concern, however, is evidence that despite their aspirations for continuing an active and full lifestyle of their choice, older people with intellectual disabilities experience few opportunities to participate in meaningful day and leisure activities of their choice (Bigby 1992, 1997; Grant, McGrath and Ramcharan 1995; Hawkins 1999). Their situation is summed up by Rogers, Hawkins and Eklund (1998, p.127): '...retirees' days were often filled with diversionary activity rather than leisure that was valued and meaningful to participants. Furthermore, they were not provided with opportunities to retain contact with previous friends or develop new social contacts.' Even opportunities for involvement in day-to-day domestic household activities tend to drop off for the older age groups (Wilson 1998).

There is little evidence to suggest that day programmes specifically developed for older participants with intellectual disabilities lead to better outcomes than age-integrated programmes. An Australian study found that staff in such programmes did not have superior knowledge of ageing issues. Such programmes run the risk of reinforcing age stereotyping and reducing individual choice by grouping people and determining the type of programme offered according to age rather than addressing issues based on individual preferences and interests (Bigby 2005).

Conclusions

Midlife and older age occupy a substantial period of the life course. Although getting older is an inevitable process, its speed and course are incredibly varied. It is as important as at any other stage of the life course that case managers adopt a person-centred approach to working with people with intellectual disabilities, placing each individual firmly in the context of his or her network of family and friends. A knowledge of the issues associated with the particular life-course stages should inform the approach of case managers and guard against negative and ill-informed stereotypical assumptions that can undermine the choices and quality of life. As people age, the task of case managers is to support individual planning, which may include the transition from living with parents, to nurture their social relationships and to ensure these are complemented by formal support services that further their sense of security, belonging, continuity, purpose, achievement and significance.

References

Allen, R. and Petr, C. (1998) 'Rethinking family centred practice.' *American Journal of Orthopsychiatry 68*, 4–15.

Ashman, A., Suttie, J. and Bramley, J. (1995) 'Employment, retirement and elderly persons with developmental disabilities.' *Journal of Intellectual Disability Research 39*, 107–15.

Bigby, C. (1992) 'Access and linkage: two critical issues for older people with an intellectual disability.' *Australia and New Zealand Journal of Developmental Disabilities 18*, 95–110.

Bigby, C. (1997) 'When parents relinquish care: the informal support networks of older people with intellectual disability.' *Journal of Applied Intellectual Disability Research 10*, 333–44.

Bigby, C. (2000) *Moving on without Parents: Planning, Transitions and Sources of Support for Older Adults with Intellectual Disabilities.* New Sydney: MacLennan & Petty.

Bigby, C. (2004) *Ageing with a Lifelong Disability: Policy, Program and Practice Issues for Professionals.* London: Jessica Kingsley Publishers.

Bigby, C. (2005) 'Comparative programs for older people with intellectual disabilities.' *Journal of Policy and Practice in Intellectual Disability 2*, 75–85.

Bigby, C., Fyffe, C., Balandin, S., Gordon, M., and McCubbery, J. (2001) *Day Support Services Options for Older Adults with a Disability.* Melbourne: National Disability Administrators Group.

Bigby, C., Ozanne. E. and Gordon, M. (2002) 'Facilitating transition: elements of successful case management practice for older parents of adults with intellectual disability.' *Journal of Gerontological Social Work 37*, 25–44.

Carter, C. and Jancar, J. (1983) 'Mortality in the mentally handicapped: a fifty year survey at the Stoke Park Group of Hospitals.' *Journal of Mental Deficiency Research 27*, 143–56.

Chappell, A. (1994) 'A question of friendship: community care and the relationships of people with learning difficulties.' *Disability and Society 9*, 419–33.

Cooper, S. (1997) 'Deficient health and social services for elderly people with learning disabilities.' *Journal of Intellectual Disability Research 41*, 331–8.

Department of Health (2001) *Valuing People: A New Strategy for Learning Disability for the 21st Century.* London: HMSO.

Erickson, M., Krauss, M. and Seltzer, M. (1989) 'Perceptions of old age among a sample of mentally retarded persons.' *Journal of Applied Gerontology 8*, 251–60.

Foundation for People with Learning Disabilities (2002) *Today and Tomorrow: The Report of the Growing Older with Learning Disabilities Programme.* London: Foundation for People with Learning Disabilities.

Fyffe, C., Bigby, C. and McCubbery, J. (2006) *Exploration of the Population of People with Disabilities who are Ageing, their Changing Needs and the Capacity of the Disability and Age Care Sector to Support them to Age Positively.* Canberra: National Disability Administrators Group.

Grant, G. (2001) 'Older People with Learning Disabilities: Health, Community Inclusion and Family Caregiving.' In M. Nolan, S. Davies and G. Grant (eds) *Working with Older People and their Families.* Basingstoke: Open University Press.

Grant, G., McGrath, M. and Ramcharan, P. (1995) 'Community inclusion of older adults with learning disabilities: care in place.' *International Journal of Network and Community 2*, 29–44.

Hawkins, B. (1999) 'Rights, Place of Residence and Retirement: Lessons from Case Studies on Aging.' In S. Herr and G. Weber (eds) *Aging, Rights and Quality of Life*. Baltimore, MD: Paul H. Brookes.

Haveman, M. (2004) 'Disease epidemiology and ageing people with intellectual disabilities.' *Journal of Policy and Practice in Intellectual Disabilities 1*, 16–23.

Hayden, M. and Heller, T. (1997) 'Support, problem-solving/coping ability and personal burden of younger and older caregivers of adults with mental retardation.' *Mental Retardation 35*, 364–72.

Heller, T. (1999) 'Emerging Models.' In S. Herr and G. Weber (eds) *Ageing, Rights and Quality of Life*. Baltimore, MD: Paul H. Brookes.

Heller, T. and Factor, A. (1991) 'Permanency planning for adults with mental retardation living with family caregivers.' *American Journal on Mental Retardation 96*, 163–76.

Heller, T., Miller, A., Hsieh, K. and Sterns, H. (2000) 'Later-life planning: promotion knowledge of options and choice making.' *Mental Retardation 38*, 395–406.

Janicki, M. (1996) *Help for Caring for Older People Caring for Adults with a Developmental Disability*. Albany, NY: New York State Developmental Disabilities Planning Council.

Janicki, M. and Ansello, E. (2000) *Community Supports for Aging Adults with Lifelong Disabilities*. Baltimore, MD: Paul H. Brookes.

Janicki, M., McCallion, P., Force, L., Bishop, K. and LePore, P. (1998). 'Area agency on aging and assistance for households with older carers of adults with a developmental disability.' *Journal of Aging and Social Policy 10*, 1, 13–36.

Knox, M. and Bigby, C. (2007) 'Moving towards midlife care as negotiated family business: accounts of people with intellectual disabilities and their families.' *International Journal of Disability, Development and Education 3*, in press.

Knox, M. and Hickson, F. (2001) 'The meaning of close friendships: the view of four people with intellectual disabilities.' *Journal of Applied Research in Intellectual Disabilities 14*, 276–91.

Krauss, M., Seltzer, M., Gordon, R. and Friedman, D. (1996) 'Binding ties: the roles of adult siblings of persons with mental retardation.' *Mental Retardation 34*, 83–93.

Laughlin, C. and Cotton, P. (1994) 'Efficacy of a pre-retirement planning intervention for ageing individuals with mental retardation.' *Journal of Intellectual Disability Research 38*, 317–28.

Lifshitz, H. (1998) 'Instrumental enrichment: a tool for enhancement of cognitive ability in adult and elderly people with mental retardation.' *Education and Training in Mental Retardation and Developmental Disabilities 33*, 34–41.

Llewellyn, G., Gething, L., Kendig, H. and Cant, R. (2004) 'Older parent caregivers' engagement with the service system.' *American Journal on Mental Retardation 109*, 379–96.

McCallion, P. and Tobin, S. (1995) 'Social workers' perceptions of older adults caring at home for sons and daughters with developmental disabilities.' *Mental Retardation 33*, 153–62.

Nolan, M., Davies, S. and Grant, G. (2001) 'Integrating Perspectives.' In M. Nolan, S. Davies and G. Grant (eds) *Working with Older People and their Families*. Basingstoke: Open University Press.

O'Malley, P. (1996) 'Group work with older people who are developmentally disabled and their caregivers.' *Journal of Gerontological Social Work 25*, 105–20.

Rogers, N., Hawkins, B. and Eklund, S. (1998) 'The nature of leisure in the lives of older adults with intellectual disability.' *Journal of Intellectual Disability Research 42*, 122–30.

Thompson, D. and Wright, S. (2001) *Misplaced and Forgotten: People with Learning Disabilities in Residential Services for Older People.* London: Mental Health Foundation.

Todd, S. and Shearn, J. (1996) 'Time and the person: the impact of support services on the lives of parents of adults with intellectual disabilities.' *Journal of Applied Research in Intellectual Disabilities 9*, 40–60.

Urlings, H., Haveman, M., Maaskant, M., Lantman, H., *et al.* (1992) '"Old?" "I'm not old". The experience of the aging process of mentally retarded persons themselves.' Presented at the ninth congress of the International Association for the Scientific Study of Intellectual Disability, Jupiter's Casino, Broadbeach, Qld, 8 August 1992.

Walker, A. and Walker, C. (1998) 'Normalisation and "normal" ageing: the social construction of dependency among older people with learning difficulties.' *Disability and Society 13*, 125–42.

Walker, A., Walker, C. and Ryan, T. (1996) 'Older people with learning difficulties leaving institutional care: a case of double jeopardy.' *Ageing and Society 16*, 125–50.

Walmsley, J. (1996) 'Doing what mum wants me to do: looking at family relationships from the point of view of adults with learning disabilities.' *Journal of Applied Research in Intellectual Disabilities 9*, 324–41.

Williams, V. and Robinson, C. (2001) 'More than one wavelength: identifying, understanding and resolving conflicts of interest between people with intellectual disabilities and their carers.' *Journal of Applied Research in Intellectual Disabilities 14*, 30–46.

Wilson, C. (1998) 'Providing quality services for individuals who are aging in community based support settings: what are the issues for service providers?' Presented at the 34th Annual Conference of the Australian Society for the Study of Intellectual Disability, Adelaide University, Adelaide, SA, 28 September 1998.

Yang, Q., Rasmussen, S. and Friedman, J. (2002) 'Mortality associated with Down's syndrome in the USA from 1983 to 1997: a population based study.' *Lancet 359*, 1019.

15

The role of the case manager in supporting communication

Susan Balandin

The aim of this chapter is to explore the role of the case manager in supporting communication for people with intellectual disabilities. Definitions of terms such as 'augmentative or alternative communication' (AAC) and 'complex communication needs' are provided, and a number of issues pertinent to effective communication are discussed, including:

- successful communication

- assessment

- behaviour and communication

- communication systems.

Although responsibility for effective communicative interactions does not rest with case managers alone, case managers do need to understand the importance of communication and how they can facilitate optimal communication for their clients. Communication is a key to successful community participation and inclusion. Indeed, it can be argued that verbal communication is a distinguishing feature of humans and an essential component of adequate quality of life. According to Light and Binger (1998), verbal communication fulfils four purposes:

- communication of needs and wants

- information transfer

- social closeness

- social etiquette.

Effective communication can be deemed a basic right (National Joint Committee for the Communication Needs for Persons with Severe Disabilities 2002).

Communication rights

People with intellectual disabilities, including those with complex communication needs, have the same communication rights as people who can speak, including the right to make choices and decisions, the right to ask for information and to have their communicative acts acknowledged, and the right to be communicated with in an appropriate and respectful manner. Case managers are integral to ensuring that the communication rights of the clients they support are respected and upheld and that their clients are given every opportunity to communicate successfully. Many people with intellectual disabilities have complex communication needs and will always experience difficulty with communication. Consequently, they will always rely on having skilled communication partners to assist them to communicate. The case manager is well placed to ensure that communication partners have the necessary support and training in order to develop the skills to interact with people with complex communication needs.

Complex communication needs

People who have little or no functional speech and require alternative or augmentative communication have complex communication needs, which are defined as a person having 'needs associated with a wide range of physical, sensory and environmental causes which restrict/limit their ability to participate independently in society. They and their communication partners may benefit from using alternative or augmentative communication methods either temporarily or permanently' (Balandin 2002, p.2).

Complex communication needs are associated with long-standing conditions such as intellectual disabilities, and people with complex communication needs require support in order to communicate effectively.

People who require support with communication

It is estimated that there are 588,700 people in Australia with intellectual disabilities. Although the severity of the impairment may vary, the majority of people with intellectual disabilities experience some restriction in the core activity of communication. Such restrictions include difficulty in being understood by familiar and/or unfamiliar communication partners and difficulty in understanding what familiar and/or unfamiliar communication partners say to them. Additionally, people with intellectual disabilities may have difficulty with literacy and access to printed information.

Case managers are likely to be required to support individuals with lifelong disabilities who experience communication difficulties, including people with complex communication needs, people with autism-spectrum disorder, people with cerebral palsy, and people with challenging behaviours. Case managers have a responsibility to ensure that they make every effort to include the person with disability in any communicative interaction. Proxies may be helpful in determining what a person wants and for assisting the person to participate optimally. A proxy is someone who knows the person well and can speak on his or her behalf. Proxies can be very helpful when planning for a person and ensuring that his or her needs and wishes are met and respected. For example, Stancliffe and Parmenter (1999) demonstrated that proxies are accurate when assisting people with intellectual disabilities with whom they are familiar to make choices.

Nevertheless, proxies are not always available or appropriate to use when communicating with a person with an intellectual disability, and therefore it may fall to the case manager to consider a variety of alternative communication methods to include the person with disability. Such methods may be as simple as allowing more time, communicating with the person in a familiar environment or providing pictures or photographs to support comprehension, for example when discussing changes in accommodation. If the case manager identifies the person's behaviours as communicative, a referral to a communication specialist will be appropriate.

Thus, it is important that case managers focus on the person and his or her needs and aspirations. This focus includes a responsibility for ensuring that the communication needs of the person with an intellectual disability are not neglected. Case managers may need to take responsibility for coordinating the selection and development of communication strategies that will foster interactions with a variety of communication partners across a range of community contexts.

Successful communication

Effective communication is essential for a good quality of life. Without effective communication, it is impossible for a person to interact with others successfully. Despite a strong focus on verbal communication within the community, it is important to recognise that people, including those with intellectual disabilities and complex communication needs or little or no functional speech, are still able to communicate a variety of messages, particularly if they have access to appropriate support (Beukelman and Mirenda 2005). Communicable messages include the expression of wants, needs, choices, hopes and dreams; asking for information; and communication for social closeness, such as having a chat with a friend. People with complex communication needs may require a third party to speak for them or require an alternative or augmentative communication system[6] (Beukelman and Mirenda 2005).

Successful or effective communication is an interaction in which both participants are satisfied that a message has been conveyed clearly. Failure to develop functional communication and the ensuing problems with message expression or understanding can have devastating effects on both the individual with disability and people who are close to or interact regularly with that person, such as family members, friends and service providers. Any difficulties with understanding or being understood by others act as significant barriers to effective communication. Sadly, many people with intellectual disabilities and complex communication needs have no alternative or augmentative communication system or, indeed, access to any functional communication system. In other words, they have no way of communicating effectively, including the use of systems such as letter boards, pictures, signs and gestures, and they must rely on others to recognise that they are trying to communicate and interpret what they are trying to say. Both service providers and others in the community may find this a difficult task, and one that most people are unable to do well without support and training.

Consequently, due to lack of training and resources, people with intellectual disabilities and complex communication needs may not be well catered for by services that are stretched to cope with large caseloads. It can take time to learn about the idiosyncratic communication of a person with intellectual disabilities and no functional communication system. It also takes time and resources to develop suitable communication systems and to train communication partners in how to use such systems effectively. Service providers may focus on the here and now of providing support and avoiding crises and rarely consider the future impact of limited communication or lack of a functional communication system on the person with intellectual disabilities. This is a cause for concern, as communication experiences, including early literacy experiences and developing a strong sense of self, are likely to influence both the future quality of life and the independence of people with intellectual disabilities.

Without an effective communication system, it is not possible for the person with intellectual disabilities to express his or her choices, needs and aspirations or to participate in a variety of contexts. Equally, it is difficult for case managers to ensure that their clients are involved in determining their own lives to the maximum of their ability. Indeed, it can be argued that case managers will be unable to adequately support people with intellectual disabilities unless they understand the importance of communication and have knowledge of a variety of ways to facilitate communication. Thus, the case manager may have to coordinate the development of communication strategies for the person with intellectual disabilities, commencing with ensuring that the person has an appropriate assessment of his or her current communication skills and future needs.

Assessment

In the past, many people with intellectual disabilities were assessed with standardised tests, and their results compared with those of a 'normal population'. Often, a mental age or language age was determined based on the person's score on the test. Thus, it was common to hear a person with a chronological age of, for example, 18 years being described as having a 'mental age' of a three-year-old. This practice led to confusion and the oppression of people with disabilities and acted as a barrier to maximising people's opportunities to participate in their community and develop skills. It also led to further marginalisation of people with disabilities, who were viewed and treated as childlike despite their obvious maturity.

An adult with a disability is quite unlike a child; rather, the adult is similar to any other adult with or without a disability. Physical and sexual maturity, life experience and ongoing learning opportunities mean that no adult is like a young child, and yet families may have some difficulty in recognising this. The case manager has a role in ensuring that a person's chronological age is respected. This recognition and respect must be communicated appropriately. Thus, it is important not to infantilise the person with disability during communicative interactions, when selecting activities and when developing communication systems. Communication systems and materials should be appropriate for an adult, and the person should be treated like an adult. This means that language can be simplified but the person should never be spoken to as if he or she were a child. Many materials are now available to support people with intellectual disabilities to acquire new skills across the lifespan. Communication materials may include photographs and symbol systems that are designed to be age-neutral and are, therefore, appropriate for a range of ages. In using these, case managers and others involved with the person must also ensure that activities and choices are age-appropriate and not those that could further marginalise the person if he or she selected to do them.

The Participation Model described by Beukelman and Mirenda (2005) provides a useful framework for the assessment and development of interventions that facilitate the participation of individuals with disabilities in activities in which their peers without disabilities participate. The Participation Model is based on the functional participation requirements of peers without disability of the same chronological age as the person with disability who is being assessed. The model is a multiphase assessment that incorporates consensus-building across a variety of people involved with the person with disability in order to assess current and future participation patterns and communication needs. At the same time, the Participation Model can be used to identify opportunity and access barriers to participation and to assist with planning appropriate intervention goals and evaluating the outcomes. Although the model is focused on people who use augmentative and alternative communication, it is appropriate for use with anyone who is experiencing difficulty in being an integrated member of the community, including people whose main barrier to participation within the community is due to problem behaviours.

Behaviour and communication

Many people with intellectual disabilities or autism-spectrum disorders have problem behaviours that can be attributed to communication difficulties. Indeed, Mirenda (1997), in a review of the research on communication and challenging behaviour, suggested that all behaviours are communicative. Consequently, it is important to consider functionally equivalent communication options when supporting people with challenging behaviours. A functionally equivalent communication option is a communication behaviour that serves the same function as the challenging behaviour. An example of functional equivalence is teaching a child to sign *more* to replace screaming or biting until more of the desired object or activity is provided. Case managers are unlikely to have to manage the intervention for problem behaviours, but they may be involved in organising comprehensive assessments of the behaviours and coordinating the intervention approach so that the person is presented with a variety of interesting opportunities that will promote engagement in the community (Beukelman and Mirenda 2005).

It is not surprising, then, that case managers who support people with intellectual disabilities may be the key service personnel to ensure that every effort is made to facilitate and support their clients' communication, including the initial assessment. It is important to remember that a person with communication difficulties will be disadvantaged in both learning and social activities unless every effort is made to ensure that he or she has an effective and functional means of communication (Beukelman and Mirenda 2005).

Therefore, case managers may need not only to consider the impact of communication on their client's ability to express choices, needs and aspirations but also to ensure that every effort is made to make certain that the client's communicative attempts are considered. Case managers may need to refer clients to a communication specialist (e.g. speech pathologist, AAC specialist) in order to seek advice on the implementation of appropriate communication systems. In addition, case managers must be prepared to use a variety of communication modes to assist their clients to participate as fully as possible in any interaction.

Supporting communication

Readers who have travelled to places where they were unable to speak the local language or who have experienced communicating with people for whom speech is a not primary or functional communication mode may understand that communicating using modes other than speech can be time-consuming and frustrating for both partners in the communicative interaction. Both partners may need to alter their usual communication pattern in order to achieve a satisfactory communication outcome. Indeed, fear of difficulty with communication is a major inhibitor of communicative interactions between people with and without disabilities.

Speech is the primary communication mode for most members of the community. Although they may supplement their speech in a variety of ways, including using gesture, facial expression and body movements, the majority of the community, including service providers experienced in working with people with intellectual disabilities, may have limited experience of communicating using modes other than speech. Indeed, researchers have demonstrated that many people, including service providers, experience difficulty in moderating their language to accommodate the communication needs of the person with intellectual disability. People with intellectual disabilities may rely on non-verbal sources of information during interactions. Non-verbal sources include the time of day when routine activities occur, the context within which a request occurs, and gestures and facial expressions. The use of non-verbal sources aids comprehension but may mask a person's communication difficulties.

Bartlett and Bunning (1997) and Bradshaw (2001) studied the interactions between individuals with intellectual disabilities and the staff members who supported them. Bartlett and Bunning (1997) assessed the verbal comprehension of each client and compared the assessed level of verbal comprehension with the staff members' expressive language output during structured and unstructured tasks. Both Bartlett and Bunning (1997) and Bradshaw (2001) identified that staff often overestimated what the adults with disabilities could understand – that is, they overestimated the communication skills of the residents with whom they worked. This overestimation resulted in many of the staff members' utterances being too complex. It is hardly surprising that people with intellectual disabilities do not respond or may respond inappropriately if they do not understand what is being said to them. Staff may deem the person to be non-responsive or non-compliant or to have challenging behaviour.

Case managers need to be aware of their own communication and the communication of others. For example, at a planning meeting, if the person with a disability sits quietly throughout the meeting, this does not always mean that he or she is understanding and participating fully in what is happening. Similarly, if a person paces the room and is disruptive, it may mean that he or she is frustrated because of not knowing what is going on. Case managers may be able to prevent these scenarios by ensuring that the person with a disability is prepared for the meeting and that every effort has been made to provide communication materials and support or at the very least that there is someone present who knows the person with a disability well and can attribute communicative intent to his or her actions. As noted already, case managers do not have to take on all these roles themselves, but they are the key personnel for advocating for the person with a disability and coordinating the various experts and service providers who can facilitate communication and ensure that the voice of the person is heard.

Useful communication systems

People with intellectual disabilities may benefit from the use of additional communication systems or multimodal communication, not only to aid them in expressing what they want to say but also to support their understanding of what is said. If people with intellectual disabilities and little or no functional speech do not have a functional communication system, they will be unable to express themselves. An inability to talk does not mean that the person has nothing to say.

Similarly, people who are acquiescent either may be anxious to please a person (e.g. service provider) who they perceive as an authority figure or may not understand what is being said and therefore may choose to agree or say nothing in order to 'save face'. Importantly, case managers need to be aware of, and prepared to use, a variety of communication modes in order to increase opportunities for people with intellectual disabilities to participate in their own decision-making and in accessing the broader community. There are a number of different communication modes and systems that can be used with people with intellectual disabilities to aid them in expressing what they want to say and in understanding (see Table 15.1).

Augmentative and alternative communication systems

AAC systems include 'low- or light-tech devices' (e.g. word- and letter-boards, pictures, photos and objects), 'high-tech devices' (e.g. speech-generating devices, computers) and unaided systems (e.g. signs) (Sigafoos and Iacono 1993). Importantly, having speech does not preclude the use of AAC. People with disabilities who have speech can still benefit from AAC systems. Indeed, we all use these from time to time, for example writing a shopping list or using a picture or product logo as a memory aid. An overview of AAC systems used by people with intellectual disabilities is provided in Table 15.1.

Some systems, such as schedules and keyword signing, can be used to support both comprehension and language expression. Case managers may be asked whether the use of an AAC system will inhibit the development and use of speech. They can be confident that the use of an AAC system not only promotes communication and understanding but also may assist in the development of speech. It is not yet clear to what extent the use of AAC influences the development of speech, but there are reports (e.g. Romski and Sevcik 1996) that some people have started to use some speech after learning to use AAC systems, such as voice-output communication aids and signs.

Augmentative and alternative communication and language

Researchers have conducted longitudinal research on the use of AAC to promote language and communication with children and young adults with intellectual disabilities. These researchers have successfully increased language production in primary-school students, adolescents in secondary school and young adults (Romski and Sevcik 1996) and very young children with intellectual

Table 15.1 Overview of high- and light-technology augmentative and alternative communication (AAC) systems

High technology	Utilises microcomputers and specialised software
	Synthesised or digitised speech
	May interface with a computer, environmental control system or telephone
	Accessed directly (e.g. using fingers or head pointer) or indirectly (e.g. scanning using a switch)
	Requires a power source (e.g. battery)
	Requires specialised repair
	Expensive to purchase and maintain
Light technology, aided	No electronic parts, but can include electromechanical switches
	Accessed directly (e.g. finger-pointing, eye gaze) or indirectly using another person to ask which symbol is required
	Examples: letter-boards, chat-books, object communication systems, schedules, symbol boards
	Talking Mats™ (Murphy and Cameron 2002, 2005)
	Easy to maintain, but setup and maintenance can be costly in time
	Useful across a variety of contexts and can be tailored to different needs (e.g. community request cards to enable the person to order a meal independently or participate actively in activities such as going to the hairdresser or choosing a gift)
Light technology, unaided	Manual signing
	Examples: Auslan, British Sign Language
	May use signed keywords to support comprehension expression
	Sign interpreters are useful with deaf people who are fluent sign-language users but may not be useful with people with intellectual disabilities who use a few keyword signs

impairments (Romski, Sevcik and Forrest 2000). Romski and colleagues suggested that in order to use AAC and develop language, it is important to understand not only the relationship between a spoken word and its referent but also the relationship between a visual symbol and the spoken word. People with limited comprehension must first learn the relationship between a visual symbol or manual sign and its referent before they can use AAC expressively. Some may never understand this relationship and will communicate using idiosyncratic gesture, vocalisations, movements and physical manipulation of others in the environment. Consequently, case managers endorsing the use of AAC to support and enhance communication must be cautious when discussing the likelihood of speech developing. AAC has been shown to assist in the development of speech for some people, but more importantly, the use of AAC ensures that people with little or no functional speech have a way to communicate and additional resources to aid their understanding.

Case managers may find simple systems that incorporate photographs or pictographs such as Picture Communication Symbols™ (PCS) useful when communicating with people with intellectual disability. It is beyond the scope of this chapter to describe the many systems available, but a discussion with a speech pathologist or searching a website such as www.isaac-online.org will provide useful information about ways to improve communication interactions. Case managers may also find techniques such as Talking Mats™ (Murphy and Cameron 2002) invaluable when assisting people with intellectual disabilities to make choices and express their hopes and dreams.

Talking Mats

Talking Mats is 'a visual framework that uses picture symbols to help people with a communication difficulty communicate more effectively' (Murphy and Cameron 2005, p.3). Using pictures to represent topics and options and a visual scale with people with little or no speech and people who have difficulty in understanding speech can assist them to express their wishes about what will occur in their own life. Service providers, including case managers, can use this tool to help the person with disability consider and discuss a variety of options. The pictures are placed on a mat so that the person with disability can look at the options and choices available and then move them using the visual scale to indicate how they feel about each option. The visual scale might include symbols for liking something, for being unsure and for definitely not liking or wanting something. More complex visual scales can be created, depending on the person's needs and abilities.

The use of a visual system such as Talking Mats gives people an opportunity not only to see their options but also to easily indicate a change of opinion. It is easy for the case manager to make a record of the decisions by photocopying or photographing the mat, and this can be used as the basis for ongoing discussion and decision-making. In order for this system to be effective, it is important that as many people as possible who are involved with the person with disability are consulted to ensure that a range of possible options are presented pictorially.

Many people with a variety of disabilities use Talking Mats successfully. Nevertheless, there are some people for whom this system is not suitable. Murphy and Cameron (2005) suggested that to use Talking Mats successfully, the person using the mat must be able to recognise picture symbols and must be able to understand at least two keywords at a time. The person must also have a reliable way of confirming his or her views so that the case manager or service provider can be sure that the placement of pictures on the mat does in fact reflect the person's views.

Case managers may also find useful tools such as the Social Networks Communication Inventory (Blackstone and Hunt Berg 2003). This inventory aids functional goal-setting and personal planning. The inventory can be used to identify a person's current and potential communication partners and the communication modes that are used with each person. This provides a means of mapping the social networks of the person with a disability and ensuring that comprehensive information about his or her communication abilities, needs and outcomes of communication interventions are tracked. This information will assist case managers to use and advocate for a variety of communication options that will facilitate the inclusion of the person with a disability in a range of activities with a range of different communication partners.

Conclusion

Communication encompasses more than the expression of wants and needs. It also includes understanding, asking for information, getting along with other people, making choices and expressing hopes and dreams. Communication is a key not only to a good quality of life but also to effective planning support for a person with intellectual disabilities. Case managers do not have sole responsibility for a person's communication or for the barriers and solutions to successful community participation. Nevertheless, the case manager, by virtue of his or her position, may be responsible for advocating for communication resources and supports for clients with intellectual disabilities. Case managers may also be the appropriate people to ensure that their clients have the opportunities and services that are needed in order to reach maximum community inclusion and participation. Communication underpins community participation. Without an understanding of the importance of communication and an idea of the resources and services available, case managers will struggle to meet their clients' needs. In addition, their own communication with their clients will be impoverished. Communication is a key to a good quality of life. Case managers who understand this will take the time to develop successful communication with their clients with intellectual disabilities and their families.

References

Balandin, S. (2002). 'Message from the president.' *ISAAC Bulletin 67*, 2.

Bartlett, C. and Bunning, K. (1997) 'The importance of communication partnerships: a study to investigate the communicative exchanges between staff and adults with learning disabilities.' *British Journal of Learning Disabilities 25*, 148–52.

Beukelman, D.R. and Mirenda, P. (2005) *Augmentative and Alternative Communication: Supporting Children and Adults with Complex Communication Needs*, 3rd edn. Baltimore, MD: Paul H. Brookes.

Blackstone, S. and Hunt Berg, M. (2003) *Social Networks: A Communication Inventory for Individuals with Complex Communication Needs and their Communication Partners.* Monterey, CA: Augmentative Communication Inc.

Bradshaw, J. (2001) 'Complexity of staff communication and reported level of understanding skills in adults with intellectual disability.' *Journal of Intellectual Disability Research 45*, 233–43.

Light, J.C. and Binger, C. (1998) *Building Communicative Competence with Individuals who Use Augmentative and Alternative Communication.* Baltimore, MD: Paul H. Brookes.

Mirenda, P. (1997) 'Supporting individuals with challenging behavior through functional communication training and AAC: research review.' *Augmentative and Alternative Communication 13*, 207–25.

Murphy, J. and Cameron, L. (2002) *Talking Mats and Learning Disability: A Low Tech Communication Resource to Help People Express Views and Feelings.* Stirling: Psychology Department, University of Stirling.

Murphy, J. and Cameron, L. (2005) *Talking Mats: A Resource to Enhance Communication.* Stirling: University of Stirling.

National Joint Committee for the Communication Needs for Persons with Severe Disabilities (2002) 'Supporting documentation for the position statement of access to communication and supports.' *Communication Disorders Quarterly 23*, 145–53.

Romski, M.A. and Sevcik, R.A. (1996) *Breaking the Speech Barrier: Language Development through Augmented Means.* Baltimore, MD: Paul H. Brookes.

Romski, M.A., Sevcik, R.A. and Forrest, S. (2000) 'Assistive Technology and Augmentative and Alternative Communication in Early Childhood Programs.' In M.J. Guralnick (ed.) *Early Childhood Inclusion*. Baltimore, MD: Paul H. Brookes.

Sigafoos, J. and Iacono, T. (1993) 'Selecting augmentative communication devices for persons with severe disabilities: some factors for educational teams to consider.' *Australia and New Zealand Journal of Developmental Disabilities 16*, 133–46.

Stancliffe, R.J. and Parmenter, T.R. (1999) 'The Choice Questionnaire: a scale to assess choices exercised by adults with intellectual disability.' *Journal of Intellectual and Developmental Disability 24*, 107–32.

16

Accessing quality healthcare

Philip Graves

The best way to achieve quality healthcare for people with intellectual disabilities is to apply the principle of inclusion and to provide the services in the same places delivered by the same people who provide healthcare for everyone in the community. This then takes advantage of the standards-maintenance systems that exist for the whole community. The standards we expect for people with disabilities should be those we expect for ourselves, our families and our friends. Case managers contribute to realising this expectation.

The medical model and the legacies of history

There are many barriers to achieving inclusion and quality healthcare. Until relatively recently, disability services, including health services, were provided from segregated facilities. That those models have been abandoned is indicative of their ineffectiveness and their inappropriateness. They did not enhance the wellbeing, dignity or quality of life of people with disabilities, and they were not conducive to quality medical care. They encouraged a view that people with disabilities did not belong in the general community.

The so-called 'medical model' has been condemned by modern disability service providers as being synonymous with historical segregated large residential services. To the extent that these were run by doctors, staffed by nurses and cared little for individual dignity and quality of life, this condemnation is appropriate. Since then, there has been separation of disability services and health. Disability services have evolved with a culture of respect for individual dignity and quality of life. There is a risk in this legacy of history being associated with a continuing culture of distrust of medical care.

What do healthcare providers think is important, and why?

Aetiology

Why is this person disabled? The issue is of concern to families because of its implications for the recurrence of disabilities in other children and future generations, and because it helps them deal with the considerable grief associated with coming to terms with disability (Mackay 1982). It is also of relevance to the person with the disability, since specific diagnostic conditions, such as Down syndrome and Prader–Willi syndrome, are associated with known physical and behavioural characteristics (O'Brien and Yule 1995) that can be anticipated, detected and treated early, thus minimising complications. At a broader population level, knowledge about causative factors such as congenital rubella and iodine deficiency can lead to their eradication through programmes such as immunisation and dietary supplementation.

Aetiology is usually investigated soon after disability is suspected but often not reviewed later in life. Improvements in investigative technology over the past two to three decades have led to increases in accuracy of aetiological diagnosis and the proportion of people with disabilities for whom accurate diagnosis is possible. In some studies, it has been possible to ascertain a precise aetiology in up to 80 per cent of people with moderate and severe intellectual disabilities and up to 50 per cent of people with mild intellectual disabilities (Stromme and Hagberg 2000). Modern diagnostic tests are also revealing errors in past diagnoses. It is, thus, appropriate to review the question of aetiology throughout life.

Early detection of disability

It is valuable to provide explanations for differences in development and behaviour to parents, and to assist children who are finding life difficult. Early intervention will also be available to assist children who have impairments that are remediable, such as deafness, and for the prevention of secondary manifestations.

Identifying the expected pathway for the person's ability pattern

Most developmental disorders are the result of a static encephalopathy – that is, the level of disability remains constant throughout life. A small proportion of developmental disorders involve ongoing neurological damage, such as San

Filippo disease.[7] Most of these degenerative disorders are hereditary and carry a recurrence risk of 25–50 per cent. For a small proportion, remedial treatments are available. For other conditions, such as Rett syndrome,[8] the rate of development may be normal early on but then slow. Other people with intellectual disabilities may deteriorate in later life due to conditions such as depression and worsening vision and/or hearing. It is good practice to consider expected development across the life course.

Maintenance of physical and mental health

Recent improvements in population life expectancy are due largely to lifestyle factors, such as diet (principally the avoidance of obesity), exercise, avoidance of drugs such as tobacco and alcohol, and having rich social networks. These measures are equally important, and harder to implement, for people with disabilities.

Management of associated conditions

Intellectual disabilities are usually the result of factors that may also affect other neurological functions and other organs. The manifestations of these include other neurological disorders such as cerebral palsy, autism and epilepsy; vision and hearing impairments; and other congenital malformations, such as cardiac, gastrointestinal and renal malformations (see Table 16.1). These conditions, and the wide range of complications that result from them, cause people with intellectual disabilities to have more health problems than the general population (Beange, McElduff and Baker 1995).

All these conditions may occur in the non-disabled population. What makes them different in people with intellectual disabilities is their increased likelihood, the nature of the intellectual disability and the way they are perceived. Management is based on the same principles as in the general population.

Understanding the person's basic ability pattern

Every person's ability pattern is different. Appreciating a person's ability profile is the key to understanding the person and making him or her feel comfortable. Nowhere is that more important than when the ability profile differs markedly from that considered normal in the community – that is, when the person has a disability. This is even more important when the differences in basic ability are not recognised, as is often the case with autism-spectrum disorders. Recognition of the underlying ability pattern will lead to greater understanding and more effective management.

Table 16.1 Associated medical conditions

System	Illnesses	Clinical issues	Comments
Central nervous system	Cerebral palsies	Cerebral palsies are a diverse group of disorders, present from childhood, which are characterised by limitations of movement and posture. Complications include deformities, dislocations, swallowing difficulties (dysphagia), gastro-oesophageal reflux	All are commonly associated with intellectual disability. The cerebral palsies are, by definition, due to a past brain injury, and hence any deterioration should raise the suspicion of ongoing or additional pathology
	Autism	Autism-spectrum disorders are the clinical manifestation of difficulties in how people relate to other people and how they see the world around them (Hill and Frith 2003). Unusual and aggressive behaviours are common. The latter may appear to be unprovoked	Autism and intellectual disability frequently coexist (Charman 2002). Autism should be considered in any person with an intellectual disability who has difficult or unusual behaviour. Autism is present from early childhood, and so the key to diagnosis lies in the early history
	Dementia	Deterioration in behaviour and/or skills, apathy, forgetfulness	Usually age-related. Likely to occur at younger age in people with Down syndrome and people with degenerative disorders such as San Filippo syndrome. May also be precipitated by non-neurological illness, e.g. urinary infection

	Vision and hearing impairments	Likely to be silent in their presentation. Should be considered in any person with behavioural problems, apathy or loss of skills	Vision and hearing should be tested regularly
	Epilepsy	Clinical features include generalised tonic<196>clonic seizures, clonic spasms, loss of postural tone, transient alterations of consciousness. Any seizure that is prolonged or unusual for the particular individual warrants medical attention and close observation	Recent advances in epilepsy include improved classification of seizure types, understanding of epilepsy syndromes (i.e. pattern of seizures throughout life) and seizure management. Epilepsy is a serious condition. Status epilepticus (i.e. seizure activity without intervening recovery and lasting more than 30 minutes) is a medical emergency and requires hospitalisation
Respiratory	Upper respiratory tract infection	High temperature, cough, runny nose, conjunctivitis	These are common and almost always of no great significance. It is important to differentiate them from potentially serious lower respiratory infections and infections elsewhere in the body
	Pneumonia	Increased breathing rate and effort, cyanosis (often manifested as duskiness around the lips)	Always serious. Usually diagnosed with a chest X-ray

Continued on next page

Table 16.1 continued

System	Illnesses	Clinical issues	Comments
	Obstructive sleep apnoea	Snoring, restless sleep, daytime drowsiness	Usually associated with obesity or nasopharyngeal incoordination (as in cerebral palsy). Potentially serious, but usually treated easily once diagnosed
Cardiovascular	Congenital heart disease	Cyanosis, shortness of breath, reduced exercise tolerance. May be present without any symptoms	Should be detected in infancy, but may be missed. Important, even if asymptomatic
	Ischaemic heart disease	Chest pain, shortness of breath, irregular heartbeat	As in the general population, warrants consideration of aggressive management, including coronary angiography and coronary artery surgery
	Hypertension	Usually symptom-free	Important as a risk factor in ischaemic heart disease and stroke
Gastrointestinal	Gastro-oesophageal reflux	Pain, regurgitation, anorexia, vomiting blood (which may have the appearance of coffee grounds), anaemia, aspiration pneumonia	Very common, particularly in the cerebral palsies. Symptoms may be non-specific
	Gastritis	Anorexia, weight loss, pain, bleeding	Very common. May be relatively symptom-free
	Constipation	Faecal soiling, anorexia, vague discomfort	May be an indicator of more severe disease, e.g. bowel cancer

Renal	Urinary tract infection	Fever, urinary frequency, non-specific ill-health	
Musculoskeletal	Spinal and other joint deformities	Deformities. In scoliosis, there may be progressive respiratory insufficiency, leading to early death	Often associated with cerebral palsy
	Fractures	Pain, swelling, immobility	May be non-specific in presentation, particularly in a person who is non-verbal and non-ambulant
Psychiatric	Depression and other mood disorders	Apathy, weight loss, behaviour disturbance, poor sleep	Treatment dependent on accurate diagnosis
	Schizophrenia	Hallucinations, delusions, behaviour disturbance	Most cases begin in adolescence or adult life, which differentiates them from autism, which presents before age 3 years
	Anxiety disorders	Behaviour disturbance, aggression, apathy	

Continued on next page

Table 16.1 continued

System	Illnesses	Clinical issues	Comments
Nutritional disorders	Obesity	Obesity*	The most common nutritional disorder. The only effective treatments are intake reduction and exercise
	Undernutrition	Underweight for length (BMI less than 18.5*)	Most commonly associated with cerebral palsy
Endocrine	Thyroid disorders	Usually underfunction. Lethargy, behaviour disturbance	Increased risk in Down syndrome
	Sex-hormone deficiencies	Usually silent. Males may have hypogonadism. Osteopenia	Detection often relies on high index of suspicion
	Diabetes	Weight loss, excessive fluid intake and urine output. Skin infection	No more common than in the general population, but common there
Haematological	Anaemia	Apathy, tiredness, shortness of breath	Causes should always be investigated
	Leukaemias	Bruising, bleeding, weight loss, infections	Particularly associated with Down syndrome

* Usually measured by body mass index (BMI): (weight in kilograms) / (height in metres). Obesity is defined as BMI greater than 30.

Use of medication

Modern pharmacology has developed a wide range of psychotropic medications that have improved the quality of lives of people with mental illness. Classes of psychotropic drugs include antidepressants, sedatives, tranquillisers, psycho-stimulants and mood stabilisers. All have a role in the management of people with intellectual disabilities who have associated conditions, such as depression, anxiety disorders and attention-deficit disorders. Problems arise when such medications are used symptomatically to control difficult behaviour, for which there may be many causes, and when used over long periods of time without adequate review. The prolonged use of major tranquillisers (e.g. haloperidol, pericyazine, risperidone, olanzapine) is of particular concern, as the dose tends to increase over time and these drugs have serious, and sometimes permanent, side effects.

Barriers to quality healthcare

Issues related to the legacy of segregation

Until the 1970s, most services tended to be provided from within large segregated centres. As a result, most healthcare providers had little or no exposure to people with disabilities during their training and little stimulus to question the prevailing attitudes. It is hardly surprising, then, that disability was regarded as a burden to society. Aggressive treatment was something seldom considered.

Medicine has made big progress over the past two decades. Advances in genetics have resulted in much greater understanding of the mechanisms of disease and its treatment. Advances in diagnostic imaging have led to improvements in the ability to detect and treat disease. Improved surgical techniques, including the ability to operate using endoscopes and improvements in postoperative care, have led to greater opportunities for intervention. Advances in pharmacology, including psychopharmacology, have led to the availability of more and safer drugs for the alleviation and cure of illness. These advances have been fuelled by environments in which scientific endeavour is encouraged and concepts such as quality control and critical thinking have some currency. For people with intellectual disabilities, the important issue is that all of this is accessible.

Increasing specialisation within medicine

Medicine is becoming increasing specialised. For people with intellectual disabilities, this presents many challenges. One person may benefit from periodic input from a wide range of healthcare providers. For example, a person with severe cerebral palsy may benefit from input from a general practitioner, neurologist, orthopaedic surgeon, physiotherapist, dietician, gastroenterologist, respiratory physician, speech pathologist, occupational therapist and orthotist.

Intellectual disability medicine is emerging as its own specialty, but it tends to be uncertain of its role and basic principles. There are very few practitioners in the field, particularly in adult medicine.

Changes within healthcare delivery systems

Worldwide, societies are becoming increasingly concerned with managerial efficiency. Public hospitals, because they are the most expensive component of healthcare, have been the major target. Public hospitals have traditionally been the major centres for training and research and for equality in healthcare provision. With the application of managerial principles, the emphasis has shifted more to inpatient throughput, away from the other aspects such as training and outpatient services, to the relative detriment of people with long-term illnesses and disabilities. In particular, the multidisciplinary services for these groups, such as adult cerebral clinics, adult intellectual disability aetiological investigation clinics, and clinics for specific diagnostic groups (e.g. women with Rett syndrome and people with Down syndrome), have not emerged.

In general practice, funding regulations that encourage short appointments do not suit people with disabilities who require more time. In Australia, new Medicare items for case conferences, management plans and extended healthcare services have been created to meet this need.

Government departments tend to disclaim responsibility for this field. Those responsible for mainstream healthcare tend to say that the responsibility lies with disability services departments, while disability services departments tend to say this is a mainstream health responsibility.

Changes in the demographics of intellectual disability

Until relatively recently, survival beyond childhood was the exception in intellectual disability (Evans, Evans and Alberman 1990). As a result, services were created for children but no plans were made for them as adults. Training in intellectual disability was provided as part of paediatrics but not adult medicine. Now, the majority of people with intellectual disabilities are adults. Services, particularly those administratively distant from disability services, such as public hospitals and professional associations, have been slow to adjust. Training in intellectual disability medicine previously was limited to departments of paediatrics.

More recently, specialised units within departments of general practice have been created within some universities.[9]

Reduced expectations of people with intellectual disability

It seems to be human nature for people to expect what has been provided in the past, rather than what might be. Hence, the demands of people with intellectual disabilities and their carers tend to lack the ambition that sometimes makes the difference between ordinary and excellent in quality of healthcare. In this context, 'ordinary' means long waiting times, lack of urgency in investigation, delays in hospitalisation and delays in referring to specialists.

Communication barriers to adequate healthcare management

People with intellectual disabilities frequently have communication impairments that limit their ability to express their concerns. They may be unaware of significant aspects of their past history and unable to comprehend healthcare instructions. Attendants may be unaware of important details in the person's health history, and systems may or may not be in place to ensure that the recommendations of doctors and other healthcare providers are carried out. In the absence of an articulate concerned patient, doctors frequently rely on and are influenced by the approach of an informed and assertive advocate. For children, this is usually a parent. For adults, the role is equally important, although there are issues related to privacy, autonomy and the availability of a suitable person.

Poverty

Poverty is known to be a significant factor in health outcomes (Ross *et al.* 2005). Most people with intellectual disabilities are dependent on social security and have little disposable income.

Lifestyle issues likely to influence health outcomes

Lifestyle factors known to affect health outcomes include smoking, exercise level, family and social networks, and nutrition. People with intellectual disabilities, particularly those who have been institutionalised, are at risk in all these areas. Public health and health promotion messages generally are not modified to suit the disabled population.

What to expect from an equitable healthcare system for people with intellectual disabilities

The starting point

A good starting point is the level of care and urgency that is available to non-disabled people in the community. In medicine, certain symptoms (e.g. chest pain, shortness of breath) and events (e.g. status epilepticus) are regarded as medical emergencies. Others suggest certain courses of action, for example iron-deficiency anaemia in an adult suggests blood loss, which is likely to be of gastrointestinal origin, possibly a malignancy, and indicates a need for endoscopy. These clinical rules apply equally to people with intellectual disabilities.

Prevention and health promotion

Prevention and health-promotion activities should be equally available to people with intellectual disabilities. These need to be informed by known hazards, such as the increased risk of hepatitis B among former institutional residents, and the reduced opportunities for exercise and recreation available to people with disabilities.

Making allowances for disability

There are some modifications to usual practice that healthcare providers need to make. Where reduced communication is a factor, a tendency to overinvestigate, particularly with simple investigations such as blood tests and X-rays, is prudent. For similar reasons, observation in hospital rather than at home may be indicated.

Regular health reviews

Because intellectual disabilities are frequently associated with additional health problems, some authors (e.g. Lennox, Diggins and Ugoni 1997) advocate the use of checklists to improve the thoroughness of routine medical reviews.

Involvement of healthcare specialists

There is frequently a need for individual specialist and specialised multidisciplinary team input. There should be a readiness to utilise referral pathways where they exist and create and/or advocate for them if they do not. Conditions such as poorly controlled epilepsy, recurrent chest infections, recurrent severe behaviour disturbance and declining wellbeing require energetic exploration.

Reviews of aetiology

Intellectual disabilities are the result of central nervous system pathology. Because of the rapidly advancing nature of this field and the possibility of degenerative disorders, issues of aetiology and deterioration due to ongoing neurological disease should always be kept in mind.

Hospital care

Once in hospital, people with intellectual disabilities should be treated with the same energy and intensity as other inpatients. This will include use of diagnostic imaging techniques and admission to intensive care units.

Keeping up to date with current legal and philosophical approaches

Several years ago it might have been acceptable to regard disability as a burden and to assume that being kind and not treating too aggressively was appropriate. This is not appropriate now. Healthcare providers should be aware that concern for individual wellbeing, dignity and autonomy are basic principles that underpin all care. They should be aware of modern disability legislation and be sympathetic to the aims of professionals working in the disability field. People with disabilities, their families and their carers can expect concern for the dignity and worth of the individual, marked by a caring and energetic approach.

Some clinical scenarios

Case study 16.1

Rebecca was born in 1960. Her parents became concerned about her from the age of two years because her language did not seem to be progressing. Initially they were reassured, but they sought further assessment six months later, when her development seemed to deteriorate. By this time, Rebecca seemed to be doing less with her hands and had lost the few words of speech that she had previously attained. She was admitted to the regional children's hospital for investigation. The paediatric neurologist told Rebecca's parents that she was most likely to have a degenerative disorder and that further deterioration and early death were likely. Extensive investigations failed to find any specific condition at this time. Rebecca was sent home with the nature and cause of her underlying condition being uncertain. Her mother continued to care for her at home, and her developmental progress remained minimal. By six years of age, she was unable to walk or talk and was dependent on others for self-care. She spent her school years in a day training centre.

In adult life, Rebecca moved into a community residential unit and attended an adult training centre.

Throughout her life, her parents harboured strong feelings of guilt and anxiety related to the uncertain nature of her disability. These were relieved when Rebecca was 30 years old and her neurologist made a diagnosis of Rett syndrome. This diagnosis was confirmed ten years later when the *MECP2* gene test was positive. Her mother described this as lifting an enormous burden.

Comment: Rett syndrome was first described in 1966 and has been diagnosed regularly only since the mid-1980s. There are likely to be a number of women with unrecognised Rett syndrome who were admitted to residential care before 1990.

Case study 16.2

Steven was born in rural Australia and grew up on the family farm. His early development was slow, but he started school at the local regular primary school. After three years, it was apparent that he was making little progress and an assessment confirmed a moderately severe intellectual disability. Investigations failed to find a cause. He continued at the local school before leaving, at the age of 12 years, and working on the family property. He was cared for by his family until his parents became quite frail. In his mid-thirties, he moved into a large residential training centre. Steven spent many hours wandering around the grounds and the local town. He enjoyed following the local football team. His family maintained regular contact and arranged for Steven along with three friends to move into a community residential unit, of which Steven became a part owner. The house had large grounds to accommodate Steven's liking for open spaces. Steven worked for a sheltered employment service until retirement at the age of 65 years.

At the age of 55 years, Steven had a bout of severe chest pain and shortness of breath. He was admitted to hospital, where he was discovered to have had a heart attack. He made a reasonable recovery, but he continued to suffer from periodic angina (ischaemic heart pain) until his death at the age of 66 years.

Comment: There are many good things about Steven's care. His early life reflected the approach at that time. Later, even before he left the institution, Steven had a reasonably good quality of life, was respected and continued to have good contact with his family, which resulted in some positive outcomes for him. It was a pity that his ischaemic heart disease was not managed a little more aggressively, perhaps by exploring the options of coronary artery surgery.

Case study 16.3

Jeremy was born in 1975, at term and after a normal pregnancy and delivery. By the end of his first year of life, it was clear that he had severe disabilities. There had been minimal motor development – he was unable to sit, crawl or walk – and he had no speech. He was also difficult to feed, regurgitated during or after most feeds and failed to thrive. By five years of age, Jeremy was an alert happy boy with no speech. He had spasticity affecting all four limbs and was dependent on others for mobility and self-care. A brain scan indicated cerebral atrophy of unknown cause. The diagnosis was cerebral palsy. Over the next seven years, Jeremy developed multiple joint deformities, dislocated hips and severe scoliosis (spinal deformity). Growth remained poor; at the age of 15 years, he weighed only 21 kilograms. He continued to vomit occasionally and had several admissions to hospital with aspiration pneumonia. Jeremy's family found him increasingly difficult to care for at home, and he moved into a community residential unit when he was 17 years old. Over the next seven years, his deformities increased, he continued to have periodic chest infections and he remained undernourished. At 24 years of age, he developed severe pneumonia, was admitted to hospital and died in spite of intravenous antibiotic treatment.

Comment: Jeremy was severely disabled and physically very frail. In spite of this, things could have been much better. His care, particularly in his later years, lacked the benefits that might have flowed from the involvement of a specialist multidisciplinary unit. Under the care of such a unit, surgical treatment of his spinal deformity, evaluation and minimisation of his aspiration risk, and measures to improve his nutrition, would have been considered.

Case study 16.4

Peter was born in 1942. He was the first child of professional parents who lived and worked in Melbourne, Australia. From infancy, he seemed different from other children. He cried a great deal and never liked being cuddled. He achieved his early motor milestones at the normal ages and seemed very good at doing things with his hands, but he did not speak until he was three years old and he preferred his own company. He was frequently quite distressed for no apparent reason and would lash out at anyone or anything within reach at these times. He used to meticulously line up his toy cars and had a fascination for insects. He seemed very bright and could remember places he had visited several years previously. Peter was not allowed to attend kindergarten or school, but he did attend a day training centre for a short time. He was eventually labelled 'mentally retarded with emotional disturbance, cause unknown'. No explanation was ever provided for his behavioural difficulties, but his parents had supportive psychotherapy for several years. Peter became increasingly difficult to manage at home. As he became bigger, his outbursts became harder to control. He would frequently hit himself and his mother and damage the house and furniture.

At 15 years of age, Peter was admitted to a large training centre, where he remained very challenging. He saw many professionals over the years and was at times labelled psychotic. He was treated with a number of major tranquillisers, most of which seemed beneficial in the short term, but he remained very challenging. He seemed best when left alone and would often wander around the grounds, apparently talking to himself. He would periodically hit out at other residents and staff. He refused to share the meal table with others. He did attend a sheltered workshop part time, and he enjoyed outings with other members of his unit. His parents visited about six times each year and took him home for a few hours each Christmas. Peter died suddenly at the age of 61 years. Several staff and fellow residents attended the funeral.

Comment: Peter's history is typical of autism. He was born before very much was known about this disorder, but the diagnosis should have been made during his time in residential care. Such a diagnosis would have provided his parents with an explanation for his unusual behaviour and ability profile and would have provided staff with management strategies informed by the vast body of autism expertise that has become available over the past two to three decades.

Summary

People with intellectual disabilities have complex and multiple associated health problems and limited access to quality services. Medical services for people with intellectual disabilities are no longer provided in-house by staff employed by disability services. The legacies of history, however, have left mainstream health services unprepared to meet the challenge of intellectual disability healthcare and left the disability service system with a degree of ignorance and distrust of what to expect from people with intellectual disabilities.

People with disabilities should expect the same levels of care that are the markers of quality for everyone else in the community. The principles of disability medicine include attention to early recognition, aetiology, management of associated conditions, and facilitation of access to multidisciplinary care. People with disabilities can expect to be treated with respect and investigated and treated with a high degree of thoroughness and energy.

References

Beange, H., McElduff, A. and Baker W. (1995) 'Medical disorders of adults with mental retardation: a population study.' *American Journal on Mental Retardation 99*, 595–604.

Charman, T. (2002) 'The prevalence of autism spectrum disorders: recent evidence and future challenges.' *European Child and Adolescent Psychiatry 11*, 249–56.

Evans, P.M., Evans S.J. and Alberman E. (1990) 'Cerebral palsy: why we must plan for survival.' *Archives of Disease in Childhood 65*, 1329–33.

Hill, E.L. and Frith, V. (2003) 'Understanding autism: insights from mind and brain.' *Philosophical Transactions of the Royal Society of London. Series B Biological Sciences 358*, 281–9.

Mackay, R.I. (1982) 'The causes of severe mental handicap.' *Developmental Medicine and Child Neurology 24*, 386–93.

O'Brien, G. and Yule, W. (1995) *Behavioural Phenotypes*. London: Mac Keith Press.

Ross, N.A., Dorling, D., Dunn, J.R., Hendricksson, G., *et al.* (2005) 'Metropolitan income inequality and working-age mortality: a cross-sectional analysis using data from five countries.' *Journal of Urban Health 82*, 101–10.

Stromme, P. and Hagberg, G. (2000) 'Aetiology in severe and mild mental retardation: a population-based study of Norwegian children.' *Developmental Medicine and Child Neurology 42*, 76–86.

17

Supporting children and their families

Susana Gavidia-Payne

Case management is an essential element of service delivery for children with disabilities[10] and their families, playing a critical role in providing supports to ensure their optimal functioning and participation in the community. Case management for this group has been characterised by inconsistent practice across different service systems and jurisdictions. Explanations of such variability are possibly rooted in sociocultural, organisational and conceptual issues. The latter, in particular, may be related to definitional concerns of case management itself, which has been part of the language commonly used in the intellectual disability field for a long time but may not be a very child- or family-friendly term (Neill 1997). Instead, in the child and family fields, and included in several pieces of legislation in different countries, terms such as 'service coordination'[11] and 'service integration' have been accepted more favourably (Bruder 2005). These terms have come to mean different things to different people, and case management with children with disabilities has become associated with a diversity of understandings and practices.

Practitioners and researchers alike have been largely preoccupied with the development of case management practices that address specific periods of the lifespan of individuals with intellectual disabilities when they have already entered the disability service system. Being part of 'the system', however, may not necessarily be the case for many children with disabilities, especially in the early years, when a definite disability diagnosis (required for formal entry into the service system) may not be available. Families of these children may be awaiting diagnosis and a corresponding service response that matches their initial developmental concern. Therefore, from the outset, families' first concerns about their children, most likely their children's development and 'where to go', may not receive a clearly articulated service response, least of all a case management response.

In discussing case management with children with disabilities, it is also evident that an overemphasis on its service and administrative functions, similar to the numerous versions for adolescents and adults with intellectual disabilities, has taken place. At best, these procedural types of service response generally focus on planning to meet individual needs. This process, however, is often compromised and implemented on a reactive basis, such as emergency respite care, restrictive behavioural supports and out-of-home placement. Although the idea of individualised and planned support fits well with contemporary practice, it begs a series of conceptual and practical questions, including what supporting children and their families really means in terms of individualised planning support. How, when and by whom are case management responses formulated? How do practitioners address the needs of children and their families in planning supports? What is the time span of these supports when considering the ever-changing nature of child and family situations, especially in the early years? What is the role of families in the process of case management? Answers to these questions have been debated; however, they have not translated into appropriate policy–practice transition, which is a major gap in the service system (Rosenau 2002).

Furthermore, it has been argued that the aims of case management in the childhood years have not been formulated coherently and have generated service outcomes that have been often unrealistic and problematic (Dunst and Bruder 2002). Case management lacks an identity in the childhood sector, and its practice may have ignored essential childhood-related issues that characterise all children and their families, regardless of the presence of a disability. Elements of a service system espoused for early childhood intervention for young children with disabilities have been explicated. Their consistent and successful application, however, continues to elude even the most dedicated of practitioners.

This chapter aims to answer some of these questions and dilemmas at three levels. First, current trends in the study of the trajectories that typify children with disabilities and their families during the childhood years are presented. Next, the values, principles and characteristics of effective case management practices in terms of service design and service delivery for children with disabilities are discussed. Lastly, current concerns and challenges in the practice of case management with this population are presented.

Theoretical basis: contexts of development

One of the tensions evident in the discussion about services for children with disabilities relates to a focus on 'development' and assumptions made about its meaning. Contemporary definitions of development in children (with and without disabilities) no longer focus on the achievement of progressive milestones as a core principle alone. This has been questioned in terms of its universality for all children (Bronfenbrenner *et al.* 1986). Hodapp, Burack and Zigler (1990), however, contend that adopting a developmental perspective, albeit an expanded version, is a useful way of conceptualising our work with people with disabilities. A revised view of development will acknowledge the importance of both the universality and the variability of the transactions between the child and his or her environment and change throughout the lifespan in a variety of contexts (Thurman 1997). It further suggests that child development trajectories are complex and that environmental and biological factors interact in a multiplicity of ways to yield a range of child and family outcomes, some of which are related to developmental milestones throughout the lifespan (National Research Council and Institute of Medicine 2000).

A focus on the contexts of development for children with disabilities and their families helps move beyond the traditional view of child development at a number of levels. First, the more distant 'policy' level that acknowledges the impact of governments' principles and visions on the lives of children with disabilities and their families is considered. An elegant example of the way this process occurs is found in a publication by the Roeher Institute (2000), as part of the Canadian National Children's Agenda. The focus of these policies is on the adoption of inclusive values and rights that ensure healthy child development, family support, economic security and fostering of inclusive communities. The various layers of influence on child development are clearly outlined and linked to other broader social policy initiatives and practices.

Second, the implementation and dissemination of practices that reflect the ideals and values underpinning policies and service delivery models is another context for consideration. This is an area where much more work remains to be done, as policies and service delivery models do not appear to be implemented effectively (Harbin *et al.* 2004). In their study of stress factors in families of children with an intellectual disability in Sweden, Olsson and Hwang (2003) found that despite the Swedish system's widespread disability policies and service systems in place, families still reported considerable difficulties in finding meaningful support for their children when navigating their way in the system. This study highlights that having services 'in place' may be necessary but not sufficient in addressing the complexity of the issues that some children with disabilities and their families may be facing. It also implies that other factors may be at work, actively acting as barriers and thus preventing the formation of an adequate service system.

Third, a more proximal context relates to the role of families in service provision to their children with disabilities. A reconceptualisation and evolution of service delivery principles now incorporates families in the development and implementation of services and programmes. Most notably, current service delivery models promote a collaborative, family-strengths approach (Werrbach, Jenson and Bubar 2002), with trends towards more family-directed services (Parish, Pomeranz-Essley and Braddock 2003), where families are meaningfully involved and in control of their own lives and resources (Parish *et al.* 2003; Turnbull and Turnbull 2001), including actual service provision. Family-centred practices are a core element of such models and are discussed later in this chapter.

In sum, the adoption of a contextual perspective is a useful theoretical framework in the examination of the various influences and their interrelationships that affect children and families. This suggests that case management, in its broadest sense, will have both a direct and an indirect effect on the lives of children with disabilities and their families, and will include policies, service delivery models and actual practical strategies. In the 'real world', this may mean a shift in the conceptualisation of all those contexts, with a reconsideration of how the main players (children, families, the service system) have been characterised. Ultimately, this will determine successful case management application, as noted in the following discussion.

Children with disabilities and the service system

Historically, children with disabilities have often been characterised in tandem with the service system that is meant to support them. Over time, services for children with disabilities have become to be known and categorised according to children's chronological age, often with their own administrative and legislative requirements. Although there is some variation in terms of the age breakdowns across countries, more commonly two distinctive systems have been recognised. One system has generally operated for children under six years of age, commonly known as 'early childhood intervention'. Children from six years of age to middle childhood, on the other hand, have traditionally been catered for by the universal and/or special education systems.

Services for children with disabilities have evolved a great deal, with contemporary approaches emphasising the social context surrounding the child. This has meant generating service responses that see supports to the child as intimately connected and as part of an individualised set of supports provided to their families and other immediate, natural environments. Also important, however, is the consideration of the child's specific characteristics and how they interface with their families and the service system. Several authors have highlighted the need to take into account the specificity of some of the variables associated with the development of children with disabilities (Burack 1990; Guralnick 1997), including, for example, the aetiology and level of disability and behavioural phenotypes. It has been noted that variations in these individual characteristics are often associated with variations in the environmental and service context surrounding the child (Gavidia-Payne and Hudson 2002). For example, the distinctive patterns of behaviour in children with autism are related to family wellbeing outcomes, such as stress and coping, when compared with children with other disabilities (Minnes 1988). This may, in turn, attract a specific service response that addresses both children's and families' concerns. The important issue is that there is not one straight trajectory but possibly multiple trajectories in framing best service options for children with disabilities. Extrapolation of these findings into the implementation of supports for children and their families means the development of flexible and individual service answers that capture the characteristics of both children and their families and their environment.

Families of children with disabilities and the service system

As stated earlier, from a theoretical perspective, families are fundamental to understanding children's wellbeing. When the discussion turns to families of children with disabilities, however, our knowledge has been largely atheoretical and focused on the disability itself as the major cause for deleterious effects on the family (Stoneman 1989, 2005). Although a considerable amount of important and methodologically sound research has illuminated our understanding of parental wellbeing, more specifically stress and coping (Abbeduto et al. 2004; Beck, Hastings and Daley 2004; Eisenhower, Baker and Blacher 2005; Tomanik, Harris and Hawkins 2004) and parent-related variables (Hastings 2002; Hastings and Brown 2002), this has continued to give a central place to the effects of the child's disability on his or her family. Less explored has been the examination of the relationship between the characteristics of the child and family systems, and variables outside such systems, with a few exceptions

(Hassall, Rose and McDonald 2005; King, King and Rosenbaum 1999). These latter studies have generally been framed around the notion of risk and resilience factors, demonstrating how the combination of powerful protective factors, such as social supports, can act as a buffer against the impact of risk factors, such as depression (Simeonsson 1994). These findings move away from the linear notion of single child or family factors affecting family wellbeing to encompass an array of service-related variables.

Adopting a family systems view moves the emphasis away from the child and the disability itself to other aspects of family life and interaction as the focus of support. In this regard, the family support movement has been instrumental in articulating the need for functional supports focused on families rather than their individual children (Bradley 1992). Turnbull and Turnbull (2000) defined family support as the entire range of government and non-government supports and services that assist families to obtain the types of life they want and need. Implicit in this and other definitions is the belief that for families of children with disabilities, these supports may be not only formal but also of an informal and community-oriented nature. This has required a paradigm shift in family support, from social welfare towards the establishment of community-based programmes, thus presenting a formidable challenge to the service system at both the conceptual and the practice level.

Despite the efforts of family support advocates, a significant gap still exists between the rhetoric and the actual practice. Several studies report that many families find the family support service system unhelpful (Brown *et al.* 2003; Harbin *et al.* 2004) and at times counterproductive to the promotion of optimal child and family outcomes. In a Canadian qualitative study, Brown *et al.* (2003) found that lack of guidance in the provision of information, and the inappropriateness and short-term nature of the support from service providers, affected the services they received. The authors concluded, however, that service responsiveness to the ever-changing nature of some families' concerns is multifaceted and may be interacting with other variables, such as families' capacity to access services in the first place.

The association between the complexity of family life and corresponding family support responses is illustrated succinctly in a longitudinal study conducted by Aniol *et al.* (2004). The authors examined the impact of residential respite care services (mean length of stay 8.78 days) on child abuse potential and family relations in a sample of parents whose children were admitted to a centre for developmental disability in the USA. Findings indicated that there was a clear and strong relationship between child abuse potential, family relations and parenting stress at three time points, but the availability of respite care did not have an ameliorating effect on child abuse potential and family relations. These findings suggest that, for some families, the limitations of certain supports, such as residential respite care, may prevail in light of more powerful family factors, including the uneven balance of risk and protective factors influencing child and family functioning. Similarly, the importance of family factors in planning for supports was demonstrated further in a study by Rimmerman and Duvdevani (1996) in Israel. The authors found that out-of-home applications by parents of children and adolescents with intellectual disabilities were predicted by high parental stress and less social (formal and informal) support available.

In summary, the above studies draw our attention to the limited adequacy of the provision of certain family support strategies, which, in light of other, more powerful considerations within and around families, may not address their needs effectively. This leads to the conclusion that if case management is to be conceptualised under the umbrella of a family support agenda, then it seems imperative to consider the variability of family life and how intra-family and individual factors work in different ways to influence families' responses to the service system, including the family support system. It is this very point that would be helpful for the service system to embrace; that is, not only the individualities of families but also how they interface with the service system need to be considered. This intersection will ultimately determine the degree of effectiveness of service responses along a continuum of support.

Case management practices with children and families

The immersion of case management practices in a broader policy context espousing family support principles is supported by the evidence provided by contemporary studies and practices that acknowledge children in the context of their families and other immediate environments. Also recognised is the uniqueness of and, hence, variability in the lives of children and families and the influence of risk and protective factors. In this way, most children and families require support at one time or another, according to the extent and strength of the associations between those various child, family and other environmental factors. Of most importance is the acknowledgement that case management responses are likely to be required when children are very young, when family concerns are first expressed, and when a formal diagnosis regarding the presence of disability is not yet made (Dworkin 2000). As subsequent service responses are triggered in the short and long term, the consideration of family support principles will be critical in ensuring the effective delivery of assistance to families and their children on an ongoing basis.

Dunst and Trivette (1994) articulated a model of case management that encapsulates the notions earlier discussed. The authors define case management as 'the use of a number of functions for mobilizing resources to meet client needs' (Dunst and Trivette 1994, p.189). They argue that the case management process 'in practice' will be ultimately successful to the extent that there is a match and strict link between what children and families need and the resources to be provided. Within the variety of case management approaches, the one characterised by an emphasis on promoting child and family capabilities as a way of improving their capacity to negotiate the service system appears most promising (Dunst *et al.* 1993). This approach coherently specifies the relationship between case manager functions (e.g. coordinator), procedural goals (e.g. identification and mobilisation of resources) and client outcomes (e.g. promoting client capacity), with an emphasis on the latter. In a series of case studies, Dunst *et al.* (1993) demonstrated that family case managers' transactions characterised by family-support principles were associated with positive family outcomes in terms of greater self-efficacy and control of their own resources.

Much of the work by Dunst and colleagues has provided the basis for the development and refinement of case management practices with children with disabilities and their families (Dunst and Bruder 2002; Dunst, Trivette and Deal 1988; Dunst *et al.* 1993). Bruder (2005) has further suggested that the ideal case management practice will encompass a combination of both a coordinated service delivery model and responsiveness to the more personal characteristics of those involved, which ultimately will lead to the establishment of partnerships among all parties. The legislation underpinning service delivery for young children with disabilities in the USA illustrates these points by specifying a triad of mechanisms as being at the centre of effective service coordination (Harbin *et al.* 2004). The first element refers to existence of a service coordinator (case manager), who will play several critical roles, namely enabler, planner, resource manager and being ready if crises arise (Dunst *et al.* 1993). The strengths of the service coordinator will include his or her ability to consult and collaborate in addition to the more technical skills required to understand disability- and age-specific issues. Within a family-centred perspective, the case manager will assist families to identify their resources, concerns, priorities and hopes regarding their child with a disability (Stepanek, Newcomb and Kettler 1996). The development of partnerships that service providers need to form with families will ensure optimal decision-making with regard to the planning and monitoring of outcomes, and will be based in mutual trust and positive relationships.

A second mechanism involves the development of individual support plans, which are characterised by agreement among all involved and inclusion of a broad range of outcomes. The case manager and agencies will have a collaborative stand, whereby there is a willingness to work together, a common vision, trust and leadership as opposed to a procedural, administrative end. The third element proposed by Harbin (2005) refers to the implementation of policies that facilitate interagency coordination and collaboration, which often rely on relationship-based approaches within agencies, outside agencies and with families. Agencies need to have staff members who are knowledgeable, informed and competent about existing resources, as children and families present with a diversity of concerns and hopes.

Although difficulties with the implementation of these elements have been identified (Harbin et al. 2004), attempts have been made to develop models that comprise some of these criteria, albeit with children with specific disabilities. One such model is the individualised wrap-around service, originally developed for children with severe emotional and behavioural disabilities, which is grounded firmly in the belief that families need to be provided with 'whatever it takes' to live as happily and typically as possible (Karp 1996). The model entails individualising supports, underpinned by a process that involves the provision of multiple services, including flexible funding and community-based services that are interdisciplinary and coordinated and focus on the strengths of both the child and the family. This is achieved through a mutually agreed plan between the service and the family, which results in a custom-made service in three or more life domains of the child and the family (Karp 1996). On the basis of the evaluation of the model, the emphasis on integrating a mix of services at the family level has been critical in ensuring the success of the programme. Although the wrap-around model focuses on populations of children with obviously complex concerns, it makes a strong case for the ways in which children and families with less complex needs could benefit from some elements of the model.

Effective case management is, therefore, multidimensional: it will entail the clear articulation and operationalisation of multiple competences (e.g. inter-agency collaboration, service provider skills, interdisciplinary team work, family-centred practices, individual planning) and clarity in the outcomes sought with children and families (e.g. quality of life, individual functioning, participation). There is general consensus (Bruder 2005; Dunst and Bruder 2002; Harbin et al. 2004; Summers et al. 2005) that there is a multiplicity of factors, broad and interactive, specific and concrete, that will facilitate the achievement of the ideal case management practice. In striving for this standard, however, barriers that prevent the enactment of these practices need to be discussed.

Challenges contributing to case management practice with children with disabilities and their families

Our current state of knowledge and practice suggests that deliberate efforts have been made to ground case management on a family-strengths-based philosophy, whereby there is a focus on family self-determination and on the essential primary nature of the client–case manager relationship (Werrbach 1996). Some reports, however, still indicate that for children with disabilities, more resources, and different ways of mobilising those resources, are needed in order to meet current demand (Parish *et al.* 2003). This has led several authors to conclude that the implementation of case management/service coordination has not been as effective as originally anticipated. Several factors have contributed to this state of affairs and need to be addressed if progress is to be made. These challenges are summarised below.

Entry into the disability system

Difficulties in links and coordination at the early stages in entering the disability service system are often experienced, especially by young children and their families. Although this has been a perennial problem, there has been very little discussion regarding the most appropriate service responses at the point where families first express a concern and, subsequently, how they find their way around the system. Service responses at this stage are powerful in determining families' access to information and support and how these will affect their future chances for fulfilment and self-determination. Addressing this problem as a system will invariably entail an analysis of the various layers of service provision in both disability and universal childhood systems, which, although challenging, are not impossible to tackle. On the basis of recent research evidence, Harbin (2005) has argued that an integrated and coordinated point of access would be an important approach to consider. It can overcome problems with the multifaceted nature of the service system and facilitate greater responsiveness to families' concerns. A common point of access is unlike many other clinically led, centralised systems flagged in the past. Rather, families are welcomed to a broad array of community resources, a coordinated organisational structure and specific referral paths, and engaged in specific tasks initiated by skilled and competent practitioners.

Identification of the outcomes and process of case management practice

Broad agreement on what case management is expected to provide has not yet been reached in the child disability field. The centrality of children's and families' experiences and concerns, if identified, often get lost among the myriad service delivery variables. This is exacerbated by the existence of a diversity of models of case management, which emphasise some aspects of case management at the expense of others, for example by focusing on the development of individualised plans as a product versus building relationships with families. In delineating the case management process more clearly, attention must be given to how it inter-sects with service responses that eventually contribute to child and family outcomes. Regrettably, the expected outcomes of case management practice have often been confused with the more generic aims of service provision. Fortunately, current research efforts in this direction (see Bruder 2005; Dunst and Bruder 2002) suggest an increasing consensus regarding the valued outcomes (e.g. family quality of life) and processes (e.g. family-centred practices and team work) of service coordination.

Policies

Much has been said about the lack of policies and the inadequacy of existing policies in addressing the specific issues relating to case management for children and families. It has been suggested that although policies regarding service provision have been articulated clearly, those concerning coordination and case management often lack sufficient specificity to guide and be distinctively linked to effective practice. Definition of the roles and responsibilities of the case manager among the various other service providers involved, as well as definition of the broad child and family goals that are important to consider in the development of plans, are just two examples that are in need of further policy development. Harbin et al. (2004) indicate that of most importance, given the developmental nature of service provision for children, is the development and implementation of policies that are based primarily on interagency collaboration (Johnson et al. 2003). Such arrangements will in turn avoid overlap, confusion, and fragmentation. Clearly, as Knitzer (1997) suggests, this kind of work requires strong leadership and a solid infrastructure in order to sustain the various tasks involved in service coordination.

Practitioners' skills, competencies and attitudes

A shift in the competencies required from practitioners has been observed in the discussion of case management practices. No longer can professionals afford to be skilful only in the 'technical' aspects of assessment, intervention and monitoring of plans. As strong research evidence indicates, relationship-building skills and an attitude that conveys an ability to adapt to change are now as critical in meeting children's and families' concerns. Unfortunately, much of both pre-service and in-service training of professionals is problematic and fails to acknowledge the challenges often faced by practitioners, as most of the work required in good case management practice involves a mix of clinical judgement, interactional styles and delivery of concrete support. Conceptualising training as a vital system of support for practitioners is critical in order to reach quality case management practices.

Conclusion

This chapter has appraised existing evidence that attests to the significance of adopting theoretical understandings behind notions such as human development, with associated risk and protective factors, family functioning, and the interplay between all of these and the service system. It has been argued that the identification and definition of, and possibly evolution in, the specific individual characteristics of children with disabilities and their families are essential in providing effective supports. This raises the issue of variability that takes places within and across families, which suggests that case management practices must be fluid, flexible and individualised enough to capture the substantial changes children with disabilities and their families experience from the moment they enter the service system – that is, when a developmental concern is first identified. It follows that some children and their families may require considerable and a great diversity of case management supports, while others will be generally self-sufficient and able to successfully access the required supports and navigate the system accordingly. In some families, the needs of the children will be paramount (e.g. life-threatening conditions) and require immediate support intervention, but in others, the needs of the parents will be overwhelming (e.g. depressive conditions) and need to be prioritised in order to address the child's needs effectively. At other times, the complexity of both the child and the family life may be such that a range of supports for the entire family is required. The recognition of this variability is at the crux of effective case management practices.

Although there is no clear consensus as to what the 'ideal' case management practice is, there is general agreement that the most promising practice incorporates a range of effective features that include the process (i.e. how to do it, when, by whom) and outcomes (i.e. what is to be achieved) with children and families. The case management process will invariably involve a number of elements, including the implementation of family-centred practices, collaboration and coordination across both generic and specialist support agencies, and team work that includes both families and service providers, all under the umbrella of clearly delineated case management policies. In terms of service responses, this translates into a combination of instrumental (e.g. seeking respite care for the family; writing an individual support plan) and less tangible (e.g. establishment of positive relationships with families; adopting a positive stand) service responses that are delivered in a timely fashion. Most importantly, it has been argued that it would be wrong to conceptualise case management practices as those that consider the role of families to be only as that of mere recipient of services. Rather, case management work that acknowledges the strengths of families and characterises them as active problem-solvers and contributors to the process and regulators of their own resources and lives will be most successful.

The outcomes of case management will embrace those children and family goals that will be viewed as complementary and strengthening of each other in the family context. Research suggests that acknowledging and understanding how families' routines and everyday activities accommodate disability within the family provide the ideal medium for identifying family and child goals (Weisner *et al.* 2005). Families' own cultural goals are central to this view and encompass the attainment of sustainable, predictable and integrated routines as a family outcome. This perspective is promising for case management practitioners in terms of providing supports that not only encompass outcomes for the family as a whole within their daily lives but also make sense to each individual family.

It is important to remind ourselves that for as long as differences in individuals and systems coexist, challenges will continue, especially if the status quo of years past persists. Children with disabilities and their families have difficult experiences when faced with the service system that is meant to support them and at a time when it is perhaps most needed. Visions of case conferences, where ten different isolated service providers discuss the life of a child and the family, may be a thing of the past only for some families. They are also a clear reminder that we cannot let go of the knowledge and practical opportunities we currently have to incorporate principles and practices that we know work well with children with disabilities and their families.

References

Abbeduto, L., Seltzer, M.M., Shattuck, P., Krauss, M.W., *et al.* (2004) 'Psychological well-being and coping in mothers of youths with autism, Down syndrome, or fragile X syndrome.' *American Journal on Mental Retardation 109*, 237–54.

Aniol, K., Mullins, L.L., Page, M.C., Boyd, M.L. and Chaney, J.M. (2004) 'The relationship between respite care and child abuse potential in parents of children with developmental disabilities: a preliminary report.' *Journal of Developmental and Physical Disabilities 16*, 273–85.

Beck, A., Hastings, R.P. and Daley, D. (2004) 'Pro-social behavior problems independently predict maternal stress.' *Journal of Intellectual and Developmental Disability 29*, 339–49.

Bradley, V.J. (1992) 'Overview of the Family Support Movement.' In V.J. Bradley, J. Knoll and J.M. Agosta (eds) *Emerging Issues in Family Support.* Washington, DC: American Association on Mental Retardation.

Bronfenbrenner, U., Kessel, F., Kessen, W. and White, S. (1986) 'Toward a critical social history of developmental psychology: a propaedeutic discussion.' *American Psychologist 41*, 1218–30.

Brown, I., Anand, S., Fung, W.L.A., Isaacs, B. and Baum, N. (2003) 'Family quality of life: Canadian results from an international study.' *Journal of Developmental and Physical Disabilities 15*, 207–30.

Bruder, M.B. (2005) 'Service Coordination and Integration in a Developmental Systems Approach to Early Intervention.' In M.J. Guralnick (ed.) *The Developmental Systems Approach to Early Intervention.* Baltimore, MD: Paul H. Brookes.

Burack, J.A. (1990) 'Differentiating Mental Retardation: The Two-Group Approach and Beyond.' In R.M. Hodapp, J.A. Burack and E. Zigler (eds) *Issues in the Developmental Approach to Mental Retardation.* Cambridge: Cambridge University Press.

Dunst, C.J. and Bruder, M.B. (2002) 'Valued outcomes of service coordination, early intervention, and natural environments.' *Exceptional Children 68*, 361–75.

Dunst, C.J. and Trivette, C.M. (1994) 'Empowering Case Management Practices: A Family-Centered Perspective.' In C.J. Dunst, C.M. Trivette and A.G. Deal (eds) *Supporting and Strengthening Families: Methods, Strategies and Practices*, Vol. 1. Cambridge, MA: Brookline Books.

Dunst, C.J., Trivette, C.M. and Deal, A.G. (1988) *Enabling and Empowering Families: Principles and Guidelines for Practice.* Cambridge, MA: Brookline Books.

Dunst, C.J., Trivette, C.M., Gordon, N.J. and Starnes, A.L. (1993) 'Family-Centered Case Management Practices: Characteristics and Consequences.' In G.H.S. Singer and L.L. Powers (eds) *Families, Disability, and Empowerment: Active Coping Skills and Strategies for Family Interventions.* Baltimore, MD: Paul H. Brookes.

Dworkin, P.H. (2000) 'Preventive Health Care and Anticipatory Guidance.' In J.P. Shonkoff and S.J. Meisel (eds) *Handbook of Early Childhood Intervention*, 2nd edn. Cambridge: Cambridge University Press.

Eisenhower, A.S., Baker, B.L. and Blacher, J. (2005) 'Preschool children with intellectual disability: syndrome specificity, behaviour problems, and maternal well-being.' *Journal of Intellectual Disability Research 49*, 657–71.

Gavidia-Payne, S. and Hudson, A. (2002) 'Behavioural supports for parents of children with an intellectual disability and problem behaviours: an overview of the literature.' *Journal of Intellectual and Developmental Disability 27*, 31–55.

Guralnick, M.J. (1997) 'Second-Generation Research in the Field of Early Intervention.' In M.J. Guralnick (ed.) *The Effectiveness of Early Intervention.* Baltimore, MD: Paul H. Brookes.

Harbin, G. (2005) 'Designing an Integrated Point of Access in the Early Intervention System.' In M.J. Guralnick (ed.) *The Developmental Systems Approach to Early Intervention.* Baltimore, MD: Paul H. Brookes.

Harbin, G.L., Bruder, M.B., Adams, C., Mazzarella, C., *et al.* (2004) 'Early intervention service coordination policies: national policy infrastructure.' *Topics in Early Childhood Special Education 24,* 89–97.

Hassall, R., Rose, J. and McDonald, J. (2005) 'Parenting stress in mothers of children with an intellectual disability: the effects of parental cognitions in relation to child characteristics and family support.' *Journal of Intellectual Disability Research 49,* 405–18.

Hastings, R.P. (2002) 'Parental stress and behaviour problems of children with developmental disabilities.' *Journal of Intellectual and Developmental Disability 27,* 149–60.

Hastings, R.P. and Brown, T. (2002) 'Behavior problems of children with autism, parental self-efficacy, and mental health.' *American Journal on Mental Retardation 107,* 222–32.

Hodapp, R.M., Burack, J.A. and Zigler, E. (1990) 'The Developmental Perspective in the Field of Mental Retardation.' In R.M. Hodapp, J.A. Burack and E. Zigler (eds) *Issues in the Developmental Approach to Mental Retardation.* Cambridge: Cambridge University Press.

Johnson, L.J., Zorn, D., Yung Tam, B.K., Lamontagne, M. and Johnson, S.A. (2003) 'Stakeholders' views of factors that impact successful interagency collaboration.' *Exceptional Children 69,* 195–209.

Karp, N. (1996) 'Individualized Wrap-Around Services for Children with Emotional, Behavior, and Mental Disorders.' In G.H.S. Singer, L.E. Powers and A.L. Olson (eds) *Redefining Family Support: Innovations in Public–Private Partnerships.* Baltimore, MD: Paul H. Brookes.

King, G., King, S. and Rosenbaum, P. (1999) 'Family-centered caregiving and well-being of parents of children with disabilities: linking process with outcome.' *Journal of Pediatric Psychology 24,* 41–53.

Knitzer, J. (1997) 'Service Integration for Children and Families: Lessons and Questions.' In R.J. Illback, C.I. Cobb and H.M. Joseph, Jr (eds) *Integrated Services for Children and Families: Opportunities for Psychological Practice.* Washington, DC: American Psychological Association.

Minnes, P.M. (1988) 'Family stress associated with a developmentally handicapped child.' *International Review of Research in Mental Retardation 15,* 195–226.

National Research Council and Institute of Medicine (2000) *From Neurons to Neighborhoods: The Science of Early Child Development.* Washington, DC: National Academy Press.

Neill, T.K. (1997) 'Integrating Services for Children with Severe Emotional Disabilities through Coordination.' In R.J. Illback, C.T. Cobb and H.M. Joseph, Jr (eds) *Integrated Services for Children and Families: Opportunities for Psychological Practice.* Washington, DC: American Psychological Association.

Olsson, M.B. and Hwang, P.C. (2003) 'Influence of macrostructure of society on the life situation of families with a child with intellectual disability: Sweden as an example.' *Journal of Intellectual Disability Research 47,* 328–41.

Parish, S.L., Pomeranz-Essley, A. and Braddock, D. (2003) 'Family support in the United States: financing trends and emerging initiatives.' *Mental Retardation 41,* 174–87.

Rimmerman, A. and Duvdevani, I. (1996) 'Parents of children and adolescents with severe mental retardation: stress, family resources, normalization, and their application for out-of-home placement.' *Research in Developmental Disabilities 17*, 487–94.

Roeher Institute (2000) *Agenda for Action: Policy Directions for Children with Disabilities and Families.* New York: L'Institut Roeher Institute.

Rosenau, N. (2002) 'Families with members with disabilities: love, money and public policy.' Policy research brief 1. Melbourne: Disability Foundation of Australia.

Simeonsson, R.J. (1994) 'Promoting Children's Health, Education, and Well-Being.' In R.J. Simeonsson (ed.) *Risk, Resilience, and Prevention: Promoting the Well-Being of all Children.* Baltimore, MD: Paul H. Brookes.

Stepanek, J.S., Newcomb, S. and Kettler, K. (1996) 'Coordinating Services and Identifying Family Priorities, Resources, and Concerns.' In P.J. Beckman (ed.) *Strategies for Working with Families of Young Children with Disabilities.* Baltimore, MD: Paul H. Brookes.

Stoneman, Z. (1989) 'Comparison groups in research on families with mentally retarded members: a methodological and conceptual review.' *American Journal on Mental Retardation 94*, 195–215.

Stoneman, Z. (2005) 'Siblings of children with disabilities: research themes.' *Mental Retardation 43*, 339–50.

Summers, J.A., Poston, D.J., Turnbull, A.P., Marquis, J., *et al.* (2005) 'Conceptualizing and measuring family quality of life.' *Journal of Intellectual Disability Research 49*, 777–83.

Thurman, S.K. (1997) 'Systems, Ecologies, and the Context of Early Intervention.' In S.K. Thurman, J.R. Corwell and S.R. Gottwald (eds) *Contexts of Early Intervention: Systems and Settings.* Baltimore, MD: Paul H. Brookes.

Tomanik, S., Harris, G.E. and Hawkins, J. (2004) 'The relationship between behaviours exhibited by children with autism and maternal stress.' *Journal of Intellectual and Developmental Disability 29*, 16–26.

Turnbull, H.R. and Turnbull, A.P. (2000) 'Family Support: Retrospective and Prospective.' In M.L. Wehmeyer and J.R. Patton (eds) *Mental Retardation in the 21st Century.* Austin, TX: Pro-Ed.

Turnbull, A.P. and Turnbull, H.R. (2001) *Families, Professionals and Exceptionality: Collaborating for Empowerment*, 4th edn. Upper Saddle River, NJ: Merrill/Prentice Hall.

Weisner, T.S., Matheson, C., Coots, J. and Bernheimer, L.P. (2005) 'Sustainability of Daily Routines as a Family Outcome.' In A.E. Maynard and M.I. Martini (eds) *Learning in Cultural Context: Family, Peers, and School.* New York: Kluwer Academic/Plenum.

Werrbach, G.B. (1996) 'Family-strengths-based intensive child case management.' *Families in Society 77*, 216–26.

Werrbach, G.B., Jenson, C.E. and Bubar, K. (2002) 'Collaborative agency training for parent employees and professionals in a new agency addressing children's mental health.' *Families in Society 83*, 457–64.

18

Review of evaluative research on case management for people with intellectual disabilities

Janet Robertson and Eric Emerson

This chapter considers the evaluative research that exists on forms of planning within intellectual disability services that approximate the functions of care management. This is done in the light of a dearth of evaluative research on care management per se for people with intellectual disabilities. After considering what forms of planning approximate care management, evaluative research on these forms of planning is reviewed in relation to coverage, quality and content, process and outcomes. The chapter concludes with recent research from the USA and the UK that has demonstrated the potential for person-centred planning (PCP) to improve the lifestyle-related outcomes for people with intellectual disabilities.

Evaluative research relevant to case management for people with intellectual disabilities

It would appear that there is no empirical evaluative research of case management per se for people with intellectual disabilities. In the UK context, Challis *et al.* (2004) conducted a systematic review of literature regarding care management for four groups of adult users of social care services: those with mental health problems; older people; people with physical disabilities and sensory impairments; and people with intellectual disabilities. The review included literature from peer-reviewed publications published since 1990. They found only 24 publications relevant to care management and intellectual disabilities. Just over half of these studies focused on different aspects of care management, with the other half including issues relating to care management as part of their multi-theme. There is no suggestion in the review that any of the studies relating to intellectual disabilities were evaluative. This low number of publications compares with 87 publications for mental health and 79 publications for older people. For people with physical disabilities, there was an even greater paucity of evidence, with only five publications being identified.

Although we have not conducted a rigorous systematic review, our own review of the literature, including studies from outside of the UK context, has failed to find any evaluative research on case management per se for people with intellectual disabilities. This is not to say that there is no relevant research to review, however. Rather, the evaluative research to be included in this chapter appears under different guises. To consider the guises under which this research can be found, we need to go back to the definitions of case management provided in Chapter 1.

In Chapter 1, case management is conceptualised very broadly as the over-arching set of functions undertaken in a service system that seeks to organise comprehensive individually tailored packages of support for people with intel-lectual disabilities. In the UK and Australia, these functions are assessment, planning and prioritisation of needs; allocation, development and negotiation of resources; and implementation, monitoring and review of support plans. How these functions are put together depends a great deal on service histories, interagency working and linkages with local communities. The varied ways of organising case management functions, however, share common features and form a continuum rather than being distinct types of service provision. At one end of the continuum is the more traditional professional model, where all the functions are vested in a professional case manager who, in conjunction with clients and their families, formulates and implements plans for support. At the other end of the continuum is a self-directed individualised funding model, wherein after processes of independent person-centred planning and independ-ent or government-based decision making about resource allocation, the person with intellectual disability and/or the person's family implements and manages a support plan by administering their own funds.

The area within intellectual disabilities research that reflects these functions, and that has been the subject of some evaluative research, can be loosely termed 'lifestyle planning'. Under this heading, a large number of types of planning can be subsumed that fulfil at least some of the functions of case management. For example, as noted in Chapter 1, although termed 'individual planning', the tasks of case management were embedded in the All Wales Strategy (AWS) for intellectual disability services in 1983 (Felce *et al.* 1998). In the Australian context, general service plans fulfil a similar role: 'General Service Plan means a comprehensive plan prepared for an eligible person which specifies the area of major life activity in which support is required and the strategies to be implemented to provide that support' (Victorian Government 1986, p.2).

It is evaluative research on such forms of planning that this chapter will review. As noted in Chapter 1, in the field of intellectual disability more attention has been paid to models of individualised planning, such as individual program and educational plans and, more recently, person-centred planning, than to ideas about case management. The evidence for the effectiveness of such forms of lifestyle planning is reviewed in relation to the areas of coverage, content and quality, process and outcomes.

Coverage of lifestyle planning

In the UK, it has been argued that, in practice, individual planning reaches only a minority of service users (Mansell and Beadle-Brown 2004a). An inspection of day services by the Social Services Inspectorate (1989) in the UK found that only 25 per cent of service users had an individual plan on file. In Wales, Felce *et al.* (1998) reported that during the implementation of the All Wales Strategy for intellectual disability services, the highest level of individual plan coverage achieved at county level was only 30 per cent of service users, the lowest being just 3 per cent. Problems in resourcing the level of individual planning required are also evident in special education, where, despite a legal mandate, half of education authorities fail to achieve the 18-week target for production of a plan (Audit Commission 1998).

Other commentators, however, have contested the assertion that individual planning has poor coverage (Emerson and Stancliffe 2004), arguing that it is supported only by the one study in Wales (Felce *et al.* 1998) and one government report on day services carried out in 1989. Indeed, more recently in the UK, the vast majority of residential service users have been found to have an individual plan (Emerson *et al.* 1999). Of a total of 560 service users involved in an evaluation of the quality of residential supports, nearly all had a plan (99 per cent in village communities, 95 per cent in residential campuses and 92 per cent in dispersed housing). High levels of coverage have also been found in the USA, where planning is legally mandated (Stancliffe, Hayden and Lakin 1999) and Australia (Shaddock and Bramston 1991).

It seems likely that the poor coverage identified in Wales was due at least partly to the evolutionary context of profound change occurring within intellectual disability services. The AWS was the first national policy in the UK to make the commitment that people with intellectual disabilities have a right to experience normal patterns of life in the community and came at a time when deinstitutionalisation dominated the agenda. The AWS signalled a wholesale restructuring of service provision and the development of new service processes at planning, management and operational levels. As well as advocating the widespread introduction of individual planning, the AWS called for the establishment of new multidisciplinary community teams (MCTs). In addition to providing specialist professional input, the MCT was to act as a single point of contact for individuals, families and generic services alike and to be a focus for local planning and the collation of information on individual need that could be fed into the county planning system.

As noted by Felce et al. (1998), the service models advocated by the AWS were relatively untried. There was resistance in the form of traditional attitudes and support of the status quo. With a vast backlog of work when first established, MCTs experienced early difficulties in progressing towards the idea of individual plans for all. It is perhaps unsurprising that within this context of profound change, the overall coverage of individual plans was initially low.

Mansell and Beadle-Brown (2004b) concur that the suggestion that plans do have a wide coverage will shortly be true: the national minimum standards for residential homes for younger adults (Department of Health 2002a) produced following the Care Standards Act 2000 require that every service user has an individual plan. They note, however, that there is the danger that in the face of limited resources, coverage will be achieved by users having plans that are notional or aspirational. When considering the effectiveness of lifestyle planning, coverage should not be seen as a sufficient indicator of planning having worked. The issues of the quality, content, process and, ultimately, lifestyle-related outcomes of planning are of central importance, and it is these issues to which we move next.

Evaluating lifestyle plan content and quality

Criticisms have been directed towards forms of lifestyle planning in respect of the content and quality of the plans that result from the planning process. These criticisms have centred on whether essential components of planning are contained within plans, the overall quality of plans and the extent to which they reflect the preferences of the person for whom the plan has been developed. This body of research is summarised below.

In Australia, Hudson and Cummins (1991) evaluated the content of general service plans (GSPs) taken from two samples: 195 people associated with the work of the Community Living Support Service Program, and 39 people associated with the work of the Intellectual Disability Review Panel. GSP content was evaluated using guidelines for the development of GSPs from the Community Services Victoria staff manual. This states that staff should consider support needs across nine areas of major life activity: living situation, education, vocation, leisure, community access, health, financial, family support, and advocacy and personal support. Staff members are required to identify support needs in each of these areas and the strategies required to provide that support under the four headings 'current situation', 'goal', 'strategy', and 'person(s) responsible'. These details are entered into a specially constructed form provided by the regulations associated with the Intellectually Disabled Person's Services Act 1986. The written GSP therefore becomes a personalised service plan for the client concerned.

Satisfaction ratings for each area were made based on whether there was a clear service-related statement and no inclusion of inappropriate information. The satisfaction rates were compared under the four headings of 'current situation', 'goal', 'strategy' and 'person responsible'. The overall figures for samples one and two, respectively, were as follows: current situation, 79.9 per cent, 72.1 per cent; goal, 63.6 per cent, 59 per cent; strategy, 47.3 per cent, 45.3 per cent; and person responsible, 56 per cent, 54.1 per cent. Hudson and Cummins (1991) note that it is surprising how low the satisfaction for 'person responsible' is, given the apparent simplicity of specifying a person to be responsible for implementing a strategy. Perhaps most worrying is that 'strategy' achieved the lowest satisfaction. If effective strategies for implementing the goals specified in plans are not put in place, then it is doubtful whether they will actually lead to any outcomes being achieved for the person. The authors suggest, however, that the problems identified are due partly to the relative newness of the GSP process and the rapidity with which it was introduced. Under these conditions, they suggest it is not surprising that early GSPs were not of the best quality.

The data from sample one were examined further by Cummins et al. (1994). They note that even at the most superficial level of analysis, a relatively high number of GSPs had marked deficiencies: 12 per cent were handwritten, with consequential problems of legibility; 32 per cent failed to present the name and status of the person in attendance; 19 per cent did not specify a review date; 30 per cent were not attended by a family member, friend or advocate; and 54 per cent were attended by six or more people.

Hudson and Cummins (1991) express optimism that continued experience with GSPs will lead to improvements in quality. In a later study, however, Cummins *et al.* (1996) analysed 163 plans from 11 community support services. Again, the average level of presentation was poor. Only 14 per cent offered any criterion for evaluating performance objectives, the average number of skill-building objectives was 3.25 per plan, and only 39 per cent of plans were current.

In a further Australian study, Shaddock and Bramston (1991) collected data on 50 individual service plans (ISPs) from community residences in New South Wales using a random sampling method. They found that only 26 per cent of ISPs referred to the results of the previous ISP, indicating a failure to appreciate the role of ISP evaluation for subsequent programming. Although all ISPs contained short-term objectives, only 48 per cent of ISPs specified long-term goals. For only 34 per cent were long-term goals complemented by short-term objectives. The authors note that without this longer-term perspective, the entire process loses much of its logic, direction and purpose. Further, analyses of short-term objectives revealed an alarming absence of measurable, behaviourally stated objectives and of specific criteria for evaluation. The authors conclude that two-thirds of ISPs were based on vaguely expressed and impossible-to-measure objectives.

A methodologically distinct study on the content of PCP was conducted by Reid, Everson and Green (1999). This study used an applied behaviour analytical approach to look at whether items and activities reported to be preferred in person-centred plans represented accurate preferences based on how individuals responded to the items and activities. Person-centred planning meetings were conducted with four people with profound multiple disabilities to develop preference maps and to identify leisure-related preferences. All lacked the communication skills sufficient to describe their preferences. A sample of the reported preferences in the plans was then assessed by presenting the preferences one at a time to participants and observing whether they approached or avoided the items. A total of 24 items and activities were assessed, representing 35 per cent of all preferences identified in plans. Each activity was categorised as 'highly preferred' (approached on at least 80 per cent of trials), 'moderately preferred' (approached on at least 50 per cent of trials) or 'non-preferred' (approached on less than 50 per cent of trials). Of the 24 sampled items, 33 per cent were identified as highly preferred, 42 per cent as moderately preferred and 25 per cent as non-preferred. In summary, the results suggest that some preferences contained within plans may not even correspond to an individual's actual preferences.

The major implication of the body of research above is that, in the absence of good-quality plans with measurable objectives, a clearly stated strategy for implementing goals and statement with regard to who is responsible for implementing the strategy, goals may not be met. Ultimately, planning has failed if it does not improve the quality-of-life-related outcomes for the people it is supposed to serve.

One study that goes beyond looking at the content of plans to consider whether stated goals are actually achieved is that of Coyle and Moloney (1999). They looked at the introduction of person-centred planning in an Irish agency for people with intellectual disabilities. This study involved the adult division of a voluntary agency in Ireland that serves around 200 people with learning disabilities. Person-centred planning, using a variant of personal futures planning (Mount 1995), was adopted to coordinate service inputs around the expressed wishes and desires of service users.

All staff in the organisation who had been involved in the PCP training were surveyed via a questionnaire. Twenty-seven replies were received from frontline staff, 16 of which had details of a completed plan for a particular individual. The remaining 11 had not yet completed the full process. Information regarding plans was analysed with respect to the types of goal set, who was given responsibility for outcomes, the numbers of people involved at each stage of the PCP process, and the timing and location of circle of support meetings. For the 16 completed plans, a total of 99 goals were identified (mean 6, range 3–10). Of these, 16 per cent concerned work, 10 per cent daytime training, 21 per cent day time leisure, 8 per cent evening-time training, 14 per cent evening time leisure, 10 per cent holidays, 6 per cent living arrangements and 14 per cent 'other' goals. The authors note that the range of goals appears to be limited to options previously available to service users and that major categories that might be expected, such as personal relationships and sexuality, are entirely absent. With respect to actually achieving goals, at the time of data collection 77 per cent of goals had either been achieved or were in the process of being addressed, i.e. a quarter of all goals remained unaddressed.

In summary, research around the content and quality of plans points to potential problems in a number of areas, including restricted range of goals, lack of long-term focus, inadequately prepared plans, lack of information on how and by whom goals are to be implemented, vaguely expressed goals, and preferred activities not corresponding to the actual preferences of service users. Most importantly, goals may remain unmet. Even if a plan does fulfil all the criteria for a good-quality plan, the whole process is rendered meaningless if the plan is not translated into action. The next section considers research on the process of lifestyle planning before moving on to look in more detail at evaluations of the outcomes of planning.

Evaluative research on the process of lifestyle planning

Other studies on lifestyle planning have looked at elements of the planning process and the satisfaction of those taking part in the planning process. Humphreys and Blunden (1987) evaluated a system of individual planning in a community-based service for people with intellectual disabilities in Wales. They looked at 19 service users (16 adults, 3 children) who had had an individual planning meeting in the past year. Interviews were conducted with 11 service users and 14 family members; 76 postal questionnaires were received back from staff who had attended the 19 individual planning meetings. Meetings were also observed.

Despite efforts to involve service users, of all participants service users contributed the least to meetings. In choosing adjectives to describe how they felt at meetings, service users used adjectives such as 'bored' and 'nervous' more than other groups of respondents and selected 'involved', 'relaxed' and 'confident' less often. Service users described themselves most often as 'pleased' and 'happy', while staff and family members used 'interested' and 'involved' more. Overall, the individual planning system received a large measure of support from its users.

The issue of service user involvement was also considered by Carnaby (1997), who looked at service user involvement in a London-based individual planning system that strives to be person-centred. Observations were made of individual planning meetings. Participants were divided into two groups: those who could speak for themselves, and those who needed others to speak on their behalf. Those who needed others to speak were excluded from discussion in meetings more frequently than they were included. Those who could speak were included more than they were excluded, being involved in discussions about 69 per cent of the time. Those who could not speak for themselves were involved to a much lesser extent than those who could.

Radcliffe and Hegarty (2001) conducted a study in the UK that aimed to provide a simple procedure for self-auditing individual planning that might be implemented easily in services. They evaluated individual planning for eight service users in one service for people with intellectual disabilities. For each person, two individual planning meetings were assessed using documentary information to see whether individual planning objectives had been met. Five objectives were achieved in both 1998 and 1999: annual individual planning meetings, a key worker report being written, presence of a multidisciplinary team, discussion of current issues, and agreed set of objectives for the future. Three objectives, however, were achieved in very few meetings: circulation of reports one week before meetings, aims and objectives of previous meetings being reviewed, and future objectives being incorporated in day-to-day programmes. This finding is notable, pointing to a tenuous link between planning and outcomes: if future objectives are not incorporated into day-to-day programmes, then it seems likely that these objectives may not be met.

Perhaps the largest-scale study of the planning process is that of Butkus *et al.* (2002). They looked at initial satisfaction with PCP following the introduction of PCP in 1998 on a state-wide basis in the South Carolina Department of Disabilities and Special Needs. An attempt was made to survey all people who had been involved in a PCP meeting over a 30-day period in spring 1999. This was done by a telephone survey in which participants in planning meetings were asked how they felt about the planning process and the independent facilitator who led the meetings. The purpose of the survey was to learn about the views of people who were actually involved in the planning process. All surveys were conducted within 14 days of the initial planning meeting.

A total of 242 interviews were conducted: 68 with family or friends, and 174 with staff. Both staff and family/friends reported moderate to high levels of satisfaction in all categories. Staff reported significantly greater levels of satisfaction overall than family friends with the PCP in which they had taken part. Overall, the lowest level of satisfaction was with 'adequacy of resources'. This result is important. Although participants may be satisfied with PCP two weeks following the initial meeting, if the goals of plans are not met, for example due to lack of resources, then satisfaction is going to decrease. Planning cannot be effective in the absence of sufficient resources to meet the goals of plans. As the authors note: 'Having a terrific plan means little unless there is the will and capacity to implement it with a high level of integrity' (Butkus *et al.* 2002, p.354). Having good planning meetings that produce good plans is only a starting point in the planning process: there must also be implementation of plans and realisation of goals that improve people's lives.

Evaluative research on the outcomes of lifestyle planning

Ultimately, the effectiveness of lifestyle planning approaches must be evaluated with respect to the impact that plans have on lifestyle-related outcomes for people with intellectual disabilities. This section considers research that has gone beyond looking at the quality and content of plans to consider the outcomes of the planning process for the service user. After reviewing the existing literature on the outcomes of planning, this section presents the results of a UK study that looked at the impact of PCP on the lives of people with intellectual disabilities.

There have been few formal evaluations of the outcomes of lifestyle planning. The first systematic review of the evidence base for lifestyle planning approaches (including care management and PCP) found only five studies, with a total of 108 subjects, which reported any outcome data for any form of lifestyle planning (Rudkin and Rowe 1999). Evidence was limited to small-scale evaluations. For example, Malette *et al.* (1992) looked at the impact of the lifestyle development process (LDP) for four people with severe learning disabilities. All four participants took part in a greater number of integrated activities, experienced at least slight increases in their unpaid social networks, and performed a greater number of integrated activities with people who were not paid to spend time with them. The sample included only those who completed LDP successfully, however, and no information is given on the proportion for whom it was not successful.

Rudkin and Rowe (1999, p.366) conclude: 'There is no quantitative evidence to support the use of lifestyle planning in general or in any individual form.' Since this review was published, little additional evidence has been produced to support forms of lifestyle planning. In relation to PCP, as noted by Holburn *et al.* (2004), research evaluating quality-of-life outcomes as a result of PCP has been qualitative, with the exception of a single case investigation by Holburn and Vietze (2002).

Concerns have been expressed that plans may remain paper exercises. As noted by Felce *et al.* (1998), planning processes of any type are likely to be ineffectual unless they are backed up by a commitment to deliver what was promised within an agreed framework of accountability. As quoted by one social worker:

> A lot of the services we are identifying in the IP [individual plan] are provided by agencies that are not accountable to me or to the CMHT [Community Mental Handicap Team] or even to social services, so I have no clout as a key worker... I can do IPs with people but the plans have no status in the sense that they are not a contract. (Felce *et al.* 1998, p.58)

There is some evidence to support such concerns. As noted in the previous section, Coyle and Moloney (1999) found that a quarter of all goals in plans studied remained unmet. The Social Services Inspectorate (1989) found evidence that plans were in case notes but not necessarily used. As reported above, Radcliffe and Hegarty (2001) found that in two and three out of eight cases they studied in 1998 and 1999, respectively, individual plan goals were not translated into the daily programme of support to service users. Hagner, Helm and Butterworth (1996) did a qualitative study of the outcomes of PCP for six people in the USA. Overall, the results point to an indirect tenuous relationship between planning and outcomes. After six months of PCP, only a few planned outcomes had been achieved, and several participants felt that 'not much had happened' (Hagner et al. 1996, p.167). Similarly, Dumas et al. (2002) interviewed 13 PCP participants and found that although needs and desires were identified, in many instances plans were not implemented because of a lack of viable service or support solutions. Further, most participants seemed to believe that they were limited to existing models of service delivery rather than being able to gain access to individualised services and supports.

More positive support for the effectiveness of lifestyle planning appeared in a study by Holburn et al. (2004) in the USA, which was the first study to examine the relationship between a comprehensive PCP intervention and a range of outcomes. They conducted a longitudinal study of the impact of PCP for a group of 19 individuals living in institutional settings in the USA. The PCP group was compared with 18 matched peers who received conventional ISP. Results indicated that PCP hastened the move to community settings, with 18 members of the PCP group moving to the community compared with only five of the contrast group. Outcome measures indicated that the quality-of-life indicators of autonomy, choice-making, daily activities, relationships and satisfaction improved more for the PCP group than for the contrast group.

More recently, a longitudinal study has been conducted in England looking at the impact of PCP on the lifestyles of people with intellectual disabilities (Robertson et al. 2005). This study is described below.

Impact of person-centred planning for people with intellectual disabilities in England

This project funded by the Department of Health sought to address the lack of evidence on the impact of introducing PCP for people with intellectual disabilities and to identify factors that may either facilitate or impede the introduction and effectiveness of PCP. The project was a longitudinal study of the impact and cost of the introduction of PCP for 93 people with intellectual disabilities living in four localities in England (Robertson et al. 2005). PCP development work was undertaken with organisations in the four localities to provide additional support to help them develop robust policies, procedures and practices to implement PCP.

The key aims of the implementation phase were to assist staff, families and self-advocates to understand and use person-centred approaches to improve each person's quality of life. There was some variation across the four sites in the type of training and tools used, but the aim was the same – for people to be supported to be contributing members of their communities and to have fulfilling lives. A central aim of the development phase was the training of facilitators who were residential workers, day-centre staff, paid advocates, parents and siblings.

Across the sites, core material and awareness training for facilitators included:

- the key principles of person-centred working

- the policy framework for person-centred working (Department of Health 2001)

- the values base

- the historical context of person-centred working and what had been learned from elsewhere

- communication styles and communication support for people with non-verbal communication

- health action planning as part of person-centred working

- an overview and more detailed focus on some of the tools (essential lifestyle planning, the McGill Action Planning System (MAPS) (Vandercook, York and Forest 1989), Planning Alternative Tomorrows with Hope (PATH) (Pearpoint, O'Brien and Forest 1993), personal futures planning, *The Personal Planning Book* (McIntosh and Whittaker 2000)).

The introduction of PCP was phased across the four localities over a 12-month period. Participants were the first 25 people with intellectual disabilities in each locality for whom an attempt was made to develop a plan. In total, 93 people took part in the project, of whom 65 (70%) had a plan developed within the timescale of the project. Information was collected at approximately three-month intervals for each participant following his or her recruitment into the study, regardless of whether or not the participant had had a plan developed.

At the initial data-collection round, a comprehensive set of background information was collected on age, gender and ethnicity, ability and additional impairments, psychiatric status, syndromes associated with intellectual disabilities, challenging behaviour, residential history (for those living in supported accommodation only), and existing arrangements for individual planning. In addition, the participant's postcode was used to derive a measure of neighbourhood deprivation: the English Index of Multiple Deprivation (Noble *et al.* 2004).

Subsequently, information was collected at three-monthly intervals. Every three months, information was collected on current scheduled day activities, physical activity, community-based activity, social networks, contact with family and friends, use of hospital-based services, health checks, community-based service receipt, and PCP activities. Every six months (in addition to the three-monthly information), information was collected on health problems; medication receipt; the person's behavioural and emotional strengths and difficulties using the Strengths and Difficulties Questionnaire (SDQ; Goodman 1999); risks, accidents and injuries; and changes in the level of choice experienced by participants. Full details of all instruments used can be found in Robertson *et al.* (2005).

The 93 participants included a wide range of people with intellectual disabilities, from people with multiple and complex support needs to those with a low level of support needs who lived semi-independently. Participants represented both those with and without sensory impairments, epilepsy, psychiatric diagnoses, challenging behaviour, and complex health needs. They also represented the full age range, from 16 to 86 years old. Participants lived in a range of types of residence, and these were situated in areas that represented the full range of neighbourhood deprivation, including some of the most and least deprived areas of England.

Change before the introduction of person-centred planning

Two approaches were used to assess whether change was evident in key outcome areas before the implementation of PCP. First, we analysed the data for all participants that had been collected before the development of individual PCPs to see whether any changes were evident over time. Second, for the 28 people for whom an individual PCP was not developed within the timescale of the project, we made comparisons between the first and last data-collection points. For both approaches, we found very little change in key outcomes before the implementation of PCP.

Change following the introduction of person-centred planning

In view of the very small number of changes evident before the implementation of PCP, we undertook simple pre- and post-comparisons to test for the impact of PCP (using the first round of data collection as the 'pre' measure). In contrast to the very limited number of changes evident before the implementation of PCP, we found statistically significant changes on a number of key outcome variables. Comparing baseline and final data points, PCP was associated with participants having a 52 per cent increase in size of social networks, a 2.4 times greater chance of having active contact with family and a member of family in their social network, a 40 per cent increase in their level of contact with friends, a 2.2 times greater chance of having active contact with friends, a 30 per cent increase in the number of community-based activities, a 25 per cent increase in the variety of community-based activities, a 33 per cent increase in hours per week of scheduled day activities, and a 2.8 times greater chance of having more choice.

The results suggest that the introduction of PCP had a positive benefit on the life experiences of people with intellectual disabilities. Overall, there was very little evidence of positive change occurring in people's lives before or in the absence of the implementation of PCP. Although PCP was associated with benefits in some domains, however, it had no apparent impact on others, such as more inclusive social networks, employment, physical activity and medication. What is striking is that this pattern of results (benefits in the number and variety of community-based and non-inclusive social activities, but no change in 'stronger' markers of social inclusion) mirrors the results of deinstitutionalisation (Emerson and Hatton 1996; Kim, Larson and Lakin 2001; Young *et al.* 1998). This suggests that rather than representing a radical departure from previous practices, the effectiveness of PCP builds on the existing capacity of services and supports. In other words, PCP may be best considered an evolutionary step in the long-standing trend towards the increasing individualisation of services.

These results are consistent with the position taken in *Planning with People* (Department of Health 2002b), which argued that PCP would be helpful but not enough in itself to promote social inclusion and that additional action to complement improved planning with individuals would be necessary. Such action is likely to include, for example, positive action to remove barriers to employment and mainstream housing options and to encourage specialist services to play a stronger role in enabling more inclusive social networks.

Another important point to note is that although PCP was found to have a positive impact for those who received a plan, 30 per cent of the people in the study did not receive a plan within the timescale of the project. This failure to implement PCP for a substantial proportion of service users occurred within the context of a well-resourced research project employing expert external consultants to provide a comprehensive training programme. Such failures may be amplified in the context of the widespread adoption of PCP to fulfil organisational obligations and requirements.

For the 28 people who did not receive a plan, by far the most common reason cited for the failure of PCP to be implemented was problems related to facilitators (64%), for example facilitators leaving or a facilitator not being available (Robertson *et al.*, in press). Anecdotally, this was due to some extent to the lack of trained facilitators within sites, which meant that if a facilitator dropped out, there was nobody available to replace them, leading to the collapse of the whole process. Further notable reported problems were lack of time, which was noted as a problem for one in four of those without a plan, and staffing issues, which were a problem for one in five of those without a plan.

The role of care managers

Although the quantitative data collected during the course of PCP implementation did not specifically address the role of care managers in the PCP process, some information on their role is available in the description of the PCP development work (McIntosh and Sanderson 2005). It was noted that care managers were initially sceptical about person-centred working and were clear that they could not act as facilitators. At the end of the project, care managers were more accepting of the concept of person-centredness, but some remained unclear about their role. Some suggested that the crisis nature of their work made it difficult to see how they could develop lasting supportive relationships with self-advocates.

Further consideration of the role of care managers is available in the analysis of the organisational factors that influenced the effectiveness of PCP (Swift 2005). Group discussions were held with a selection of care managers, community teams and frontline support workers to explore their understanding of the concept of PCP, their experience of it (e.g. as facilitators or members of circles), how it fitted with their respective roles, and whether it had altered the way in which they approached their work. The overriding concern for care managers across the sites was one of conflict, both about their accountability and about their proper relationship to service users, circles of support and the planning process. The issue of accountability boiled down to an acknowledgement of 'our core business' (care management), which entailed tasks, such as the gatekeeping of resources, that could not be reconciled easily with some of the tasks associated with PCP. For most, it was a question of striking 'a balance of intrusion and input – some people are happy with us just doing the bit they need us to' (Swift 2005, p.97). This care manager summed up the sentiments expressed by colleagues at each of the four sites:

> We need to have a huge change in the way that we work and I think all of us would say that we want to work and we try to work in a person-centred planning way but the processes that we have within care management are not person-centred as such because they are about needs and it is about resources and the way the resources are then allocated. (Swift 2005, p.97)

The most commonly cited obstacles to care managers becoming more engaged in PCP or feeling able to work in person-centred ways with individuals related to the bureaucratic strictures of their employing agencies. There were several elements to this. First, the weight of their caseloads invariably meant that they had limited time to spend with any one individual. Second, eligibility criteria under Fair Access to Care (Department of Health LAC 2002) determined that priority for care management services was given to people with the most immediate needs and ran counter to the ethos of long-term planning. Third, the infrastructure to assessment and care management (the assessment processes, local authority financial requirements and data-recording systems) were not conducive to a person-centred approach. Finally, care managers complained about the 'dead hand of management' (Swift 2005, p.99) that too often frustrated attempts to find innovative solutions to the problems thrown up by PCP.

Conclusion: implications of research on lifestyle planning

In this chapter, we have considered the evaluative research that exists on forms of lifestyle planning for people with intellectual disabilities. Many criticisms have been levelled at lifestyle planning, at both an individual and a systemic level, particularly in terms of the coverage and outcomes of planning. Research is now emerging, however, that suggests that planning, and in particular person-centred planning, can be effective in improving lifestyle-related outcomes for people with intellectual disabilities. This section summarises the implications of the research reviewed above for those involved in planning with people with intellectual disabilities.

With respect to coverage, there is a danger that plans will be developed en masse for people with intellectual disabilities in the UK to meet national minimum standards and *Valuing People* (Department of Health 2001) stipulations that PCP should be introduced for everyone that uses services. It is important, however, that plans are not developed only to 'tick boxes' in order to meet legislative requirements. Merely having a plan is not an indicator of planning having worked. The issues of the quality, content, process and, ultimately, lifestyle-related outcomes of planning are of central importance.

If plans are going to improve the lives of people with intellectual disabilities, then attention needs to be paid to the quality and content of the plans. Research around the content and quality of plans points to potential problems in a number of areas, including restricted range of goals, lack of long-term focus, inadequately prepared plans, lack of information on how and by whom goals are to be implemented, vaguely expressed goals, and preferred activities not corresponding to the actual preferences of service users. Plans should have measurable objectives, a clearly stated strategy for implementing goals, and a statement with regard to who is responsible for implementing the strategy. Without these, goals may remain unmet.

Even if a plan does fulfil all the criteria for a good-quality plan, the whole process is rendered meaningless if the plan is not translated into action. The research reviewed suggests that in some instances, plans are not implemented because of a lack of viable service or support solutions. Indeed, participants in PCP in the USA reported lowest levels of satisfaction for 'adequacy of resources'. If resources are not available to meet the goals of plans, then once again the process is rendered meaningless. Further, it is important that planning does not limit people with intellectual disabilities to existing models of service delivery but enables them to gain access to individualised services and supports.

In conclusion, the effectiveness of forms of lifestyle planning must be evaluated with respect to the impact that the plans have on the lives of people with intellectual disabilities. Research in the USA and the UK on PCP indicates that planning can indeed improve lifestyle-related outcomes for people with intellectual disabilities. The research on PCP in the UK, however, suggests that planning may not be sufficient to promote stronger markers of inclusion, such as more inclusive social networks, employment, and access to mainstream housing. Additional action may be needed to remove barriers to these aspects of inclusion.

The UK study also failed to lead to plans being developed for nearly a third of participants. This was due to some extent to the lack of trained facilitators within sites, which meant that if a facilitator dropped out, there was nobody available to replace them, leading to the collapse of the whole process. In parallel with the arguments concerning coverage and the AWS presented earlier in this chapter, it seems likely that such problems stem from the early stage of the development of PCP within services for people with intellectual disabilities. It is hoped that as PCP training becomes more widespread, the problems associated with attempts to develop plans will lessen. The question of how to promote more inclusive social relationships and employment via planning remains to be addressed, however.

References

Audit Commission (1998) *Getting in on the Act: A Review of Progress on Special Educational Needs.* London: Audit Commission.

Butkus, S., Rotholz, D., Lacy, K., Abery, B. and Elkin, S. (2002) 'Implementing Person-Centered Planning on a Statewide Basis: Leadership, Training and Satisfaction Issues.' In S. Holburn and P. Vietze (eds) *Person-Centered Planning: Research, Practice and Future Directions.* Baltimore, MD: Paul H. Brookes.

Carnaby, S. (1997) 'What do you think? A qualitative approach to evaluating individual planning services.' *Journal of Intellectual Disability Research 41,* 225–31.

Challis, D., Xie, C., Hughes, J., Jacobs, S., *et al.* (2004) *Social Care Services at the Beginning of the 21st Century: Findings.* Manchester: Personal Social Services Unit, University of Manchester.

Coyle, K. and Moloney, K. (1999) 'The introduction of person-centred planning in an Irish agency for people with intellectual disabilities: an introductory study.' *Journal of Vocational Rehabilitation 12,* 175–80.

Cummins, R., Jauernig, R., Baxter, C. and Hudson, A. (1994) 'A model system for the construction and evaluation of general service plans.' *Australia and New Zealand Journal of Developmental Disabilities 19,* 221–31.

Cummins, R., Baxter, C., Hudson, A. and Jauernig, R. (1996) 'A model system for the evaluation of individual program plans.' *Journal of Intellectual and Developmental Disability 21,* 59–70.

Department of Health (2001) *Valuing People: A New Strategy for Learning Disability for the 21st Century.* London: Department of Health.

Department of Health (2002a) *Care Homes for Younger Adults and Adult Placements. National Minimum Standards: Care Home Regulations.* London: The Stationery Office.

Department of Health (2002b) *Planning with People: Towards Person-Centred Approaches.* London: Department of Health.

Department of Health LAC (2002) *Fair Access to Care Services: Guidance on Eligibility Criteria for Adult Social Care.* London: Department of Health.

Dumas, S., de la Garza, D., Seay, P. and Becker, H. (2002) 'I Don't Know how They Made it Happen but They Did: Efficacy Perceptions in Using a Person-Centered Planning Process.' In S. Holburn and P. Vietze (eds) *Person-Centered Planning: Research, Practice and Future Directions.* Baltimore, MD: Paul H. Brookes.

Emerson, E. and Hatton C. (1996) 'Deinstitutionalization in the UK and Ireland: outcomes for service users.' *Journal of Intellectual and Developmental Disability 21,* 17–37.

Emerson, E. and Stancliffe, R. (2004) 'Planning and action: comments on Mansell & Beadle-Brown.' *Journal of Applied Research in Intellectual Disabilities 17,* 23–6.

Emerson, E., Robertson, J., Gregory, N., Hatton, C., *et al.* (1999) *Quality and Costs of Residential Supports for People with Learning Disabilities: A Comparative Analysis of Quality and Costs in Village Communities, Residential Campuses and Dispersed Housing Schemes.* Manchester: Hester Adrian Research Centre, University of Manchester.

Felce, D., Grant, G., Todd, S., Ramcharan, P., *et al.* (1998) *Towards a Full Life: Researching Policy Innovation for People with Learning Disabilities.* Oxford: Butterworth Heinemann.

Goodman, R. (1999) 'The extended version of the Strengths and Difficulties Questionnaire as a guide to child psychiatric caseness and consequent burden.' *Journal of Child Psychology and Psychiatry 40,* 791–801.

Hagner, D., Helm, D. and Butterworth, J. (1996) 'This is your meeting: a qualitative study of person-centered planning.' *Mental Retardation 34,* 159–71.

Holburn, S. and Vietze, P. (eds) (2002) *Person-Centered Planning: Research, Practice and Future Directions.* Baltimore, MD: Paul H. Brookes.

Holburn, S., Jacobson, J., Schwartz, A., Flory, M. and Vietze, P. (2004) 'The Willowbrook Futures Project: a longitudinal analysis of person-centered planning.' *American Journal on Mental Retardation 109,* 63–76.

Hudson, A. and Cummins, R. (1991) 'General service plans: an evaluation of their content within two service delivery systems.' *Australia and New Zealand Journal of Developmental Disabilities 17,* 401–11.

Humphreys, S. and Blunden, R. (1987) 'A collaborative evaluation of an individual plan system.' *British Journal of Mental Subnormality 33,* 19–30.

Kim, S., Larson, S.A. and Lakin, K.C. (2001) 'Behavioural outcomes of deinstitutionalisation for people with intellectual disability: a review of studies conducted between 1980 and 1999.' *Journal of Intellectual and Developmental Disability 26,* 35–50.

Malette, P., Mirenda, P., Kandborg, T., Jones, P., *et al.* (1992) 'Application of a lifestyle development process for persons with severe intellectual disabilities.' *Journal of the Association for Persons with Severe Handicaps 17,* 179–91.

Mansell, J. and Beadle-Brown, J. (2004a) 'Person-centred planning or person-centred action? Policy and practice in intellectual disability services.' *Journal of Applied Research in Intellectual Disabilities 17,* 1–9.

Mansell, J. and Beadle-Brown, J. (2004b) 'Person-centred planning or person-centred action? A response to the commentaries.' *Journal of Applied Research in Intellectual Disabilities 17,* 31–5.

McIntosh, B. and Whittaker, A. (2000) *Unlocking the Future: Developing New Lifestyles for People who have Complex Disabilities.* London: King's Fund.

McIntosh, B. and Sanderson, H. (2005) 'Supporting the Development of Person-Centred Planning.' In J. Robertson, E. Emerson, C. Hatton, J. Elliott, *et al.* (eds) *The Impact of Person-Centred Planning.* Lancaster: Institute for Health Research, Lancaster University.

Mount, B. (1995) *Capacity Works: Windows for Change using Personal Futures Planning.* Manchester, CT: Communitas.

Noble, M., Wright, G., Dibben, C., Smith, G., *et al.* (2004) 'Indices of deprivation 2004.' Report to the Office of the Deputy Prime Minister. London: Neighbourhood Renewal Unit.

Pearpoint, J., O'Brien. J. and Forest, M. (1993) *PATH: A Workbook for Planning Positive, Possible Futures and Planning Alternative Tomorrows with Hope for Schools, Organizations, Businesses and Families.* Toronto: Inclusion Press.

Radcliffe, R. and Hegarty, J. (2001) 'An audit approach to evaluating individual planning.' *British Journal of Developmental Disabilities 47*, 86–97.

Reid, D., Everson, J. and Green, C. (1999) 'A systematic evaluation of preferences identified through person-centered planning for people with profound multiple disabilities.' *Journal of Applied Behavior Analysis 32*, 467–77.

Robertson, J., Emerson, E., Hatton, C., Elliott, J., *et al.* (2005) *The Impact of Person-Centred Planning.* Lancaster: Institute for Health Research, Lancaster University.

Robertson, J., Hatton, C., Emerson, E., Elliott, J., *et al.* (in press). 'Reported barriers to the implementation of person-centred planning for people with intellectual disabilities.' *Journal of Applied Research in Intellectual Disabilities,* in press.

Rudkin, A. and Rowe, D. (1999) 'A systematic review of the evidence base for lifestyle planning in adults with learning disabilities: implications for other disabled populations.' *Clinical Rehabilitation 13*, 363–72.

Shaddock, A. and Bramston, P. (1991) 'Individual service plans: the policy-practice gap.' *Australia and New Zealand Journal of Developmental Disabilities 17*, 73–80.

Social Services Inspectorate (1989) *Inspection of Day Services for People with a Mental Handicap.* London: Department of Health.

Stancliffe, R., Hayden, M. and Lakin, K. (1999) 'Effectiveness and quality of individual planning in residential settings: an analysis of outcomes.' *Mental Retardation 37*, 104–16.

Swift, P. (2005) 'Organisational Factors Influencing the Effectiveness of Person-Centred Planning.' In J. Robertson, E. Emerson, C. Hatton, J. Elliott, *et al.* (eds) *The Impact of Person-centred Planning.* Lancaster: Institute for Health Research, Lancaster University.

Vandercook, T., York, J. and Forest, M. (1989) The McGill Action Planning System (MAPS): a strategy for building the vision. *Journal of the Association for Persons with Severe Handicaps 14*, 205–15.

Victorian Government (1986) *The Intellectually Disabled Persons' Services Act 1986.* Melbourne: Victorian Government.

Young, L., Sigafoos, J., Suttie, J., Ashman, A. and Grevell P. (1998) 'Deinstitutionalisation of persons with intellectual disabilities: a review of Australian studies.' *Journal of Intellectual and Developmental Disability 23*, 155–70.

Notes

1 Needs are subject to many different interpretations (Bradshaw, J. (1972) 'The concept of social need.' *New Society 496*, 640–43). In this book, the term 'needs' refers to judgements made by others based on both professional assessments and the views of the person and others that know them well, about what the person with a disability requires in order to achieve a quality of life commensurate with that of others in their community. Wants and aspirations are the ideals or dreams expressed by the person about things they would like in order to achieve a maximum quality of life.

2 This story is not based solely on any individual or family with whom I worked. Rather, it is an amalgamation of stories and experiences I had as a case manager working with families who faced issues of relinquishment.

3 This has since been extended to people over 65 years and to 16- and 17-year-olds and carers.

4 Note the role is described as 'planning support', indicating that the role is not to plan for people but to support them and their networks in order to plan for themselves.

5 To follow the development of CLBC, see www.communitylivingbc.ca

6 An integrated group of components, including the symbols, aids, strategies and techniques used by individuals to enhance communication. The system serves to supplement any gestural, spoken and/or written communication abilities (American Speech–Language–Hearing Association 1991). 'Report: augmentative and alternative communication.' *ASHA 33* (Suppl. 5), 9–12.

7 In San Filippo disease, the child usually presents in early childhood with what appears to be a static encephalopathy. The diagnosis usually becomes apparent by mid-childhood, when the child begins to lose skills and develop coarsening of facial features. Death is usually in the late teenage years.

8 Rett syndrome occurs exclusively in girls. Characteristically, the child develops normally for the first year or two of life. There is then a plateau in developmental progress, followed by a loss in hand and language skills and, thereafter, very slow developmental progress. There is now a specific diagnostic test for this disorder, but the diagnosis can be suspected only by recognition of the variable rate of development in the early years.

9 One textbook of developmental disability medicine has been produced largely as a result of the emergence of these units (Lennox, N.G. (ed.) (2005) *Management Guidelines: Developmental Disability.* Melbourne: Therapeutic Guidelines).

10 The term 'disabilities' in this chapter is used in the generic sense to encompass characteristics of disabilities in both children under six years of age who may not have a formal diagnosis of intellectual disability and children over six years of age for whom the term 'intellectual disability' applies.

11 The terms 'service coordination' and 'case management' are used interchangeably in this chapter, as much of the available early childhood intervention literature does not distinguish between the two.

Subject Index